LEADERSHIP IN SUSTAINABILITY

Perspectives on Research, Policy, and Practice

Published in the United States of America.

Fielding University Press is an imprint of Fielding Graduate University. Its objective is to advance the research and scholarship of Fielding faculty, students, alumni and associated scholars around the world, using a variety of publishing platforms. For more information, please contact Fielding University Press, attn. Jean-Pierre Isbouts, 2020 De la Vina Street, Santa Barbara, CA 93105. Email: jisbouts@fielding.edu. On the web: www.fielding.edu/universitypress.

Library of Congress Cataloging-in-Publication data
Leadership in Sustainability: Perspectives on Research, Policy, and Practice
1. Social Sciences - Sustainable Practices

Leadership in Sustainability

Perspectives on Research, Policy, and Practice

Edited by
Richard P. Appelbaum, Frederick Steier, Paul Stillman
and David Blake Willis

FIELDING UNIVERSITY PRESS

Leadership in Sustainability:
Perspectives on Research, Policy, and Practice

Editors
Richard P. Appelbaum, Frederick Steier, Paul Stillman,
and David Blake Willis

Contributors
Richard P. Appelbaum
Karen Smith Bogart
Henry Fowler
Four Arrows, aka Don Trent Jacobs
Laurence Habib
Agnes Dewi Hartkamp
Jean-Pierre Isbouts
Kerul Kassel
Kevin LeGrand
Alice E. MacGillivray
Flávio Mesquita Da Silva
Shelley Mitchell
Isabel Rimanoczy
Katrina S. Rogers
Frederick Steier
Paul Stillman
Sergej van Middendorp
David Blake Willis

Table Of Contents

Leadership in Sustainability: *An Invitation and Introduction*

Richard P. Appelbaum and Frederick Steier
Fielding Graduate University

This volume brings together chapters that combine a focus on both leadership and sustainability. While the volume is titled *Leadership in Sustainability*, we also hope to make the reader aware of sustainability in leadership – not only how sustainable leaders can be effective, but also how such leadership can sustain itself. The chapters call for understanding the reciprocal relationship between leadership and sustainability, and what happens when the two are brought together in a turbulent world.

Obtaining an understanding requires a systems approach, and the chapters in this volume offer a variety of ways of doing so that honor the interconnections and interdependencies between leadership and sustainability. One key to this perspective is how a system – be it a community, an organization, an eco-system, or a nation – balances stability and change. What is the role of leadership in managing multiple perspectives when differences exist regarding what should be maintained and what can be changed within the system and its environment? Who is holding on? Who seeks change? How might bringing leadership and sustainability together afford a better understanding of the seemingly intractable "wicked problems" that we face today (Churchman, 1967, Rittel and Weber, 1973; Camillus, 2008)? Does such an approach suggest a shift from "leadership of" to "leadership with?"

The chapters in this volume address these issues in many different contexts – some organizational, some cultural, and some national. What is significant is that they share an understanding of how sustainability and leadership might inform each other, particularly in a world where attention to both social and ecological justice is so critical. We recognize that while much has been written over the years about leadership and sustainability, much less scholarship has addressed the effort to bring the two concepts together in a systematic fashion.

This volume engages that challenge, arguing that the ways in which leadership and sustainability inform one another depends, in large part, on what, specifically, the organization is seeking to sustain.

In Chapter 1, Appelbaum sets the overall framework by laying out both ecological and social issues, then showing how there is a need for sustainability leaders in business, government, NGOS, and education.

Chapters 2 and 3 turn our attention to the ecological challenges that we currently face by identifying dire problems that require immediate solutions. In Chapter 2, Isbouts shows that we are at a critical tipping point in climate change, posing an existential threat that requires immediate action on the part of sustainability leaders in government and business. In Chapter 3, Willis, Four Arrows, Rogers, and Fowler extend this argument by examining unsustainable human practices involving animals, natural habitat destruction, and complex global networks; posing the question, "What does Anthropocentrism mean for sustainability leadership?"

Chapters 4-7 are studies that address these concerns at the organizational level, providing case studies on sustainability leadership in action – leaders and organizations that try to "walk the talk." In Chapter 4, Rogers uses an Environmental, Social, Governance (ESG) framework to show how one ecologically-oriented outdoor corporation has sought to realize its goals for environmental sustainability. In Chapter 5, in similar fashion, Stillman examines four enterprises in different sectors (consumer retail, specialty foods, higher education, and eco-technology), identifying common values and practices that enable them to best achieve their goals. In Chapter 6, Bogart also employs an ESG framework to better understand how corporate social responsibility (CSR) principles and stakeholder engagement creates both risks and opportunities for the firm. In Chapter 7, MacGillivray argues that healthy biodiversity can hold lessons for organizational leadership by showing parallels in the transformation of an Oklahoma police department from a rigid hierarchy to a more inclusive model of shared leadership.

Chapters 8-12 identify ways of thinking and new approaches that are needed today. If sustainability leadership is to be effective, changes in psychology, consciousness, culture, and worldview are necessary. In Chapter 8, Kassel, Mitchell, and Rimanoczy employ an original Sustainability Mindset Model (SMM) to better understand the tension that firms face as they seek to balance the need for short-term profit and growth and the need for long-term social, environmental, and economic impacts, as well as other stakeholder concerns. In Chapter 9, LeGrand also employs an original measure, the Environmental Activism Propensity (EAP) scale, to argue that leading sustainability leaders are more likely to be self-directed individuals. In Chapter 10, Four Arrows argues forcefully that sustainable development education is missing a crucial link. It fails to acknowledge that the root of our present environmental and social crises is the dominant Eurocentric worldview, which needs to be replaced with an indigenous worldview. In Chapter 11, Willis looks to Indian social activists in the Gandhian tradition - Dalits, Muslims, Hindus, Christians, Atheists – who have much to teach us about sustainability leadership. In Chapter 12, Middendorp, Habib, Hartkamp, Da Silva, and Steier draw on examples from Norway, the Netherlands, and Brazil to examine the importance of collaborative support networks in creating sustainability leadership, including the use of World Cafés to engender widespread participation.

Finally, in the Afterword, Steier and Isbouts make connections between systems approaches and the very idea of wicked problems with implications for whole systems design.

In her landmark book, *Male and Female,* Margaret Mead (1949) stresses the importance of seriously considering "the questions that we ask." For example, we might recognize that, while in many settings we think of questions as inviting answers and information, we might also think about what our questions do. Might they create movement toward new forms of understanding? Might they also create an opportunity to reflect on the very assumptions that underpin our understanding, such as ways of thinking about sustainability leadership in diverse contexts? In this volume, we honor the idea of asking powerful questions that allow readers to reflect on what was learned from a chapter, but also allow them to consider what new ideas might be brought forth. To that end, each chapter also contains questions for the reader that open doors for learning. This learning might also involve presenting situations in which the readers are involved to in considering the lessons learned from each chapter, and across chapters.

The focus on questions is significant in that another important feature of the volume is opening a path to different levels of learning about sustainability leadership. Following the ideas of Gregory Bateson (1972; see also Visser, 2007; Bateson, M.C., 2010), we try to bring in both first order learning – learning about our worlds – as well as "deutero-learning' or second order learning – learning about our learning process itself. This becomes especially important as we invite the readers to engage in the very same second order learning processes that are being described in the various chapters.

References

Bateson, Gregory. 1972. *Steps Towards an Ecology of Mind.* San Francisco: Chandler.

Bateson, Mary Catherine. 2010. *Willing to Learn: Passages of Personal Discovery.* Hanover, NH: Steerforth.

Camillus, John C. 2008. "Strategy as a Wicked Problem, *Harvard Business Review* (May) (https://hbr.org/2008/05/strategy-as-a-wicked-problem)

Churchman, C. West. 1967. "Wicked Problems," *Management Science **14** (4) (December): B-141–B-146.*

Mead, Margaret. 1989. *Male and Female.* New York: William Morrow & Company

Rittel, Horst W. J. and Webber, Melvin M. 1973. "Dilemmas in a general theory of planning," *Policy Sciences* 4(2), 155-169.

Visser, Max. 2007. "Deutero-Learning in Organizations: A Review and a Reformulation," *Academy of Management Review* 32:2: 659-667.

CHAPTER 1

Why Sustainability Leadership is Needed

Richard P. Appelbaum
Fielding Graduate University

Preamble

The subject of this chapter. In the United States, two-thirds of all adults believe that the federal government is not doing enough to reduce the effects of global climate change (Funk and Hefferon, 2019). A global survey of twenty-six countries reports that the same percentage of respondents regard climate change as a major national threat (Pew, 2019). Given that the need for sustainable development is now widely accepted, leaders in business, government, non-profits, and education must have more than a sustainability mindset; it is also important that they understand the systemic connections between social and ecological sustainability. Although the idea of sustainability remains poorly understood, the United Nations calls for achieving seventeen sustainable development goals by 2030 (UN, 2020). Is this reasonable or is it a lofty ambition? Is the very notion of sustainable development a contradiction in terms? In this chapter, we address these issues, arguing that there is a need for sustainability practitioners who are grounded in a systemic understanding of social and ecological sustainability.

The nature of the study. In order to understand the significant environmental and social challenges to achieving sustainable development, this chapter draws on both existing research and original studies conducted by the author. On the environmental side, I look at the scientific research on human-caused climate change, including the most recent findings of the Intergovernmental Panel on Climate Change (IPCC). On the social side, I draw on my own research on the global production systems that drive economic development, with harsh consequences for both planet and people. My conclusions are based on several decades researching global production systems, including factory field studies and interviews with workers in the United States, Vietnam, Bangladesh, and

China; public hearings conducted by the Los Angeles Jewish Commission on Sweatshops (1999), which I organized and chaired; and my work as Advisory Council Chair for the Workers' Rights Consortium, the leading anti-sweatshop nongovernmental organization in the United States (WRC, 2020).

The outcome of this chapter. IPCC studies and other scientific research clearly show that we are heading for a major human-caused climate crisis; but, as this chapter seeks to show, current approaches to sustainable development are flawed. These approaches currently rely on businesses voluntarily adopting "best practices" in hopes of reducing their ecological footprint and providing decent and safe working conditions throughout their global networks of contract factories. Evidence shows that neither of these outcomes is likely to be achieved. Corporate social responsibility – the so-called "triple bottom line" of profits, planet, and people – has failed to adequately protect either the planetary environment or factory workers. In today's global economic system, profit-making inevitably drives business strategies, often at the expense of people and planet, however lofty a firm's aspirations. Self-regulation is insufficient, and so public oversight is needed. I conclude with some suggestions for a systemic rethinking of sustainability leadership, addressing the need for such leadership in businesses, nonprofit organizations, government, and higher education.

Introduction: Sustainable Development – What Could Possibly Go Wrong?

The call for sustainable development is now more than three decades old. The term was first coined in the Brundtland Report, issued by the World Commission on Environment and Development in 1987 (former Norwegian prime minister Gro Harlem Brundtland chaired the Commission). According to the Report, sustainable development is best defined as "development that meets the needs of the present without compromising the ability of future generations to meet their own needs." The definition itself was a compromise in that it sought to appease both anti-growth environmentalists and the pro-growth business community:

> The concept of sustainable development does imply limits - not absolute limits, but limitations imposed by the present state of technology and social organization on environmental resources and by the ability of the biosphere to absorb the effects of human activities. But technology and social organization can be both managed and improved to make way for a new era of economic

> growth. The Commission believes that widespread poverty is no longer inevitable. Poverty is not only an evil in itself, but sustainable development requires meeting the basic needs of all and extending to all the opportunity to fulfil their aspirations for a better life. A world in which poverty is endemic will always be prone to ecological and other catastrophes (UN, 1987).

Stated simply, from this viewpoint, sustainable development means that today's business and political leaders – and by association, all of us – should leave our planet in good health for our children and grandchildren. These are truly noble sentiments, but are they really achievable? Has a "new era of economic growth" really emerged and, if so, is it even compatible with "the ability of the biosphere to absorb the effects of human activities?" As the report acknowledged, poverty is certainly "an evil in itself," and it was clearly prescient in predicting "that widespread poverty is no longer inevitable." According to the World Bank (2020), the percentage of the world's population living in dire poverty (less than $1.90USD /day) declined from 36 percent at the time the Report was issued, to less than 10 percent today; but, at what cost? Much of the decline in global poverty has resulted from the explosive economic growth of China, India, and a handful of other countries – growth that has taken a considerable ecological toll. The economic growth of these countries is tied to their role in supply chains that originate in the U.S., Europe, Japan, and a small number of other countries that made their industrial transitions decades ago. The greenhouse gases from those earlier transitions brought the world to its present position, while the greenhouse gases that are now being off-loaded to the developing countries that power global supply chains are sealing our fate.

The Brundtland Report's primary focus is on environmental challenges. It does not give much attention to the global workforce whose labor drives the global economy or to the role of global supply chains in driving environmental degradation. While unsafe working conditions are mentioned, the assumption is that industrial production and free trade will provide sufficient (and decent) employment in globalized production systems, and that the principle challenge is to find ways to do so sustainably. In many ways the Brundtland Report created division among activists that remains largely true today. Environmental activists, who focus on the future of the planet are often ignorant of, and all too often indifferent toward, workers' rights. Labor activists focused on abuse of workers may acknowledge the looming environmental crisis, but see workers' rights as the more immediate and pressing concern. The possibility that the system, by its very nature, might produce widespread labor abuses is seldom considered.

In this chapter, I will argue that an adequate model of sustainability must address both environmental protection and workers' rights. Only then can we hope to develop a shared understanding that will bring activists on both sides together in a common struggle for a truly sustainable future. I will begin by describing the current state of affairs regarding both sides of the coin – environmental and workers' rights activists. I will then offer suggestions for an educational program that brings systematic attention to both issues, in hopes of training a cadre of new leaders who can enact truly sustainable change.

Global Warming and Climate Change: Welcome to the Anthropocene

For a half of a million years, before settled agriculture became the norm, hunting and gathering societies were sustained by what their immediate natural environment provided; they made little attempt to significantly change the world around them. In fact, there were very few humans around to change the planet: it is estimated that prior to agriculture, the global population numbered fewer than 10 million people, roughly the same number that occupy a large-sized metropolitan area today (Kahn, 2020). With the advent of agriculture some 10-15 thousand years ago, all of this changed. Trees were felled, land was cleared, crops were planted, and the loss of natural habitats to farming and grazing proved to be inexorable. Settled agriculture, which provided larger and more stable sources of food, resulted in population growth and development of cities. By the time of Christ, there were 300 million people in the world – a significant increase from pre-agricultural times, but still relatively few. It took approximately another eighteen centuries for humanity to number one billion, only 130 years to reach the second billion around 1930, and only another 30 years to reach the third billion in 1960. Since that time the world population has increased by a billion people every twelve years, reaching 7.8 billion today (Worldometer, 2020; Quora, 2020). Now, most of us live in large urban areas, including some thirty-three megacities whose populations exceed 10 million (UN, 2018). Exponential population growth and the explosion of enormous metropolitan regions have effectively shredded much of what was once the planet's non-human environment.

The Industrial Revolution, which occurred only three hundred years ago, effectively sealed the fate of the planet. It resulted in the massive production of goods and services, a global profit-driven economic system, and mass consumerism. It also led to an accelerating demand for energy and raw materials and, by relying on carbon-based energy sources, now threatens our planet's climate and ecosystems. With the invention of the microchip and its commercialization in 1971, these processes have gone global. Thanks to modern information technology, giant transnational firms are now able to source materials, hire workers, and manage their supply chains and marketing operations anywhere in the world. Profit maximization almost always means cost minimization by means of the cheapest labor and fewest enforced environmental regulations. While most of the damage to date has been done by advanced industrial nations, the rest of the world is eager to catch up, rapidly adding to global ecological challenges. The rapid rise of China, which makes up almost a fifth of the world population, is the most obvious case in point. China is merely following in the footsteps of Southeast Asian countries and India is not far behind. During the first two decades of the 21st century, per-person income, one indicator of consumption, increased by nearly two-fifths in the world as a whole; in China, the increase was more than fourfold (World Bank, 2019). As China achieves economic parity with the United States and other advanced industrial countries, the environmental impact of such massive consumption will be extreme and long-lasting.

The most recent reports of the Intergovernmental Panel on Climate Change (IPCC) are truly alarming. The IPCC's October 2018 Special Report noted that greenhouse gas emissions continue to rise, despite pledges from virtually every country to lower them, concluding that since the second half of the 19th century "we are already seeing the consequences of 1°C (1.8°F) of global warming through more extreme weather, rising sea levels and diminishing Arctic sea ice, among other changes" (IPCC, 2018). The IPCC Report gave the world until 2030 to achieve the 1.5°C goal (2.7°F), after which it predicts far greater risks of droughts, floods, and extreme heat waves, resulting in poverty for hundreds of millions of people (reported in Watts, 2018). An IPCC report the following year noted significant shrinkage of glaciers, snow cover, and arctic sea ice; ocean warming; and melting of the northern permafrost, all of which are contributing to sea level rise that would prove catastrophic if the Greenland and Western Antarctic ice sheets, already melting, were to melt entirely (IPCC, 2019). Current research has found that, contrary to the claims of climate skeptics, previous scientific studies have significantly under-estimated the degree of climate change that was occurring (Oreskes, Oppenheimer, and Jamieson, 2019; Oppenheimer et al, 2019; Linden, 2019). Debra Roberts, CoChair of the IPCC working group on impacts, warns that "it's a line in the sand and what it says to our species is that this is the moment and we must act now… This is the largest clarion bell from the science community, and I hope it mobilizes people and dents the mood of complacency" (reported in Watts, 2018). We are now clearly well into an urgent climate emergency that must be addressed (Gills and Morgan, 2019; IPCC 2018; Watts, 2018). There is a growing scientific consensus that human impacts on the planetary environment are of such significance that we have entered a new geological era: the Anthropocene ("human epoch").

The term Anthropocene was used informally as early as the mid-1970s, but was popularized some fifteen years ago by Paul Crutzen, an atmospheric chemist and recipient of the Nobel Prize in Chemistry (Oldfield *et al.*, 2013; Crutzen and Stoermer, 2000). The International Union of Geological Sciences has since convened to decide whether the Holocene Epoch – the period that began some 12,000 years ago following the last ice age within which modern human societies emerged – has been officially superseded by the Anthropocene (Stromberg, 2013); a formal proposal will be made to the official geological organizations next year. The distinction is important, both because it acknowledges that human activities are now significantly altering the planet, and also, it calls for interdisciplinary knowledge, "from engineering and environmental science to the social sciences and humanities," if we hope to get an adequate understanding (Oldfield *et al.*, 2018).

Supply Chains and Workers' Chains: Key to Understanding Climate Change and Sustainability

The nature of production has changed over the past fifty years, and not in ways that auger well for our planet or its people. These changes, which reflect larger, systemic processes of globalization are symbolized by the half-century shift in fortunes between the world's largest corporations (Lichtenstein, 2005).

The emblematic late 20th century corporation was General Motors, whose revenues at the time made it the world's largest firm. General Motors was a giant manufacturer; it not only designed and sold motor vehicles, but it also made them. Most of GM's work was done in-house by its own workforce, including more than 600,000. unionized U.S workers (Associated Press, 2019). As unionized workers, they were able to, and did effectively, bargain for a share of the growing American economic pie: higher wages, shorter working hours, and a safe and healthy working environment.

Today, however, the manufacturing world has significantly changed. The emblematic 21st century firm is not GM, but Walmart – a giant retailer whose revenues exceed a half trillion dollars, outstripping every other firm (Fortune, 2020), as well as the GDP of all but twenty-five or so countries on Earth. Walmart sells other firms' products, firms that do not manufacture anything, but instead outsource their production to independent contractors through supply chains that circle the globe. In today's business model, the global corporations that were called "manufacturers" a half century ago are better understood as "branded marketers." They design and market products, but the actual manufacturing occurs in millions of independently owned contract factories throughout the world. Corporations that use these factories have no legal responsibility for the social or environmental problems that inevitably arise as a byproduct of production. Because of competitive pressures, businesses often source from factories in countries where environmental and labor standards are weak or nonexistent, and, if these standards do exist, they are seldom enforced.

Brand competition at the top means that factories now compete globally for clients by cutting wages and creating working environments that are harsh, unhealthy, and unsafe. The repercussions are usually hidden from public view. Whether you are buying cheap clothing or the latest model iPhone, you have no way of knowing where and under what conditions the product you purchase was made. Occasionally, abuses are so significant that they cannot be hidden, such as when the eight-story Rana Plaza industrial building in Dhaka, Bangladesh collapsed in 2013, killing 1,134 garment workers and injuring another 2,500 (Nova and Wegemer, 2016; Ross, 2016), or the harsh working conditions in the giant Foxconn electronic assembly plant in Shenzhen, China led to 14 suicides in 2010. Rana Plaza was making clothing for virtually every name-brand apparel maker in Europe and North America; Foxconn was Apple's principal assembly plant for iPhones (Chan, Pun, and Selden, 2016).

In the age of GM, unionized workers in advanced industrial countries had some degree of power, thanks to a three-party system of governance involving unionized labor, corporations, and the government; the latter being tasked with making and enforcing labor-management rules and regulations. In today's age of Walmart, this tripartite "social contract" has been replaced by a "social accountability contract" that involves three very different parties: corporations, the contract factories they hire, and independent auditing companies that monitor factories and report back to the corporations that use them. Missing from this new tripartite approach are the workers themselves and their union representation, and government enforcement. What was once public regulation has given way to a system of private enforcement, which critics dismiss as the fox guarding the chicken coop. It is worth noting that the many factories in the Rana Plaza industrial building were part of social compliance auditing schemes and that Foxconn had Apple auditors (Esbenshade, 2016; Appelbaum, 2018).

In the 1990s, anti-sweatshop activists brought public attention to sweatshops in global supply chains. Prominent brands like Nike and Gap became targets of student-led, anti-sweatshop campaigns in Europe and the U.S. In response, many corporations moved to self-regulation, hoping to avoid governmental regulation by countries where they sourced their production, or interference by international organizations such as the UN International Labor Organization. "Corporate Social Responsibility" (CSR) had become a buzzword by the early 21st century, a three-legged stool in which businesses pledged to value "people, planet, and profits." Firms established CSR divisions, hired staff to implement social audits, and trumpeted their successes in public relations publications and product advertising. On the three-legged stool, one leg has proven to be foundational: profits. Publicly-traded firms cannot afford to sacrifice profits for noble concerns, however well-intended. As environmental concerns became more publicly fashionable, the environmental leg was found to have good public relations value, and might even contribute occasionally to the bottom line. As Walmart has shown, cost savings can be realized by cutting a firm's carbon footprint (Sturcken and Bonini, 2018; Hertzberg, 2020).

The third leg, however, has proven to be the weakest: providing safe and healthy factories, or paying a decent wage, added cost and cut into profits. Perhaps for this reason, talk about CSR has morphed into more general talk about sustainability, with its strong environmental association, rendering the notion of actual corporate responsibility for workers' well-being largely invisible. Public oversight – government regulation of global businesses – has given way to self-regulation.

We need leaders to have a far better understanding of these dynamics if they are to develop strategies for achieving environmental and social sustainability differences in a globalized world. Some balance between self-regulation and novel forms of government oversight is needed, posing both theoretical and practical challenges for sustainability education in the 21st century.

Sustainability Leadership: Some Suggestions for Rethinking Education

Net Impact, an organization that defines itself as, "a community of more than 60,000 student and professional leaders creating positive social and environmental change in the workplace and in the world," surveyed more than 3,000 graduate students in one hundred leading business and management graduate schools. Nine out of ten respondents reported that learning about social and environmental business was a personal priority, but only half reported that they were "very" or "completely" satisfied with what they were learning in their graduate programs.

The overwhelming majority claimed that they would take a pay cut if they could find work after graduation in an organization that reflects their social and environmental values (Net Impact, 2014). The Net Impact study findings are reinforced by international studies as well. The UK's National Association of Students surveyed more than 21,000 first and second year UK college students between 2010 and 2013 and reported that "eight in every ten students consistently believe that sustainable development should be actively incorporated and promoted by universities. Approximately two-thirds of students would be willing to sacrifice £1000 from the average starting salary to work for a company with a positive social and environmental record, whilst over two-fifths would be willing to sacrifice £3000" (Drayson, Bone, Agombar, and Kemp, 2014).

A program in Sustainability Leadership should go beyond providing surface understanding of sustainability issues and practices, and should also address the need for high-level education that engages scholarly literature on social and ecological sustainability. The curriculum is aimed at producing leaders in businesses, non-profits, government, and educational institutions who have a systemic understanding of the history and practice of sustainability efforts. It would accomplish that by critically examining what has worked and what has failed, both environmentally and socially, and by looking at empirical evidence regarding corporate claims for effective "best practices." Empirically-grounded case studies would provide insight into the effectiveness of stakeholder engagement, both when firms "go it alone" and when they partner with international governmental organizations such as the World Bank, the International Labor Organization, the U.S. Agency for International Development, or the UN Global Compact. Students would learn how organizational development skills can be mobilized in the service of sustainability, the creation of human resource management systems for sustainability, and how social media can be effectively used to promote sustainable practices.

There are four critical areas that pose significant challenges for sustainability leaders: businesses, nonprofits, governments, and educational institutions.

Businesses. Sustainability is clearly seen as a necessary strategic aspect of most firms' corporate plans. Notwithstanding, the evidence that CSR efforts are often aspirational rather than effective, at best. One recent global survey found that 81 percent "felt strongly that companies should help to improve the environment. This passion for CSR is shared across gender lines and generations" (Nielson, 2018a). Another survey found that half of US consumers claimed they would "definitely or probably change their consumption habits to reduce their impact on the environment" (Nielson, 2018b). It's worth noting that both studies focused exclusively on environmental issues and not social concerns. A statement recently issued by the CEOs of 181 major corporations that comprise the Business Roundtable claimed to set a "modern standard for corporate responsibility" in asserting a "fundamental commitment to all of our stakeholders," including shareholders, employees, suppliers, communities, and customers (Fitzgerald, 2019). All major corporations now have codes of conduct pledging environmental stewardship along with safe and healthy workplace conditions throughout their global supply chains, as well as CSR staff tasked with implementing such policies. Yet, to the extent that such staff has any formal – as opposed to on-the-job, training it is usually in MBA programs that offer courses and certificates in CSR that assume businesses can be trusted to regulate themselves, that free market solutions, exclusive of government regulation, will solve all problems. A large scholarly literature indicates that this approach is a failure (Appelbaum and Lichtenstein, 2016).

A program in Sustainability Leadership aimed at corporate CSR staff would teach about the larger social forces that have stymied solutions, as well as specific skills from practices that have proven effective. It would be closely tied to studies in organizational systems design, in order to provide a broader understanding of organization structures and cultures. This program would yield a systemic understanding of how different managerial roles can be used to foster and evaluate meaningful changes in CSR practices.

Nonprofits. CSR typically fails because it is structured to enable businesses to self-regulate across global supply chains, effectively avoiding public oversight. In order to achieve compliance with social and environmental CSR aspirations, businesses often hire non-governmental organizations (NGOs) to monitor and report on supply chain compliance, flagging violations and suggesting corrective measures. This process lacks transparency, accountability, and independent enforcement.

A program in Sustainability Leadership would provide the same sort of systematic understanding designed for corporations, although tailored for the growing number of NGOs that are concerned with monitoring and compliance. Through case studies of best practices of firms and NGOs that have been successful, it would identify how truly independent auditing and reporting can most effectively be achieved.

Governments. The challenges of social and environmental sustainability are global, while regulation and enforcement are local. Global governmental organizations concerned with social and ecological sustainability issue many aspirational edicts, but they lack enforcement power. The UN's International Labor Organization (ILO) has numerous conventions governing workplace issues, many of which have been ratified by almost all countries, the U.S. being the principal exception. These conventions lack any enforcement mechanism. In a similar vein, the UN Global Compact's Ten Principles address such issues as human rights, workers' rights, the environment, and corruption. As of March 2021, a total of 16,809 organizations in 160 countries had signed on to the Global Compact including 13,589 companies and business associations, 296 public sector organizations, 690 academic institutions, 394 foundations, 125 cities, 1,687 NGOs, but only 28 unions (UN Global Compact, 2021a, 2021b). The reason for the low level of organized labor participation is evident. As its website indicates: "The UN Global Compact is a purely voluntary initiative. It does not police or enforce the behaviors or actions of companies. Rather it is designed to stimulate change and to promote corporate sustainability efforts and encourage innovative solutions and partnerships" (2021c). The same can be said for the UN Environmental Program (UNEP), its Millennium Development Goals (MDGs), and its Framework Convention on Climate Change (UNFCCC): all provide excellent guidelines, useful educational resources, and countless stakeholder meetings to achieve social and environmental objectives. But, since no country is willing to give up sovereignty to an international institution, such institutions remain aspirational in nature. Enforcement is local, but countries that seek to enforce local social and environmental laws and regulations run the risk of losing business to less compliant countries.

Given the unique challenges that confront national and international governmental efforts to reach sustainability goals, a program in Sustainability Leadership would, ideally, partner with specialists in the field of international relations to offer courses that critically examine the challenges faced by international governmental organizations and, in particular, the limitations of current approaches.

Educational Institutions. A growing number of community colleges, four-year colleges, and universities now have sustainability working groups devoted to their campuses' environmental practices. Though the staff that is tasked with improving their institutions' sustainability practices typically lacks formal training in sustainability. They are usually found within the administrative unit concerned with business operations, and are recruited to address sustainability issues. The Association for the Advancement of Sustainability in Higher Education (AASHE, 2017) surveyed 452 college and university staff concerned with sustainability issues. Based on the questions and position descriptions in the report, the large majority were concerned with environmental rather than social aspects of sustainability. The survey found that sustainability staff tended to be young, with nearly three out of five under 40; female, by a factor of slightly more than three out of five; and overwhelmingly white, at nearly nine out of ten. While almost all had BAs, and nearly three out of five had MAs, only those in top leadership positions were likely to have PhDs. Four out of five positions surveyed were full-time and salaried. Median salaries ranged from $46,000 to $82,000 depending on the type of position, indicating a sizeable group of administrators at various levels concerned with sustainability issues. Among those who responded to a question concerning what kind of position their predecessor had moved into, most had moved into other sustainability positions in higher education, non-profits, business, or government. The AASHE study concludes: "While campus sustainability positions are relatively new within higher education, they are growing and evolving...There are significant opportunities for continued growth in higher education sustainability staffing positions moving forward" (38).

A program in Sustainability Leadership would draw on the experience of sustainability efforts at universities that have successfully implemented sustainable practices, and partner with AASHE in developing courses designed specifically for higher education.

The Growing Need for Sustainability Leadership

George Basile, Senior Sustainability Scientist and Professor of Practice at Arizona State University's Global Institute of Sustainability, notes that the advantage of a sustainability degree, as opposed to incorporating sustainability concerns in, for example, an MBA, "is that most organizations have a host of exceptional MBA holders, yet they still have a growing suite of challenges and increasing market needs that the MBA does not address directly." He goes on to assert, based on market research, that specialized knowledge is required beyond on-the-job training: "The combination of organized degree efforts and field experience provides the integrated learning/leadership-growth platform needed to expand one's knowledge base in foundational areas key to sustainability, as well as having the hands-on opportunities to experiment for oneself in this rapidly evolving arena" (quoted in Glouderman, 2014). Martha Willard, executive director of the International Society of Sustainability Professionals, claims that the value of a degree in sustainability is "increasing as each day passes...it's no longer enough to have a degree in organizational development, environmental studies, or engineering. It doesn't sound specific enough. And higher education has responded by offering more degrees that have sustainability in the title" (quoted in Glouderman, 2014).

There is a large and growing demand for scholar-practitioners who understand the complex linkages that underlie successful sustainability efforts. If there is any hope for significant advancements in global social and ecological sustainability, educational institutions at all levels need to take a hard look at the challenges we face, and the hard evidence that examines claims of true success in sustainability. The clock is running out; the urgency is great. The need for informed sustainability leadership has never been greater.

Questions for Discussion

1. What is the widely-accepted Brundtland Report definition of sustainability, and what challenges are raised by this definition?
2. Do you believe that we have entered a new geologic era, the Anthropocene? What evidence can you cite in supports of your belief?
3. What three values does CSR espouse, and what is the evidence for the success of each?
4. What is meant by the claim that General Motors is a template for 20th century capitalism, while Walmart now plays that role for the 21st century?
5. How do global supply chains affect the achievement of sustainability goals?
6. What do you believe is the best strategy to balance social and ecological sustainability concerns?
7. How would you construct a program to prepare leaders committed to balancing social and ecological sustainability?

About the Author

Richard P. Appelbaum, Ph.D., is Professor at Fielding Graduate University's School of Leadership Studies, where he chairs the Doctoral Concentration in Sustainability Leadership. His research focuses on social and ecological sustainability, workers' rights, and the impact of technology on globalization. His two most recent co-authored books are *Innovation in China: Challenging the Global Science and Technology System* (Polity, 2018), and *Achieving Workers' Rights in the Global Economy* (Cornell University Press, 2016). He is the author or co-author of twenty books and 150 articles; is a Fellow of the American Association for the Advancement of Science (AAAS); has been a resident fellow at the Rockefeller Foundation Bellagio (Italy) Center; and he chairs the Advisory Council of the Workers' Rights Consortium. He is Distinguished Research Professor Emeritus at the University of California – Santa Barbara, where he co-founded UCSB's Global Studies Department.

References

AASHE. 2017. *Salaries & Status of Sustainability Staff in Higher Education 2017.* The Association for the Advancement of Sustainability (https://www.aashe.org/wp-content/uploads/2017/09/AASHE-Staffing-Survey-Report-2017.pdf).

Appelbaum, Richard P. 2019. "Labor," entry in Juergensmeyer, Mark, Saskia Sassen, Manfred Steger, and Victor Faessel (eds.), *Oxford Handbook of Global Studies.* Oxford, England: *Oxford University Press.*

Appelbaum, Richard P. and Nelson Lichtenstein (eds.). 2016. *Achieving Workers' Rights in the Global Economy.* Ithaca, NY: Cornell University Press.

Associated Press. 2019. "A brief history of General Motors Corp" (April 4) (https://www.mlive.com/business/2008/09/a_brief_history_of_general_mot.html).

Chan, Jenny, Ngai Pun, and Mark Selden. 2016. "Apple, Foxconn, and China's New Working Class," pp. 173-189 in Richard P. Appelbaum and Nelson Lichtenstein (eds.), *Achieving Workers' Rights in the Global Economy.* Ithaca, NY: Cornell University Press.

Crutzen, P.J. and Stoermer E.F. 2000. The "Anthropocene," International Geosphere-Biosphere Programme, *IGBP Newsletter* 41 (May): 17–18. (http://www.igbp.net/download/18.316f18321323470177580001401/1376383088452/NL41.pdf)

Drayson, Rachel, Elizabeth Bone, Jamie Agombar, and Simon Kemp. 2014. "Student attitudes towards and skills for sustainable development," National Union of Students (November). (https://www.heacademy.ac.uk/sites/default/files/resources/Student%20attitudes%20towards%20and%20skills%20for%20sustainable%20development.pdf).

Esbenshade, Jill. 2016. "Corporate Social Responsibility: Moving from Checklist Monitoring to Contractual Obligation?" pp. 51-69 in Richard P. Appelbaum and Nelson Lichtenstein (eds.), *Achieving Workers' Rights in the Global Economy.* Ithaca, NY: Cornell University Press.

Fitzgerald, Maggie. 2019. "The CEOs of nearly 200 companies just said shareholder value is no longer their main objective," CNBC (August 19) (https://www.cnbc.com/2019/08/19/the-ceos-of-nearly-two-hundred-companies-say-shareholder-value-is-no-longer-their-main-objective.html).

Fortune. 2020. "Fortune Global 500," Fortune Rankings (https://fortune.com/global500/).

Funk, Cary and Med Hefferon. 2019. "U.S. Public Views on Climate and Energy," Pew Research Center (November 25) (https://www.pewresearch.org/science/2019/11/25/u-s-public-views-on-climate-and-energy/).

Gills, Barry and Jamie Morgan. 2019. "Global Climate Emergency: after COP24, climate science, urgency, and the threat to humanity," *Globalizations* (September 24). (https://www.tandfonline.com/doi/full/10.1080/14747731.2019.1669915)

Glouderman, Nikki. 2014. "Is a Sustainability Degree Worth It? Here's a Crash Course," *Greenbiz* (June 11) (https://www.greenbiz.com/blog/2014/06/11/are-sustainability-degrees-worth-it) Sheila Bonin.

Hertzberg, Richie. 2020. "Walmart Calls It 'Project Gigaton' But This Isn't Science Fiction," The Hill: Changing America (January 8) (https://thehill.com/changing-america/sustainability/climate-change/476060-walmart-calls-it-project-gigaton-but-this-isnt).

IPCC. 2018. *Special Report: Impacts of 1.5°C of Global Warming on Natural and Human Systems"* IPCC Special Report on Global Warming of 1.5C, ch. 3 (October) (https://www.ipcc.ch/site/assets/uploads/sites/2/2019/06/SR15).

IPCC. 2019. *The Ocean and Cryosphere in a Changing Climate: Summary for Policymakers* (September 24): p. 16 (https://report.ipcc.ch/srocc/pdf/SROCC_FinalDraft_FullReport.pdf).

Kahn.2020. "The Dawn of Agriculture," Kahn Academy (https://www.khanacademy.org/humanities/world-history/world-history-beginnings/birth-agriculture-neolithic-revolution/a/where-did-agriculture-come-from).

Lichtenstein, Nelson. 2005. "Wal-Mart and the New World Order: A Template for Twenty-First Century Capitalism?" *New Labor Forum* 14:1; 21-30.

Linden, Eugene. 2019. "How Scientists Got Climate Change So Wrong," *The New York Times* (November 8) (https://www.nytimes.com/2019/11/08/opinion/sunday/science-climate-change.html?smid=nytcore-ios-share).

Los Angeles Jewish Commission on Sweatshops. 1999. American Jewish Congress of Los Angeles (January).

Net Impact. 2014. 2014 *Business as Unusual:* The social & environmental impact guide to graduate programs – for students by students." (https://netimpact.org/sites/default/files/documents/business-as-unusual-2014.pdf)

Nielsen. 2018a. "Global Consumers Seek Companies That Care About Environmental Issues," report from Nielsen Company surveys (November 9). (https://www.nielsen.com/us/en/insights/article/2018/global-consumers-seek-companies-that-care-about-environmental-issues/).

Nielsen. 2019b. "Was 2018 the Year of the Sustainable Consumer?" report from Nielsen Company surveys (December 17) (https://www.nielsen.com/us/en/insights/article/2018/was-2018-the-year-of-the-influential-sustainable-consumer/).

Nova, Scott and Chris Wegemer, 2016."Outsourcing Horror: Why Apparel Workers Are Still Dying One Hundred Years After Triangle Shirtwaist," pp. 17-31 in Richard P. Appelbaum and Nelson Lichtenstein (eds.), *Achieving Workers' Rights in the Global Economy.* Ithaca, NY: Cornell University Press.

Oldfield, Frank *et al.* 2018. *"The Anthropocene Review:* Its Significance, Implications, and the Rationale for a New Interdisciplinary Journal," The Anthropocene Review 6:3 (December 11) (https://journals.sagepub.com/doi/full/10.1177/2053019613500445).

Oreskes, Naomi, Michael Oppenheimer, and Dale Jamieson . 2019)."Scientists Have Been Underestimating the Pace of Climate Change," *Scientific American* (August 19)(https://blogs.scientificamerican.com/observations/scientists-have-been-underestimating-the-pace-of-climate-change/).

Quota. 2020. "What Was the World's Population Around the Time of Jesus?" downloaded from https://www.quora.com/What-was-the-worlds-population-around-the-time-of-Jesus.

Pew. 2019. "Publics Around the World Increasingly See Climate Change, Cyberattacks, and American Power as Threats," Pew research Center: Spring 2018 Global Attitudes

Survey (February 7) (https://www.pewresearch.org/global/2019/02/10/climate-change-still-seen-as-the-top-global-threat-but-cyberattacks-a-rising-concern/pg_2019-02-10_global-threats-2018_0-03/).

Stromberg, Joseph. 2013. "What is the Anthropocene and Are We In It?" *Smithsonian Magazine* (January) (https://www.smithsonianmag.com/science-nature/what-is-the-anthropocene-and-are-we-in-it-164801414/).

Sturcken, Elizabeth and Sheila Bonini. 2019. "Why Walmart's Project Gigaton Gives Us Hope," *GreenBiz* (April 15) (https://www.greenbiz.com/article/why-walmarts-project-gigaton-gives-us-hope).

UN Global Compact. 2021a. "The Ten Principles of the UN Global Compact," United Nations (https://www.unglobalcompact.org/what-is-gc/mission/principles).

UN Global Compact. 2021b. "Our Participants," United Nations (https://www.unglobalcompact.org/what-is-gc/participants/search?)

UN Global Compact. 2021c. "Frequently Asked Questions," United Nations (https://www.unglobalcompact.org/about/faq).

UN. 1987. "Our Common Future: Report of the World Commission on Environment and Development," UN World Commission on Environment and Development (eds.). Oxford: Oxford University Press (also downloadable at http://www.un-documents.net/wced-ocf.htm).

UN. 2018. "The World's Cities in 2018: Data Booklet." United Nations, Department of Economic and Social Affairs, Population Division (https://www.un.org/en/development/desa/population/publications/pdf/urbanization/the_worlds_cities_in_2018_data_booklet.pdf).

UN. 2020. "About the Sustainable Development Goals" (https://www.un.org/sustainabledevelopment/sustainable-development-goals/)

Watts, Jonathan (2018) "We have 12 years to limit climate change catastrophe, warns UN," *The Guardian* (October 8) (https://www.theguardian.com/environment/2018/oct/08/global-warming-must-not-exceed-15c-warns-landmark-un-report).

Worker Rights Consortium. 2020. "Our Work" (https://www.workersrights.org/our-work/).

World Bank (2009) "World Development Indicators, GNI per capita, all countries, 1960-2018 (constant 2010 US$)" Calculated from http://api.worldbank.org/v2/en/indicator/NY.GNP.PCAP.KD?downloadformat=excel

World Bank. 2020. "Poverty headcount ratio at $1.90 a day (2011 PPP) (% of population), calculated from WB Databank, Microdata (https://data.worldbank.org/indicator/SI.POV.DDAY).

Worldometer. 2020. "World Population by Year." Downloaded from https://www.worldometers.info/world-population/world-population-by-year/.

CHAPTER 2

The Tipping Point in Climate Change: *A Call to Leadership*

Jean-Pierre Isbouts
Fielding Graduate University

Preamble

The subject of this chapter. While for many people, climate change has always been an abstract concept, 2020 was the year in which the devasting impact of growing climate change slammed our planet. In addition to the devastation wrought by the COVID-19 pandemic, the beginning of the century's third decade witnessed millions being affected by catastrophic floods, drought, wildfires, and hurricanes. These major weather events should convince even diehard skeptics that climate change poses an existential threat to life on earth.

The nature of the study. This chapter offers an overview of the sheer scope of climate change events in 2020, and what humankind can do to mitigate the rise of even more devastating phenomena. While it shows that climate change has always been a part of the story of earth and of the rise of homo sapiens, it also argues that the current changes in our climate are far more corrosive because of the toxic impact of human-generated emissions.

The outcome of this chapter. The chapter presents the argument that only a concerted effort of all nations could conceivably limit the damage of climate change and begin to initiate a process of recovery. We are not powerless, and climate change is not inevitable; but the need to take action is urgent.

Introduction

Between June and July of 2020, a record *five* tropical storms barreled across the Atlantic Ocean and slammed into the Caribbean and the southern coastline of the United States. One of these storms, Isaias, cut a swath of destruction across the Eastern seaboard, spawning tornadoes, widespread flooding, and power outages for millions of people. According to the National Oceanic and

Atmospheric Administration (NOAA), the 2020 hurricane season was the most devastating on record, with at least 25 named storms (National Oceanic and Atmospheric Administration, 2020). July and August 2020 were also the hottest months on record for scores of American states, placing great strain on the power grid and threatening farmers with drought. In California, over 9,000 wildfires burned nearly 4.5 million acres and more than 10,000 homes, forcing thousands of people to evacuate.

Meanwhile, China faced its worst flooding in decades, with 8 to 12 inches of rainfall *per day* in many areas, displacing millions of people and prompting the second-highest level of the national-emergency response (Myers, 2020). In East Africa, millions suffered from another plague: huge swarms of voracious locusts that can eat as much in a day as the entire population of a large country like Germany. As a result, millions face the acute threat of famine amidst the upheaval of the COVID pandemic.

Are all of these disasters related in some way? The answer is yes; 2020 will be remembered not only for the COVID pandemic, but also as the year that climate change finally hit our planet with full force and with devastating results. Therefore, it is difficult to believe that large segments of the American population, including former President Trump, continue to deny that global warming has become an existential threat to life on Earth. For years, climate change was the subject of heated discussions on the political stage: Democrats warned it was coming, Republicans dismissed it as a clear and present danger, while others were undecided. But 2020, the year of the COVID pandemic, was also the year that climate change finally became a reality, with devastating effects. "Climate change is tough for people to grasp," says Marshall Shepherd at the University of Georgia, "but its DNA can now readily be seen in today's tropical systems, heat waves, droughts and rainstorms" (Flavelle & Foundatin, 2020).

The timing couldn't be worse. With all nations entrenched in fighting the coronavirus, most were wholly unprepared to deal with the ferocious impact of climate change. Many scientists, including Yale's Beth Gardiner, draw an explicit link between climate change and the coronavirus: "The virus has shown that if you wait until you can see the impact [of climate change]," she wrote, "it is too late to stop it" (Gardiner, 2020).

All of these threats are unfolding as the world is facing unprecedented challenges, some of which are predictable and others that will be new and unfamiliar. The century-long pre-eminence of the United States in the fields of science, technology and defense is now being challenged by resurgent powers in China and Russia. As a result, many nations are reverting to a Cold War posture; some will align themselves in an Anglophile orbit (including the U.S., Canada, Britain and Australia), others will join the Sinophile sphere of influence (including China and much of South East Asia), while the third bloc, the European Union, is diminished by Britain's decision to leave the EU. This will greatly hamper a globally coordinated response to climate change, which is what scientists believe is the only way to confront global warming. And yet, regardless of their geographical or geopolitical positions, all countries will face the same threats—and opportunities to resolve these threats.

Climate Change Has Always Been a Fact of Life

Today, very few scientists, irrespective of their ideology, challenge the idea that our planet is experiencing a fundamental change in the global climate. And indeed, why should they? Climate change has always played a seminal role in shaping our planet. Some nine billion years after the Big Bang, the planet we call Earth was simply one of many objects left over from the collapse of a giant molecular cloud. Eventually, that cloud coalesced into a sun, while other objects kept bouncing around like billiard balls on a pool table. One of these was the primordial Earth while another, a large body called Theia, slammed into Earth to form the Moon. Bits and pieces of that collision were discovered by the crew of Apollo 14.

Then, the Earth began to cool, allowing microorganic life to form—scientists in Western Australia have discovered the fossilized remains of ancient microorganisms in sandstone strata that appear to be 3.48 billion years old. But the atmosphere still lacked oxygen, and without that, true life could not begin. Fortunately, as the Earth cooled, clouds began to form, which in turn produced the rain that sustains the oceans. But it still took another 2 billion years for complex, multi-cellar life to make its appearance during the so-called Cambrian Explosion (Isbouts, 2021).

Unfortunately, these budding life forms were threatened by predators far larger and more powerful than they, including a great variety of dinosaurs. That changed some 66 million years ago, when a massive asteroid struck today's Mexico with a speed of 14 miles per second, gouging the huge Chicxulub crater out of the Earth's surface. Since it entered at a 60-degree angle, the vaporized rock was blasted back into the air, blocking all sunlight, depriving plant life of photosynthesis, and ultimately causing the extinction of the dinosaur species. "A very bad day for dinosaurs," says Gareth Collins at Imperial College in London, "but good news for us today" (Crane, 2020). Indeed, with the threat of large predators now reduced, the first humanoid species, the *Homo erectus,* was allowed to develop. Since they walked upright, these humanoids were free to wield tools and weapons with their hands. This gave them access to a richer diet, which in turn accelerated their brain development. As a result, the species *Homo sapiens* began to emerge almost simultaneously in Europe, Africa, and Asia between 250,000 and 100,000 B.C.E.

Fig. 1. Skull of Homo Sapiens, dated around 100,000 B.C.E. (Author photo)

These early humans were tested once more by another climate event: the Ice Age, reaching its most severe level, the Glacial Maximum, some 22,000 years ago. The sharp climate changes challenged early humans to develop new survival strategies. Fortunately, with the formation of ice and the drop of sea levels, so-called "land-bridges" appeared between Europe, the Americas, and even parts of Asia (such as Australia) that allowed large migrations, prompted by the search for new hunting areas, to occur. The cooler temperatures also forced humans to learn to manage fire as a source of warmth, and as a means to cook their food, prompting major changes in their diet.

But another major threat soon emerged. When the last glacial age ended some 11,000 years ago, the climate began to warm, the ice receded, and the oceans stabilized, reaching their present form. The warming of the Earth also caused many animal species to become extinct, not only because of warmer temperatures, but also because of changes in vegetation and water supply—a dangerous precursor to what we are witnessing today. These changes would have killed off the fragile early humans, were it not for the warmer climate, which allowed entirely new edible crops and plants to prosper in the wild like never before. That is a very important lesson, which could have significant ramifications for us today.

This raises an important question: Can global warming also have a positive dimension? Could we, for example, develop new food resources in places that were not suitable for agriculture before? According to a study by the University of Guelph, some 30% of today's global surface could begin to grow high-yield crops if current warming trends continue. Researchers refer to these as "frontier soils," particularly in Canada and Russia, which could be unlocked to produce vast quantities of wheat, maize, and potatoes. In Canada alone, the amount of arable land could increase by as much as 40%, according to agriculture expert Ian Jarvis, Program Director of the GEO Global Monitoring (GEOGLAM) Initiative. "Canada is in a better situation than much of the rest of the world," he says (University of Guelph, 2020).

The downside is that many of these regions are currently habitats for a wide variety of wildlife (known as "biodiversity hotspots") and that the inevitable use of agricultural fertilizers and pesticides could affect local water sources. Writing in *Anthropocene Magazine,* researcher Emma Bryce also warns that such cultivation would inevitably release vast amounts of carbon dioxide from the soil (Bryce, 2020). However, other researchers have countered that argument, saying that high latitude lands are already releasing high levels of carbon due to warming, particularly due to the melting of the permafrost.

Another opportunity that has arisen from climate change in northern territories is that large swaths of land will now become available for archaeology and forensic study. The payoff would not be limited to finding artifacts from previous cultures; "Archaeology has the potential to provide both data for, and methods of, addressing challenges the global community faces through climate change," Marcy Rockman and Carrie Hritz wrote in *PNAS*, the Proceedings of the National Academy of Sciences. We just need to find ways to "fully realize the multiple potential uses of archaeology for the challenges of climate change," they add (Rockman & Hrtiz, 2020).

In sum, climate change has always played a major role in shaping life on Earth. The problem is that, today, climate change is not just driven by natural evolutionary forces but by the growing release of carbon-dioxide in the atmosphere. The quadrupling of the human population during the 20th century, despite two world wars, accelerated this trend to the extent that today, humankind emits *twenty times* the amount of carbon dioxide compared to the beginning of the 20th century. Increasing deforestation, particularly in the Amazon, which serves as the "Earth's lungs," has also accelerated the trend. So where does that leave us? Are there other strategies we can develop to mitigate the impact of climate change?

What Will the World Look Like in 5-10 Years?

Many people associate global warming with higher temperatures. Indeed, the summer of 2020 was unprecedented in the severity of its heat. Baghdad experienced record temperatures of 125 degrees; Death Valley clocked in at 130 degrees, the highest temperature ever recorded in the U.S.; and much of Northern Europe also suffered in sweltering heat, with London routinely pushing temperatures above 100 degrees. Australia experienced massive wildfires, fueled by a prolonged drought, turning the sky a fiery red. All these phenomena are the inevitable result of a 150-year period of relentless industrial revolution, fueled by the combustion of coal, oil and gas. These fossil fuels have released so many heat-trapping gases into the atmosphere that average global temperatures are much higher, and for more prolonged periods, than they were in the 1950's. This increase in heat places some 40% of humanity at acute risk. Millions of people in Africa, India, Latin America and the Middle East do not have access to air conditioning, or to a reliable supply of potable water. Indeed, the problem of securing clean drinking water across the planet has become one of the most urgent issues today.

The extreme heat also poses a grave risk to the ability of these continents to grow food and sustain their economic development. In Guatemala, for example, many farmers have seen their harvest of corn and beans wither for three years in a row because of high temperatures and lack of water. Scientists predict that annual rainfall in this region will decrease by as much as 60% in the next 50 years, which will make nations like Guatemala no longer viable for human habitation. In Zambia, the water levels of the Kariba Reservoir dropped 8.3% in 2019, its lowest level in a quarter century. In Greece, the number of days with excessive heat has jumped from 50 in the 1980's to 120 in the 2010's. Even in the United States, many large urban concentrations—such as Houston, Texas—face such a rapid increase in temperatures that they may no longer be livable in one or two decades, if current trends continue.

The New Mass Migrations

The inevitable result, scientists say, will be a mass migration of people on a scale not seen since the end of the last Ice Age. Even moderate projections suggest that by 2030—just ten years from now—some *two billion* people will be on the move. In some ways, it will be a repeat of the massive migration that took place after another major climate change event: the eruption of the volcano on Thira, which devastated trade in the Mediterranean basin and prompted a catastrophic invasion of the Near East by the *Peuples de la Mer*, the "Sea Peoples," or *Shiqalaya* as they are called in Ugaritic texts. Driven by famine on a vast scale, this great mass of poor and marginalized folk went on a desperate search for food that, once bolstered by success, soon degenerated into a naked quest for loot and plunder. They raped, pillaged and killed their way through modern-day Turkey and the Levant, and even came close to destroying the Egyptian Empire led by King Ramses III. Indeed, an off-shoot of these migrants, the Philistines, would very nearly destroy the nascent communities of ancient Israel.

Similarly, many experts believe that the mass migration in the wake of the 2011 Arab Spring was largely driven by drought, famine and systemic unemployment. These effects cascaded around the world, prompting Chancellor Merkel to accept one million refugees (which nearly led to the collapse of her government) while convincing Britons that they would be better off without the European Union.

Projections by Princeton's Michael Oppenheimer show that a similar mass migration could happen in every populated continent in the world, but on a far greater scale. Some models show that some 30 million migrants will head towards the U.S. over the next 30 years, overwhelming border controls. South Asia, where a quarter of the world population lives, will be greatly affected as well. Some 8.5 million people have already fled the region, mostly heading for the Persian Gulf. In all, the World Bank estimates that climate change will produce 143 million more migrants and refugees from Africa, South America, and Southeast Asia by 2050 (Mealy, 2018).

These mass migrations can be stemmed if the region's governments—with the support from the World Bank and the International Monetary Fund—agree to invest massively in creating sustainable employment. Some researchers speak of a "Marshall Plan" for South Asia and the Middle East, which is similar to the way Europe was able to recover from the destruction and displacement caused by World War II through a massive injection of funds. Already, 193 countries have adopted a "Sustainable Development Goals" program that, among other things, aims to improve education and work with global partners to ensure a stable food supply.

The problem is that many governments in these regions are autocratic and beset by corruption. These regimes have traditionally relied on stop-gap measures, such as large infrastructure projects, to temporarily relieve the pressure of systemic unemployment. This is where First World technology and know-how, in addition to funding, can make a critical difference. There are ways to make Third World cities far more livable and affordable, including the provision of sustainable jobs, but the leaders of these nations must embrace such solutions as their utmost priority.

The Rising Seas

Global warming has another devastating effect: melting icecaps near the poles—where the rise in temperatures is now twice as high as anywhere else in the world—will lead to a rise in ocean levels. New research has shown that the displacement of rising tides has been underestimated by a factor of three, affecting 150 to 300 million people globally. These projections indicate that by 2050, much of Vietnam as well as parts of China, Thailand, the Nile Delta, and all of southern Iraq will be under water. In the United States, coastal cities like Miami and Atlantic City will also most likely be inundated. In India, this has led to another change: a shift in the cycle of monsoons, which means that it now rains when the crops are most vulnerable, washing them away or deluging them altogether. Together with the growing threat of global famine, this will prompt another wave of migration into the cities, particularly those at higher sea levels.

Fig. 2. The waterfront of Hong Kong. Estimates suggest that by 2050, much of Asia will be under water.

Today, more than half of the world's population lives in cities, according to the World Bank. That number will rise to 67% by the 2050's. This process has already begun, and by the end of this decade, four out of every ten urban residents will live in slums. At the same time, migrants will move north to escape ever-rising temperatures. Today, most people live within a narrow band where a temperate climate allows for abundant food production. As we have seen, that band will shift inexorably towards the north, and the population will move with it. Much of Latin America will no longer sustain high-volume cultivation, as is the case in West Africa and central China.

The signs are everywhere, such as the massive flooding in the United States as a result of excessive rainfall. According to government data, the U.S. lost some 1.5% of its G.D.P. in 2017 due to weather-related events—and flooding has only increased since then. An even more striking sign is the near-collapse of China's Yangzi basin managed by the Three Gorges Dam. This massive project, completed at eye-popping expense in 2006, was supposed to curtail the growing danger of flooding in the Yangzi basin. The truly biblical scale of flooding in 2020, however, brushed the dam aside and displaced millions of people while destroying some 28,000 homes.

The source of all these rainstorms and hurricanes is the excessive evaporation of the oceans because of global warming, and this can have many unanticipated effects. The rapid rise in moisture levels, for example, is what prompted the explosion of locust swarms in much of Eastern Africa in 2020, which caused over $8.5 billion in damage, according to the World Bank. Even more worrying is the fact that the zone of devastation is expanding, according to estimates by *The Economist* (July 2, 2020).

Some fear that the swarms, which can breed by a factor of 20 in each new generation, may jump the Red Sea and invade Yemen and Saudi Arabia to the northeast, as well as Sudan, Uganda and Tanzania to the west—areas where they will be even more difficult to control. In April of 2020, locusts had already ravaged three million acres of cultivated fields, threatening some 20 million people with famine.

What Can We Do?

What can we do to stop this seemingly inexorable wave of catastrophic effects? Have we waited too long to stem the release of greenhouse emissions? Is the collapse of much of our human civilization a fait accompli?

Here, the scientific community is divided. On the one hand, there are scientists who acknowledge the reality of climate change, but believe it has gone too far to be fully reversed. For example, a NASA *Newsletter* once asked the question, "Is it too late to prevent climate change?" and provided a disturbing answer: "Even if we stopped emitting greenhouse gases today, global warming would continue to happen for at least several more decades, if not centuries,...

because it takes a while for the planet (for example, the oceans) to respond, and because carbon dioxide – the predominant heat-trapping gas – lingers in the atmosphere for hundreds of years." The solution, NASA argued, is a "two-tier approach" involving both mitigation (reducing greenhouse gases) and adaptation ("learning to live with, and adapt to, the climate change that has already been set in motion"). The Intergovernmental Panel on Climate Change also acknowledges that some amount of future global warming is inevitable, and recommends mitigation measures such as cyclone and flood shelters, early warning systems, and sea walls (IPCC, 2018).

Others go even farther, arguing that climate change is here to stay, and that it serves no useful purpose to try to combat it. That is the view of political scientist Bjorn Lomborg, former director of the Danish government's Environmental Assessment Institute and President of the Copenhagen Consensus Center. Lomborg's just-released book, *False Alarm,* claims that we stand to waste trillions of dollars to fight the effects of climate change, and to little effect. "[Climate change] is not like a huge asteroid hurtling towards earth," he writes; "it is instead a long-term chronic condition that needs attention and focus, but one that we can live with." (Lomborg, 2020). The proper response, he argues, is to pump all funds allocated to fighting global warming into turbo-charging the global economy instead. As Lomborg puts it, the private sector has always responded to rapid change, and it will do so again, provided it is unbound by government regulation. After all, he says, it is in the interest of the private sector to preserve and sustain the markets on which it depends. Similarly, Jem Bendel, Professor of Sustainability Leadership at University of Cumbria in Britain, argues that we need to learn to live with climate change through "Deep Adaptation," recognizing that human resilience will enable societies to prevail, so long as we relinquish the belief that endless economic growth is sustainable and restore a simpler way of life (Bendel, 2018).

Most climate scientists vehemently attack such positions as too extreme, arguing that doing nothing will merely accelerate the damage that climate change will inflict on life on our planet. They point out that current carbon dioxide concentrations in the atmosphere are unprecedented since the Pliocene Epoch three million years ago. Among others, these scientists urge the immediate closing of coal-burning electricity generators and other coal-burning facilities. They also appeal to Fortune 1000 corporations—which by themselves are responsible for 14-32% of total emissions—to take immediate action to curtail their own emissions and carbon footprint.

The answer to climate change is far from simple, and requires a systemic approach on all fronts. The private sector needs to embrace leadership in sustainable development, which is the subject of this book. The good news is that some companies are indeed doing so. A major food producer, Unilever, has pledged to use only materials from sustainable sources by 2020, to eliminate single-use plastic packaging by 2025, and to be entirely carbon neutral by 2030. Unilever was prompted to do so after research revealed that it is one of the firms most responsible for plastic pollution in India, the Philippines, and Indonesia. Similarly, another global food producer, Nestlé, has pledged to use sustainable sources and to deploy satellite technology to ensure that no deforestation is taking place anywhere in its supply chain. The Swedish furniture retailer Ikea has also banned single-use plastic products and wants to use 100% renewable energy by 2021 and emission-free home deliveries by 2025. To that end, it has invested $2 billion towards renewable energy projects, including the installation of 750,000 solar panels on Ikea properties. In the United States, former President Trump's decision to withdraw from the 2017 Paris Agreement served as a call to action for many American Fortune 500 companies. Over 2,200 businesses and investors, including Walmart and Apple, formed "We Are Still In," pledging a continued commitment to the Paris Accord—including a goal of net-zero emissions by 2050. Amazon has pledged to bring its emissions down to zero by 2030. In 2021, President Biden signed an executive order whereby the U.S. rejoined the Paris Agreement.

Yet, can private businesses be trusted, on their own, to solve the crisis? As other chapters in this book argue, strong government action is also needed, with the Paris Agreement being one important step in that direction. As an illustration of what we as a global community can accomplish, in 2020 COVID-19 lockdowns around the world lead to a decrease of 2.4 tons of global CO_2 emissions.

Of course, these emissions will rise as the global economy continues to recover, but it shows the potential of a coordinated effort on the part of governments throughout the world to combat climate change. A concerted effort by all nations could conceivably be able to limit the damage of climate change and begin a process of recovery.

These are all hopeful signs, but they will only serve to reduce the ongoing

COVID lockdown causes record decrease in CO_2 emissions for 2020

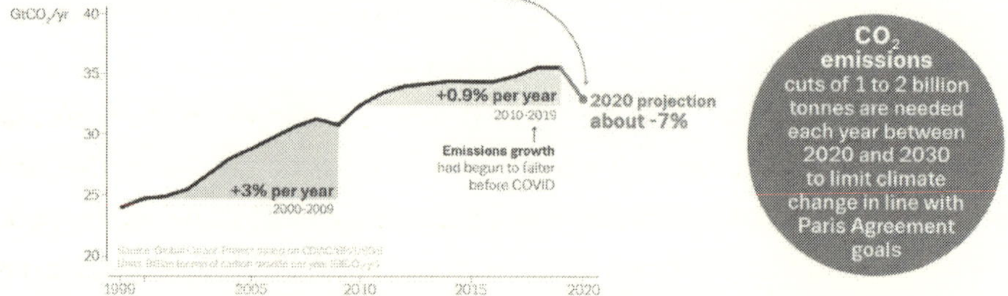

Emissions from road transport cause the largest share of the global 2020 decrease

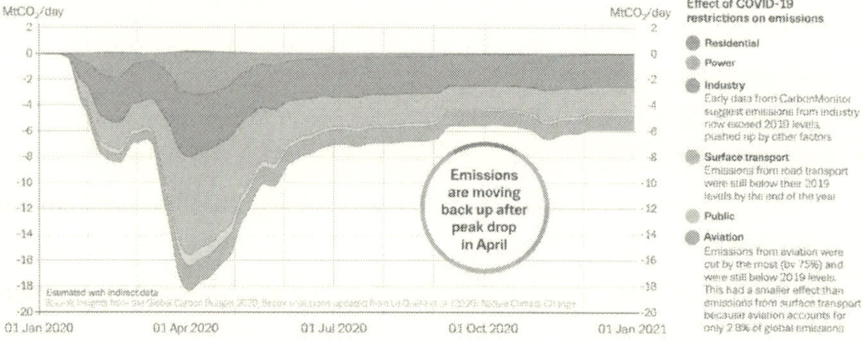

Fig. 3. Reduction in emissions as a result of COVID-19 lockdowns in 2020 (NASA)

effects of climate change. To truly protect the earth from its devastating impact, entirely new technologies will be needed as well. For example, the airline industry—one of the largest producers of carbon emissions—will need to radically embrace a goal of operating zero-emission aircraft in the foreseeable future. The COVID-19 pandemic—which in 2020 grounded as much as 50% to 70% of global air traffic—will give them the painful, but necessary, opportunity to do so. For example, Lufthansa received a $1.7 billion aid package from the German government on condition that part of the funds be used to purchase or lease reduced-emissions aircraft. For Boeing and Airbus, the duopoly of global aircraft manufacturing, this serves as a wake-up call to abandon wasteful jets like the Airbus 380 and focus on creating new airliners that can progressively reduce the carbon footprint of air travel.

Another hopeful sign is a crop of new technologies that aims to tackle one of the most urgent needs today: to secure clean drinking water for all people on the planet. Innovative water treatment and filtration techniques have advanced by leaps and bounds in the last few years, including the use of pressure membranes, nanotechnology filters, and ultraviolet irradiation.

The challenges we face as a result global warming are dire. But the pandemic has given us the opportunity to pause, to reflect on the fragility of human life, and to develop a unified action plan. Ever since the meteor that killed the dinosaurs, human beings have always found ways to respond to catastrophic changes in our climate. This gives us hope that together, we can rise to the challenge and ensure the survival of our species.

Questions for Discussion

1. What role did climate change play in the formation of the Earth?
2. How did humans cope with climate change in the past?
3. Other than rising temperatures and sea levels, what indirect effects can climate change have on our planet?
4. What are the greatest obstacles to implementing a global action plan to combat climate change?
5. What is the private sector doing to mitigate the effects of climate change?
6. Can each of us as citizens play a part in mitigating the effects of climate change?

About the Author

Jean-Pierre Isbouts, D.Litt. is a historian and National Geographic author. He served as professor in the Media Psychology and Human Development Ph.D. programs at Fielding Graduate University and the managing editor of Fielding University Press. Isbouts is the author of more than 15 National Geographic hardcover and softcover books, including the upcoming *Ultimate Visual History of the World.*

References

Bendel, J. (2018) "Deep Adaptation: A Map for Navigating Climate Tragedy," IFLAS Occasional Paper 2, University of Cumbria, UK: Initiative for Leadership and Sustainability(https://mahb.stanford.edu/libraryitem/deep-adaptation-map-navigating-climate-tragedy/)

Bryce, E. (2020, February 14). "If agriculture advances north under climate change, the emissions cost will be huge." *Anthropocene Magazine.*

Crane, L. (2020, May 26). "Asteroid that killed the dinosaurs hit just right for maximum damage." *New Scientist.*

The Economist. (2020, July 2). "Locusts have hit east Africa hard."

Flavelle, C., & Foundatin, H. (2020, August 4) "Hurricane, Fire, Covid-19: Disasters Expose the Hard Reality of Climate Change." *The New York Times.*

Gardiner, B. (2020, March 23). "Coronavirus Holds Key Lessons on How to Fight Climate Change." *Yale Environment 360.*

IPCC (2018) *Special Report: Impacts of 1.5°C of Global Warming on Natural and Human Systems"* IPCC Special Report on Global Warming of 1.5C, ch. 4 (October) (https://www.ipcc.ch/sr15/chapter/chapter-4/)

Isbouts, J. P. (2021). *The Ultimate Visual History of the World. National Geographic*, pp. 30-35.

Lomborg, B. (2020) *False Alarm: How Climate Change Panic Cists Us Trillions, Hurts the Poor, and Fails to Fix the Planet.* Basic Books, pp. 17-18

Mealy, E. (2020, March 19, 2018). "Climate Change Could Force Over 140 Million to Migrate Within Countries by 2050: World Bank Report." *The World Bank.*

Myers, S. L. (2020, August 25). "After Covid, China's Leaders Face New Challenges from Flooding." *The New York Times.*

NASA (n/d) "Is it too late to prevent climate change?" Global Climate Change: Vital Signs of the Planet (https://climate.nasa.gov/faq/16/is-it-too-late-to-prevent-climate-change/)

National Oceanic and Atmospheric Administration. (2020). "2020 Atlantic Hurricane Season takes infamous top spot for busiest on record." November 10.

Rockman, M., & Hritz, C. (2020, April 14). "Expanding use of archaeology in climate change response by changing its social environment." *Proceedings of the National Academy of Sciences of the United States of America.*

University of Guelph. (2020, February 12). "Climate Change to create farmland in the north, but at environmental costs, study reveals." EurekaAlert.org.

CHAPTER 3

Sustainability Leadership and the Problem of Anthropocentrism

David Blake Willis, Four Arrows, and Katrina S. Rogers
Fielding Graduate University
Henry Fowler
Navajo Technical University

Preamble

The subject of this chapter. The Age of the Coronavirus has unleashed a new normal on the world. Unsustainable practices involving animals, natural habitat destruction, and complex global networks highlight the disregard of and depredations by humans toward the environment and have resulted in catastrophic losses. While terrible on their own, these impacts may well pale by comparison with what may be coming next. We now need to do some serious soul-searching for the causes, consequences, and potential solutions for our behavior as *anthropos*, as humans, that can move beyond a singular focus with ourselves at the center. What does Anthropocentrism mean for Sustainability Leadership?

The nature of the study. The goal in this chapter is to situate an understanding of Sustainability Leadership within the context of deep reflection on Anthropocentrism, the cause of many of our problems (including COVID-19). Our disrespect of biodiversity as well as diversity among our fellow human beings has wreaked havoc on our planet. The term *Anthropocene* itself was first used by scientists in the early 2000s (Appelbaum, in this volume) and has now been proposed for our epoch to the International Commission on Stratigraphy for consideration in 2021. How might we date the Anthropocene to delineate our present geological age? Perhaps from the dramatic rise of human population, the accelerated pace of industrial production or the use of agricultural chemicals? Or might it be the nuclear markers of atomic-bomb detonations (Anthropocene vote…, 2019)?

The outcome of this chapter. We hope in this chapter to open the eyes of all of us, especially those who may not yet know the richness and value of Indigenous Wisdom and Traditional Ecological Knowledge. Anthropocentrism and its related concept, the Anthropocene, include philosophical, spiritual, worldview, educational, and policy orientations that reflect deep and abiding influences that need examination and a critical perspective for Sustainability Leaders in the 21st century. Recognition of the impacts of these orientations is reflected in the founding of the journal *Anthropocene* in 2013, whose editors noted at the time that "virtually no place on Earth is left untouched now by human activity" (Chin, Fu, Harbor, Taylor, and Vanacker, 2013), and the creation of *The Anthropocene Review* in 2014. How we understand the choices before us and what we decide to do about them reflect a compelling need to review what we mean by "Sustainability Leadership."

Introduction: An Understanding of Choices - Sustainable Development and Leadership

> *"The grim prognosis for life on this planet is the consequence of a few centuries of forgetting what traditional Indigenous societies knew and the surviving ones still recognize."*
>
> - Noam Chomsky (2013, p. i)

Clear environmental threats and the need for an understanding of the environment that reaches beyond simple cause-and-effect relationships are rapidly moving to center stage for Sustainability Leaders and the consciousness of sophisticated planners, whether they be civilian, governmental, or military. Nearly every predicted indicator of climate change appears to have been deeply under-estimated. The consequences of not planning and not acting when faced with these "wicked problems" are simply unfathomable for Sustainability Leaders (Satterwhite, Miller, and Sheridan, 2015).

At the same time, the fragility of the connections between these environmental problems was long ago appreciated in the wisdom of Indigenous cultures around the planet, communities as diverse as the Kogi of South America (Reddy, 2013; Ereira, 2012; *Aluna*, 2012); the Maasai and Kikuyu of East Africa (Maathai, 2003); and the Aboriginal peoples of Australia, India, and the polar regions. Effective traditional responses include Sahelian herders and their practices, the

Kaitaikitanga ecosystem of environmental management of the Maori (Fulvio, 2020), and the practices of the New Kulanui University (Gaudelli with Ching Fu-Lan, 2016, pp. 107-118). How might we think "outside of the Neo-Darwinian box" (Fuller, 2011)?

The choice for us is between different mental models, with culture representing "patterns of sense-making" a key factor, has been proposed by Hikaru Komatsu, Jeremy Rappleye, and Iveta Silova in their article "Culture and the Independent Self: Obstacles to Environmental Sustainability?" (2019, p. 2). This insightful essay aims to bridge empirical scientific data between the EF (the Ecological Footprint of Consumption) and data on individualistic cultures in order to move us away from the present "apocalyptic trajectory." Culture does affect environmental impacts, which means that it should be a central point of discussion when it comes to sustainability, something indigenous leaders have long known and advocated.

Sustainability Leadership can no longer ignore, dismiss, or sidestep Indigenous Worldviews and their successes in balancing and sustaining natural habitats. Respecting all sentient beings, and the belief that most everything is sentient, may help us to realize that the boundaried relationships between human and other-than-human entities, taken for granted by humans, may no longer be tenable apart from Nature. How might we re-examine the wide philosophical support for a human-centered world from ancient to contemporary philosophers? What non-anthropocentric assumptions exist as outliers in the world? Especially those that are still embraced by traditional Indigenous cultures? Sustainability Leaders can bring forth non-anthropocentrism in their organizations. How might Sustainability Leaders' implement real-life policies in their institutions with an awareness of the assumptions that we have long held?

The Roots of Anthropocentrism

We ask our readers to consider, first of all, the foundational concepts which have brought us to this stage, beginning with a recognition that the Industrial Age – preceded by a Mercantile Age of savage and unforgiveable depredations in the name of God, King, Queen, and human greed for treasure – have brought catastrophic consequences to our diverse and lively world societies. Many of the cultures that remain today, estimated to be approximately 15,000 (Union of International Associations UIA, 2019) are as endangered as the animals, plants, insects, and other members of our larger Biome, that massive, living wonder that is our planet.

Our primary focus for the rest of the 21st Century will be the problem of *Anthropocentrism,* the central cause of disrespecting biodiversity, as well as diversity among human beings. Our prejudice begins with how we have ignored, dismissed and side-stepped Indigenous worldview perspectives which challenge boundaries and borders between ourselves and Nature. The dilemmas of history have led us to "civilization" as problematic, revealing the Anthropocene as a human-dominated era where our numbers and activity have had dramatic, far-reaching impacts, imperiling us as a species. Like earlier geologic eras, the Anthropocene is a specific geological time, in this case either after or part of the late Holocene, which began about 8000 BCE, at the end of the last glacial period (Meyer, 2018). The difference is the human-influenced, or anthropogenic, nature of this era. The word combines the root *anthropo* (human) with *-cene,* the suffix for epoch (please see the three sites mentioned in the References that all begin with 'Welcome to the Anthropocene,' 2011, 2012, 2013; also, the journal *Anthropocene*). It also implies deep-rooted beliefs about nationalism (Bagchi, 1996). Humans may have changed the way the world works, but we now have to change the way we think about how the world works, too.

What are the philosophical, spiritual, educational, worldview, and policy orientations that reflect this influence of anthropocentrism on the world? What colonialisms, external and internal, have been deeply embedded in our souls, to the extent that we are literally killing ourselves, profligately over-consuming and over-extracting the bountiful resources of our planet?

Before the advent of cities, human belief systems were cyclical, derived from the rhythms of the seasons, the migrations of animals, and the repeating patterns of the sun and the moon. Orderliness in this pre-history meant a confidence in the return of phenomena and an appreciation of the roles of all players. Life was seen as an ensemble cast and drama rather than one of heroic protagonists and the story arc of an epic journey. We note here the emphasis on *his*-story, the idea of a heroic journey that begins with the telling of stories, the great epics, that are in the beginning cyclical but that are gradually replaced by singular male-heroic stories. In this sense, Aphrodite and Isis are gradually displaced by Apollo and Osiris, with matriarchal societies pushed to the margins by the patriarchal order. Gods come to dominate theologies rather than Goddesses, and a concern with

Fig. 4. The Blue Marble - First Image of the Earth as a Whole
(NASA, Apollo 17, December 7, 1972)

the existential questions of fate and judgment that parallels the development of cities and civilization evolves into a hierarchy with dominance, a valued and sanctioned approach to society, rather than a communal and balanced view.

What we have lost, too, is an understanding of the role of language, which has become codified and seemingly made permanent by text, rather than by telling. This privileging of the written version of events has empowered only the tellers who have had access to the code. For most of human history, oral, rather than textual, traditions were the primary mode of communicating the order of the universe. We can see this with Sanskrit, and how it is still handed down primarily as a memorized and repeated oral tradition. Humans begin first with oral traditions and our "Mother tongue," and then text, but the modern era has upended this ordering and marginalized the power of the voice.

As humans settled in urban communities, the city, the *civ,* became identified with stability, power, and culture, while those people still living nomadically in cyclical patterns and speaking incomprehensibly were seen as "beyond the

Fig. 5. Aluna, A Message to Little Brother from the Kogi People (Alexander Rieser, 2012)

pale." Without "Barbarians," the wandering souls or tribes who speak a *"ba-ba"* tongue, we cannot have "Civilization," the "people of the city." Moreover, when cultural traditions became associated with the supposedly inerrant traditions of *The Book (The Bible)*; the *Analects*; and then, later, the Charter of the Company, beginning with the Dutch East Indies Company and, soon afterwards, the British East India Company, the received wisdom became male, linear, and predatory.

The Age of Colonialism or Imperialism is also the beginning of what might be called the Capitalocene (Hayman, 2018, p. 78). Predatory Capitalism utilizes a clear dictum in the Bible, which has been affirmed by Christians, Jews, and Muslims alike that clearly indicates and dictates human separation from and dominance over Nature:

> *God blessed them and said to them, 'Be fruitful and increase in number; fill the earth and subdue it. Rule over the fish of the sea and the birds of the air and over every living creature that moves on the ground* (Genesis 1:28).

It is worthwhile to take a moment here to reflect on the significance of religious and spiritual beliefs, to understand more clearly the role they play in the maintenance of anthropocentrism. Rebirth or reincarnation has been featured in most Indigenous traditions. Beliefs in reincarnation can be found from India, Amerindians, and elsewhere, cyclical epistemologies prevalent in the "pre-history" of humanity (Olson,1949). In contrast, all of the major Abrahamic religions offer inconsistent or unclear ideas about whether or not animals or plants have souls. Even where such a belief exists, humans are generally regarded as superior beings in the scheme of things. Most have fully dismissed the idea of reincarnation; interestingly, the separation of humans and animals was reinforced by the removal of the concept of reincarnation from Christianity at the Council of Nicea in 325.

Rebirth, the Problem of Sentience, and the Dance of Time

The widespread philosophical support for a human-centered world from ancient to contemporary philosophers is now giving way to a return to pre-textual, pre-historical visions that include this idea of rebirth, cycles, and our natural connections with the non-human world. The interplay of the human and plant worlds is spoken of, for example, by the ubiquitous depictions in South Asian art of the beautiful Ashoka tree intertwined with female deities, the *yakshi* or *shalabhanjika*. Frequently seen in South Asian art, this belief has it that a tree blossoms only when it is kicked hard by a *shalabhanjika*, a young maiden (Tudge, 2006, also remarked on this in his treatise on trees and fertility; see also Gupta, 1971, p. 96).

The associations of trees with good fortune and fertility ("touch wood, knock on wood") are of course well known and deeply embedded in Shinto, Buddhism, and Hinduism. It is also related to health and well-being, as we see in the Japanese concept of *shinrin yoku* or forest bathing. Sufi and Zen have similar traditions, as revealed in the writings of Peter Matthiessen (*The Snow Leopard,* 2008) and Jonathan Balcombe (2011, 2017), who explore the journey of altering our consciousness about creatures ordinarily seen as simply having been created for our exploitation. As with many Indigenous traditions, animals are, in fact, sentient in the Great Chain of Being, a chain no longer seen as hierarchical and created solely for our exploitation (see Lovejoy, 1933, 2010) but as horizontal and interwoven with connections suggesting an ensemble cast instead of a prime hero at the center of the narrative. Seemingly inanimate "objects" like trees and creatures supposedly devoid of consciousness like fish take on a whole new realm of consciousness in this understanding (Wohlleben, 2016 a, b; Balcombe, 2017).

We note here, too, that there is a body of theoretical literature in environmental education about the dangers of anthropocentrism, yet little of this has found its way into the discussion on diversity and inclusion: In fact, it is almost entirely absent. Diversity is consistently conceptualized as being exclusively about honoring human differences in race, ethnicity, sexual orientation, gender, socio-economic status, age, ability, and unique experiential background, religious or political beliefs. In other words, diversity is seen as a human issue alone. This, despite the fact that many of the great activists of our time— Wangari Maathaai, J. Krishnammal, S. Jagannathan (Coppo, 2004), and other recipients of the Right Livelihood Award (2020, the Alternative Nobel Peace Prize), have blended their views on the environment with concepts about human societies.

Unlike Abrahamic religious beliefs, Buddhism, Hinduism, and other South Asian spiritual traditions view humans as having lived before as other-than-human entities and all life forms as sentient, similar to Indigenous Peoples (See the *Jatakas* and the *Panchatantra*). Certain other Eastern religions, especially Jainism, view not only humans but animals and even plants as endowed with consciousness and belonging to a larger order of sentient existence. This karmic eschatology in Indic traditions represents a much stronger affiliation with non-human life than the oft-stated compassion put forth in Abrahamic traditions. Indic traditional beliefs, of course, also see human incarnation as *karmic progress* from insects, plants and animal to human; or in reverse, depending on one's karma. Furthermore, both Eastern and Western religious teachings tend to see escape from the Earth and from earthly existence as the primary goal of life on Earth.

Most Indigenous cultures have similar rebirthing eschatological beliefs, which influence how other-than-human sentient beings are treated, but that are somewhat different from these Indic ones (though they also discuss the transmigration of souls). The constant blurring of human-animal categories and the empathy that humans are expected to have toward animals are based on the important eschatological assumption of "an originally undifferentiated universe in which the boundaries between the human and nonhuman, the spiritual and material, were shifting and permeable," quite unlike the Christian assumption that animals have no souls (Obeyesekere, 2002, p. 45). In fact, many Indigenous cultures see non-human sentient beings as teachers with intimate, protective, and benevolent qualities. Antonia Mills and Richard Clobodin's scholarly work on reincarnation beliefs among North American Indians reports that transmigration would be expected because of "the basic premise that animal life forms are as sentient and evolved as human" (Mills 2008, p. 34).

Aside from eschatological assumptions, Western philosophy itself has supported our current anti-nature and exclusively human-centered behavior. Although European thinkers see the Greeks as their intellectual forebears, the pre-Socratic Greeks themselves looked toward the East for sources of wisdom. Most Greek scholarship related to the founding of Western philosophy, however, has focused and continues to focus on ideas that separate human life from non-human life.

Sustainability Leadership and *Phronesis* (Practical Wisdom)

Traditional Indigenous Wisdom in many cultures thus focuses on a circular logic of renewal and rebirth, which our recent concern with sustainability has revived. Sustainability returns logic to our past, renews more matriarchal understandings of life, and provides a powerful metaphor for our predicament as a species in the Age of the Anthropocene. The extent of the challenges and the rapid timing with which Sustainability is teaching us indicates that the time has come to begin the hard work of balancing human needs with those of other species and of our physical and geological home. Yet the powerful dominance of hero-centered narratives continues to be the predominant image even in Sustainability Leadership. Even luminaries like Greta Thunberg are put into this perspective, despite their views to the contrary.

We may want to give new attention to the Greek idea of *phronesis*, or practical wisdom, as a way to reveal actionable values, practices, and processes associated with Sustainability Leadership (Stillman, 2015; see also the Center for Practical Wisdom at the University of Chicago). Values and norms for activism and conservation (LeGrand, 2015) revive traditional understandings of the universe when it comes to environmental sustainability. Thus we face a stark, existential question as Sustainable Leaders: *Can societies encourage sufficient changes in human lifestyles to avert ecological collapse?*

What is needed now is a "deep sustainability leadership"(Schein, 2015) and the motivation to influence behavior and capacity leading to large-scale transformational change. Schein explored this through interviews with 65 Corporate Sustainability Leaders in more than 40 multinational corporations, NGOs, and consultancies. Utilizing fields as diverse as integral ecology, deep ecology, and eco-psychology, he saw the need to move away from "the ecocentric–anthropocentric continuum" or what he calls anthropocentric blindness to "the eco-psychological foundations" for thought and action.

Moreover, this holistic way of seeing is what Four Arrows, his daughter, and his grandson saw early on, with the words and title of a collaborative article they did together in 2010 reflecting this: "Anthropocentrism's Antidote: Reclaiming Our Indigenous Orientation to Non-human Teachers." The need for leadership to move to this vision of ecological sustainability, with the understanding that financial, social, and natural systems are interconnected, has also been foregrounded by Alice MacGillivray (2015). In her work, also found in this volume, *boundary* is seen as the central concept in systems thinking, with an emphasis on how leaders understand and work with boundaries.

The edges of organizations and groups can be seen as places for the mixing of diverse ideas to enable learning and innovation, just as the edges in nature can be places for the mixing of diverse nutrients and species to enable high productivity. On a local level, the emergence of women who are sustainability entrepreneurs, as reported by Jo-Anne Clarke (2015), gives us pause and hope for enhancing community and improving the health of our planet, too. Sustainability Leadership is, therefore, not only about the environment, ecological fragility, and balance (viz. Willis, Steier, and Stillman, 2015), but also about a return to Indigenous Wisdom. This, of course, threatens the established patriarchal order, not least in the corridors of economic power. Cultivating a systemic understanding, a holistic way of seeing and acting that is so often identified with Indigenous perspectives, stands in stark contrast to a more industrial-era, reductionistic way of knowing.

This way of understanding appears as cyclical in most cultures regardless of their spiritual or religious orientations. The wisdom of the *Tandava*, the classic Dance of Shiva of the God Nataraja, that Ananda Coomaraswamy (1918) has described so well, speaks of the power of the moment, as does the Japanese concept of *ichigo-ichie*, those once in a lifetime meetings, moments, and chances, as the being and becoming that continually unfolds. Likewise, in China, Japan, and Korea, the back and forth flow of powerful centers alternates with times of fragmented states, continually returning, helping us understand that it is indeed the circle, the cycle, that we are a part of, and will always return to, as members of human societies. We will have to evolve further with the changing climate and environmental conditions of the Anthropocene, a psycho-cultural transformation that authors like Susanne Moser model as an archetypal death-rebirth process. Or should we say 'Anthropocenes" (Geological, Biological, Social, and Cultural), as Tuukka Toivonen and his colleagues suggest to us (2017). Put in scientific language, this is a "tripartite progression of severance, threshold, and reincorporation (which) provides a map for navigating the *terra quasi-incognita* of this transformation" (Berzonsky & Moser, 2017).

Fig. 6. Nataraja - The Tandava Dance of Time of the God Nataraja, Lord of the Dance (Art Gallery, Thanjavur, India, David Blake Willis)

This does not mean, however, that we should simply accept our fate, a view nineteenth century European colonials had of Indians and other Asians which they termed fatalism. Such interpretations, of course, privilege Western interpretations and do a disservice to local agency and action. We thus embrace circulation as cultural *process* and search here for new imaginations and, even more critically, interrogations, probing for new vistas and perspectives to help us understand what has been happening. This is a reimagining for Sustainability Leaders with the 21st century in mind, a new era that has moved us to approaches to social phenomena that are multilateral, multipolar, and multicultural. As mixing, mashing, hybridities, and creolizations assert themselves, like the destructive yet creative Dance of Shiva, newness springs up and the possibility emerges to realize that what is "new" is actually "old."

Sustainability Leadership and Worldview Reflection: The Indigenous Perspective

Traditional Indigenous approaches to learning about life skills and values have much to teach us about Sustainability Leadership. They had as their paramount idea that humans are intimately related to non-human life forms. Honoring and learning from animals, plants, birds, bodies of water and the fish that dwell in them were inseparable from any learning experience and from any life application of that learning. Moreover, from the Indigenous perspective, humans are the younger brothers and sisters of the non-human elders of creation and the non-human elders are our teachers. In describing how Indigenous cultures see us as "lesser beings in the democracy of species," in her book *Braiding Sweetgrass,* Robin Wall Kimmerer asks what the world would be like if educators and scientists saw plants and animals as teachers rather than subjects (2013, p. 347). She, like Noam Chomsky, and a growing number of scholars, believes that if we continue to reject this view, our prospects for survival are marginal. Instead, acknowledging interrelatedness and reciprocity with an attitude of giving that reflects a sense of interconnectedness and interdependence with nature enables us to establish a sustainable "return of the gift" (Fulvio, 2020).

Four Indigenous precepts related to living in ways that are not anthropocentric can inform Sustainability Leaders; these include:

1) Respect for the significance of all life.

2) Believing in the complementarity of opposites.

3) Avoidance of hierarchy.
4) Taking only what is needed from our non-human relations.

This is "a paradigm shift toward a solidarity economy" (Boggs, 2011, 2012, p. 169) which facilitates, at its foundation, the production and exchange of goods that communities really need to sustain themselves. What might "practices to promote interdependent selfhood" (Komatsu, Rappleye, and Silova, 2019) be that lead us collectively to sustainability?

First, when one lives in a way where they see a tree as a relative (rather than a resource), diversity and inclusion, as relates to fellow human-beings, follows. Couple this with the concept of Earth as our Mother and with the prevalence of matriarchal cultures and we can understand why most pre-contact cultures were "gender-egalitarian and consensus-based societies, actively promoting peace and sustainability by various well-conceived guidelines relating to their economic, social, political and cultural features" (Goettner-Abendroth, 2018, p. 4). The scholars who contributed to Goettner-Abendroth's (2009) earlier edited volume *Societies of Peace* reveal that such societies were also non-violent and practiced great respect for all living creatures without exploitation of humans, animals or nature. They "revered women as sources of knowledge, cultural progenitors and influential decision-makers because of their ability to bear children, teach the family and contribute to their communities" (Smith, 2008, p. 575; see also Smylie, Olding, & Ziegler, 2014). Prior to European contact, "violence against women was nearly unheard of but was dealt with seriously when it did occur" (Smith, 2008).

Second, re-embracing such notions of diversity requires re-learning a new level of respect for other-than-human life in a "complementary duality." Hillary S. Webb (2012) contrasts this with Western binary models that see opposites as incompatible "and are therefore engaged in an eternal antagonism and struggle for dominance" (p. 2). This idea of complementarity is foundational to the Indigenous Worldview and its understanding that all forms of Nature have varying degrees and kinds of sentience. "The Twinned Cosmos pervades every facet of Indigenous philosophy... "Everything that exists exists by halves... inseparable and mutually reinforcing...When the Twinship stops, the Cosmos crumbles" (Mann, 2016, pp. 242-243). Consider the natural symbiotic dynamics of blood and breath, air and water, or male and female.

This is not a claim that everything is automatically in balance. To the contrary, balance points are always shifting. Creative tensions are always happening between complementary opposites, and this is where Sustainability Leaders need to focus their attention. Consider, for example, the tension between dominant and Indigenous worldviews as it relates to human-centeredness. We are not trying to find a balance between them, *per se,* but rather are trying to understand where complementarity exists. It is like seeing the differences in blood and breath, finding the problem in the blood that can put it back into harmony with the breath. The Cherokee Indians in 19th century Georgia adopted settler lifestyles in ways that still allowed them to hold onto their traditional beliefs. This allowed for a relative balance between cultures. At least until the Euro-Americans discovered gold, leading to a mindset of materialism, greed, and, ultimately, the Trail of Tears.

Third, the prevalent idea of hierarchy in the dominant worldview is also problematic. Hierarchical worldview leads to domination of others, not inclusion. Harmony does not result from people following the directions of "superiors," but rather from following "Pathways." Indigenous Pathways can be seen as a structural metaphor for learning to live life optimally and for the greater good: "In traveling a Pathway we make stops, encounter and overcome obstacles, recognize and interpret signs, seek answers and follow the tracks of entities that have something to teach us" (Cajete, 1994, p. 55). Internalizing what is learned comes from critical thinking, planning, implementation of resultant choices and reflection, for assuring the right path is being followed. Learning does not come from authoritarian mandates.

In this context, the concept of humility is an important quality that can be embodied by Sustainability Leaders. A number of research studies have concluded that humble leaders, inspire great teamwork and focus on organizational goals and listen more effectively than leaders who do not score high on humility (Hyman, 2018). Behaviors that are seen as humble include such actions as asking for feedback, active listening, and generating among others an understanding of employee needs. Friedman et. al. outlined the six characteristics of humility in leadership: listening, delegating, accepting responsibility, compassion/altruism, desire to contribute, and not retaliating in the workplace (2017, p. 60). All of these qualities are aligned with many of the tenets noted above in Indigenous thinking about listening, understanding, and caring for others.

Furthermore, this learning journey is based on assumptions about the beautiful gift of diverse and inclusive life on Mother Earth. For example, the Navajo believe that good life resides in every angle of the morning light with a promising sense of beauty, hope and determination for every individual. The Navajo understand that with a sense of the complementary and the supplementary, an individual will feel beauty above, below, around and before, and behind - from every angle. This perspective stems from the natural surroundings; plants, animals, rivers, mountains, and sky. These are what bring forth the energy of spirit that aligns with the purpose of life, to keep balance, harmony and respect with the natural order.

The only true authority for living life well comes from this Spiritual energy, although wise elders who still remember the old ways can help with their knowledge of songs, prayers, ceremonies, and oral storytelling of the Navajo Creation Story. This story frames the Navajo epistemology as coming from the womb of Mother Earth, Father Sky, Sacred Mountains, Darkness and Day, White and Yellow Corn, Corn Pollen Boy, Beetle Girl, Changing Woman, First Man and Woman, Fire, Water, and Air. It comes from realizing that every aspect of life is an integral part of the whole that includes tiny insects, rivers, trees, mountains, and canyons, all of which are part of the elements that complete the natural order of the universe.

Finally, the fourth precept has to do with connecting life to an absence of greed. Indigenous understandings including knowing that life must consume life in order to continue, but taking more than one needs, without great respect and expressed gratitude leads to dire consequences. The consequences include developing hierarchy, forgetting complementarity, disrespecting diversity, and restricting inclusion. This is why the taking of animals, birds, fish, and plants for food is accompanied by stories about the wisdom of each life-giver and ceremonies to remind of our oneness with them and to give deep gratitude for the sacrifice made.

The Pueblo Indians' stories teach us, for example, that each animal has a spirit village. When hunted and killed, their spirits return to this village and tell how they were treated by the hunter. If treated inappropriately, the village might decide to stop giving themselves to humans. The Hopi, with a deep understanding of the corn plant and its spiritual power, practiced elaborate, artful ceremonies in honor of each stage of planting and harvesting.

Whether killing a deer, harvesting corn, picking berries, digging up roots, or consuming our relations, traditional Indigenous cultures prioritize thinking about ways of consuming that are just. Robin Wood Kimmerer (2013) expresses the idea beautifully in *Braiding Sweetgrass* when talking about gathering wild berries:

> I live vicariously through the through the photosynthesis of others. I am not the vibrant leaves on the forest floor-I am the woman with the basket and how I fill it is a question that matters. If we are fully awake, a moral question arises as we extinguish the other lives around us on behalf of our own. Whether we are digging wild leeks or going to the mall, how do we consume in a way that does justice to the lives we take? (p. 177)

What intentional actions can Sustainability Leaders do now to start this process, that can help us live in ways that truly see how Indigenous understandings of biodiversity create social systems that reflect great respect for human diversity and inclusion?

A Radical Indigenous Policy Framework for Sustainability Leadership

"If we are going to heal, let it be glorious" - Beyoncé (Villanueva, 2018)

Critical awareness about humanity's place in the ecosystem and employment of Indigenous worldviews will enable Sustainability Leaders to tap into our ancestral knowledge and promote international and collaborative partnerships. Evolution builds from what is already available, and the wisdom of our ancient ancestors, which is still available to us, can be a special teacher if we listen carefully. Thus, to reshape anthropocentrism from continuing to allow the destruction of life systems that disregard the intrinsic value of non-human life forms, we can re-embrace the worldview that kept us from destroying the planet for thousands of years. The key is to draw from the deep well of Indigenous knowledge still available in the world. Stepping up to this challenge and opportunity can best be approached by setting policy frameworks that see leadership as being informed by Indigenous Knowledge.

Committing to traditional Indigenous leadership requires sensitivity to those who still, against all odds, possess the knowledge. This means adopting a simultaneous commitment to protecting Indigenous rights, ending settler colonization that continues to oppress First Nations sovereignty, and accessing Indigenous sources whenever possible. Books such as *Teaching Truly: A Curriculum to Indigenous Mainstream Education* (Four Arrows, 2013) and *Indigenous Sustainable Wisdom: First Nation Know-how for Global Flourishing* (Narvaez and Four Arrows, 2019) can be of use, especially when there are local Indigenous People present.

Here, we speak for leaders throughout organizations and societies, advocating similar steps for Sustainability Leadership. Elsewhere, we have argued for the importance of an Indigenous policy framework for education and educators (Four Arrows, Rogers, Willis, & Fowler, 2020). One example in education is the green strides program that emerged from the Green Ribbon Schools Program, which was created as a result of the advocacy of 80 non-governmental organizations (ED Program, 2018). Originally an award program, the "Green Strides Initiative" was added to connect all school communities with free, publicly available resources from a variety of sources. The Green Strides portal was created for access to resources, webinars, case studies, promising practices, and collaboration so that all schools could make progress toward achieving the goals of the award. Supporting environmentally responsible practices by saving energy and water, improving indoor air quality, and fostering an appreciation among future generations of environmentally sustainable practices should be something all Sustainability Leaders practice in their organizations.

Sustainability Leaders and citizens can also advocate for Sustainability Leadership in many ways in their own Commons and Public Trusts, whether it be local, regional, or national:

1) Appreciate Indigenous perspectives on ways of living together and using resources sustainably.
2) Appreciate the role of Indigenous Knowledge and traditional ways of learning in maintaining the sustainability of a community.
3) Understand the role of "modern" education and media in undermining Indigenous Knowledge and ways of teaching and learning.
4) Identify opportunities for integrating relevant aspects of Indigenous Knowledge and approaches to teaching and learning in school curricula and in organizational practices.

Four different approaches to sustainability have been envisioned by Preiser, Pereira, and Biggs (2017), which they frame as the eco-modernist paradigm, the planetary stewardship paradigm, the pathways to sustainability approach, and the critical post-humanist paradigm. They suggest seeing "the Anthropocene as responsibility" as a deeper underlying frame which enables us to engage with an ethic of responsibility for being human and acting on the planet, something we have been advocating here for Sustainability Leaders, as well. A good example is the FSSD, the Framework for Strategic Sustainable Development, a resource for supporting the shift to sustainability that has been applied to the ecomunicipality of Whistler, B.C., Canada (Baugher, Osika, and Robèrt, 2016).

In all of these approaches, reciprocity and caretaking are emphasized in what Mazzocchi Fulvio (2020) calls a "polycentric laboratory for sustainability… a pluralist space in which multiple cultural expertise can interact and mutually enrich, yet maintain distinction and integrity." We propose further to see "the future as cultural fact" (Appadurai, 2013), an era and a charge for Sustainability Leaders of aspiration, anticipation, and imagination. Here, again, the power of Indigenous Wisdom enables us to peer seven generations ahead just as it helps us to see seven generations behind as well.

How might we move, then, beyond what has been called "the techno-human condition" (Allenby and Sarewitz, 2011) or the converging technologies of "Humanity 2.0" (Fuller, 2011) to what the great social activist Grace Lee Boggs (2011, 2012) envisioned as sustainable activism for the 21st century? Soedjatmoko, the first Rector of the United Nations University and Indonesian revolutionary, reminds us here of the roles of power and morality, of different ways of knowing, and of our capacity for transcendence in global transformation (Newland and Soedjatmoko, 1994). Soedjatmoko's main life goal was something we should be reaching for now: an ethical framework for a common humanity.

Biology, theology, and spirituality will need to be reinvented, as Fuller (2011) reminds us, just as we will also need realignment and radical adjustment in what is certainly an age of "wicked complexity" (Allenby and Sarewitz, 2011). This suggests, of course, nothing less than a map for global citizenship as practice and praxis (Gaudelli, 2016) that will need to focus on decolonizing wealth, with Indigenous wisdom leading the way in healing divides and restoring balance. It includes what Edgar Villanueva (2018) calls "bringing the oppressor into the circle of healing" with compassion by drawing on Native traditions with the seven steps for how to heal: grieve, apologize, listen, relate, represent, invest, and repair. Such an approach also embraces the deep sense of interconnectedness with all life in the universe that the Lakota sacred prayer invokes when they say *Mitákuye Oyás'iŋ*, which means all are related.

Three conceptual domains need to be prominent if we are to grapple with the needs of this "era of deep transformation": liminality, performance, and dialogue (Holzmer, 2013). Indigenous communities have long emphasized all three of these in the creative, yet practical, functioning of their societies. Generative tension is central to dialogue as transformative process, something commemorated and ritualized by Indigenous societies.

The prospects are good. Michael Tomasello's (2019) magisterial, data-driven study titled, *Becoming Human: A Theory of Ontogeny,* identifies eight pathways for human cognition and human sociality that give us hope: Social Cognition, Communication, Cultural Learning, Cooperative Thinking, Collaboration, Prosociality, Social Norms, and Moral Identity. That these represent the preponderance of what it means to be human became very clear during the COVID-19 pandemic of 2020. We have, on important occasions, been able to come together, in shared agency, to address deep, even catastrophic circumstances, particularly outside the United States. Moreover, this shared agency has also occurred at times of emerging, transformational leadership that has moved beyond command-and-control and the hero model (Satterwhite, Miller, and Sheridan, 2015, p. 65, Table 1, p. 71; Schuyler, Wheatley, Scharmer, Schein, Quinn, and Senge, 2016). We await that time in the United States, and in other nations that are challenged as well, revealing the need for "new models of leadership practice" (Schuyler, et al, 2016) that aim to create meaning and coherence in the midst of upheavals and uncertainty.

Thus we advocate for the integration of applied Indigenous Knowledge and Indigenous Wisdom into Sustainability Leadership practices. Initiatives going forward should be framed more broadly to include Indigenous knowledge. Resources for leaders for their ongoing professional development are a key to this success. At the local, organizational, or regional levels, it will be important to make the case that Indigenous knowledge is a component of diversity and inclusion as well. Knowledge needs to be holistically understood and diverse perspectives cultivated in order to create a sustainable future for all of humanity. It is a radical shift, one that requires our full attention as Sustainability Leaders

Fig. 7. Worldviews - Reaching for the Sky (Word Press, 2013/07/17/worldview/)

as we move beyond anthropocentrism towards a deeper understanding of our place and our role on our planet.

Questions for Discussion

1. What do Sustainability Leaders need for their next steps in transitioning to a balance that will empower and support the rest of the planet?
2. What will it take for humanity to support a transition to a collaborative view of sharing for our planet?
3. How might Sustainability Leaders convince naysayers who argue for a continued focus on development and exploitation of resources, both human and natural?
4. What steps are needed to bring all parties into the circle of change required for sustainability?
5. Traditional Indigenous spirituality embraces the idea that other-than-human life forms are the greatest teachers for human beings. Can you think of any

examples how this might be so?
6. Why is self-interest versus intrinsic value of non-humans not the best way to implement a non-anthropocentric perspective?
7. What would it mean for sustainability leaders to approach their work in the spirit of humility?

*An earlier version of this chapter, which we have edited and adapted here for this book, appeared as Four Arrows, Rogers, K., Willis, D., & Fowler, H. (2020). Our Human-Centered Focus Is Killing Us, in *Toward Critical Environmental Education: Where are we now? Current and Future Perspectives.* Eds. Steinberg, S., Gkiolmas, R.S. and Skordoulis, C.S. (eds.). Amsterdam: New York: Springer Publishing. We have also substantially drawn from Four Arrows (2019), The Media Have Missed a Crucial Message of the UN's Biodiversity Report, *The Nation*, May 20, 2019; Hikaru Komatsu, Jeremy Rappleye, and Iveta Silova. (2019), Culture and the Independent Self: Obstacles to Environmental Sustainability? *Anthropocene* 26, pp. 1-13; and Richard Appelbaum's chapter at the beginning of this book.

About the Authors

David Blake Willis, PhD, is Professor of Anthropology and Education at Fielding Graduate University and Professor Emeritus of Anthropology at Soai Buddhist University in Japan. His interests in anthropology, sustainability, social justice, and immigration come from 37 years living in traditional cultural systems in Japan and India. He researches and writes on transformational leadership and education, Creolization, comparative education, citizenship, transcultural communities, and Dalit/Gandhian liberation movements in South India. His publications include *World Cultures: The Language Villages* (Tertium Quid, 2016); *Modern Strategies for Sustainability Leadership* (Fielding, 2016); *Reimagining Japanese Education: Borders, Transfers, Circulations, and the Comparative* (Oxford Studies in Comparative Education, 2011); *Transcultural Japan: At the Borders of Race, Gender, and Identity* (Routledge, 2007); and *Japanese Education in Transition 2001: Radical Perspectives on Cultural and Political Transformation* (Adelaide Shannon, 2002).

Four Arrows, identifying as Irish, Cherokee and Lakota, is internationally known for his work in promoting Indigenous worldview and critical inquiry. Formerly Dean of Education at Oglala Lakota College, he is currently in the School of Leadership Studies at Fielding Graduate University. His publications include *Unlearning the Language of Conquest* (University of Texas, 2008); *The Authentic Dissertation: Alternative Ways of Knowing, Research and Representation* (Routledge, 2008); *Critical Neurophilosophy and Indigenous Wisdom* with Greg Cajete and Jongmin Lee (Sense, 2010); *Teaching Truly: A Curriculum to Indigenize Mainstream Education* (Peter Lang, 2013); *The Red Road: Linking Diversity and Inclusion Initiatives to Indigenous Worldview* (IAP, 2020).

Katrina S. Rogers, PhD, is President of Fielding Graduate University in Santa Barbara, CA. As faculty, she has taught in her field in global environmental politics and policy, social movements, research, and theory. In the course of her career, Rogers has served in many roles, including executive, board member, and teacher. She led the European campus for Thunderbird School of Global Management in Geneva, Switzerland for a decade, working with international organizations such as the Red Cross, World Trade Organization, United Nations Development Program, and the European Union. She also developed externships for students at several companies, including Renault, Nestle, and EuroDisney (now Disneyland Paris). She holds doctorates in political science and history. In addition to many articles focused on organizational leadership in sustainability, Rogers currently serves on the Boards of Prescott College, the Master's in Sustainability Advisory Group for Northern Arizona University, the Toda Institute for Global Policy & Peace Research, and the Public Dialogue Consortium. She has also worked with the Arboretum at Flagstaff and Grand Canyon Trust. She received a Presidential post-doctoral fellowship from the Humboldt Foundation and was a Fulbright scholar to Germany where she taught environmental politics and history.

Dr. Henry Fowler is Dean of Graduate Studies and Faculty Member at Navajo Technical University, teaching mathematics and Diné studies. He was recently appointed to Navajo Nation Board of Education (NNBE) as the Diné culture and language specialist. Each year, Dr. Fowler presents the Navajo Math Circles for students ages 11-18, a two-week mathematics learning camp that brings together Navajo culture with math. He is the co-founder and co-chair of the summer camp that aims to increase enthusiasm for the often-challenging subject to Navajo students. Originally from Tonalea, AZ, Dr. Fowler has been influential in helping students on the Navajo nation to become fluent with math while integrating the traditional aspects. His clans are Tódich'ii'nii (Bitter Water Clan) born for Tóbaahi Náneesht'ézhí (Zuni Edgewater clan). His maternal grandparents are Tł'ízí lání (Manygoats clan) and his paternal grandparents are Táchii'nii (Red running into the water clan). He earned his Bachelor's and Master's degrees in math from Northern Arizona University and an Educational Doctorate from Fielding Graduate University.

References

Allenby, Braden R., and Sarewitz, Daniel. (2011). *The Techno-Human Condition.* The MIT Press.

Anthropocene Vote, Pollution Cover-Up and Quark Pioneer. (2019). The Week in Science: 24–30 May 2019, *Nature,* 29 May, https://www.nature.com/articles/d41586-019-01677-7

Appadurai, Arjun. (2013). *The Future as Cultural Fact: Essays on the Global Condition.* Verso.

Bagchi, Alaknanda. (1996). Conflicting Nationalisms: The Voice of the Subaltern in Mahasweta Devi's Bashai Tudu. *Tulsa Studies in Women's Literature*, Vol. 15, no. 1, pp. 41-50.

Balcombe, Jonathan. (2011). *Second Nature: The Inner Lives of Animals*. St. Martin's Griffin.

Balcombe, Jonathan. (2017). *What a Fish Knows: The Inner Lives of Our Underwater Cousins.* Farrar, Straus and Giroux.

Baugher, John Eric, Osika, Walter, and Robèrt, Karl-Henrik. (2016). Ecological Consciousness, Moral Imagination, and the Framework for Strategic Sustainable Development, pp. 119-142, in Schuyler, Kathryn Goldman, Baugher, John Eric, and Jironet, Karin. (Eds.). (2016). *Creative Social Change: Leadership for a Healthy World.* Emerald Group Publishing.

Berzonsky, Carol, and Moser, Susanne C. (2017). Becoming Homo Sapiens: Mapping the Psycho-Cultural Transformation in the Anthropocene, *Anthropocene,* Vol. 20, December, pp. 15-23, https://doi.org/10.1016/j.ancene.2017.11.002

Boggs, Grace Lee, with Kurashige, Scott. (2011, 2012). *The Next American Revolution: Sustainable Activism for the Twenty-First Century.* University of California Press.

Cajete, Greg. (1994). *Look to the Mountain: An Ecology of Indigenous Education.* Kivaki Press.

Center for Green Schools. (2018). *What We Do.* Retrieved from http://centerforgreenschools.org/what-we-do.

Center for Practical Wisdom, University of Chicago (2020). Center for Practical Wisdom, Home Page, See https://www.uchicago.edu/research/center/the_center_for_practical_wisdom/

Chomsky, Noam. (2013). Cover Endorsement for Four Arrows. *Teaching Truly: A Curriculum to Indigenize Mainstream Education.* Peter Lang.

Chin, Anne, Fu, Rong, Harbor, Jon, Taylor, Mark P., and Vanacker, Verle. (2013). Anthropocene: Human Interactions with Earth Systems, *Anthropocene*, Vol. 1, September, pp.1-2.

Clarke, Jo-Anne. (2015). The Integrative Entrepreneur: A Lifeworld Study of Women Sustainability Entrepreneurs, pp. 202-233, in Willis, David Bake, Steier, Fred, and Stillman, Paul, Eds. *Modern Strategies for Sustainability Leadership.* Fielding University Monographs, Volume 5. Fielding University Press.

Coomaraswamy, Ananda. (1918). *The Dance of Shiva.* https://babel.hathitrust.org/cgi/pt?id=nyp.33433082246665;view=1up;seq=10

Coppo, Laura. (2004). *The Color of Freedom: Overcoming Colonialism and Multinationals in India.* Common Courage Press.

ED Program. (2018). *U.S. Department of Education Green Ribbon School.* Retrieved from https://www2.ed.gov/programs/green-ribbon-schools/index.html.

Ereira, Alan. (2012). *Aluna (Conscience)/The Kogi.* www.alunathemovie.com/the-kogi/

Four Arrows, Jacobs, Jessica London, and Ryan, Sage. (2010). Anthropocentrism's Antidote: Reclaiming Our Indigenous Orientation to Non-Human Teachers, *Critical Education,* Vol. 1, No. 15, March, pp. 1-20.

Four Arrows, Rogers, K., Willis, D., & Fowler, H. (2020). Our Human-Centered Focus Is Killing Us, in *Toward Critical Environmental Education: Where are we now? Current and Future Perspectives*. Eds. Steinberg, S., Gkiolmas, R.S., and Skordoulis, C.S. (eds.). Springer.

Four Arrows (2019). The Media Have Missed a Crucial Message of the UN's Biodiversity Report, *The Nation*, May 20, 2019.

Friedman, H.H., Fischer, D., & Schochet, S. (2017). Humility and Tone at the Top. *International Leadership Journal*, 9(2), 54-79.

Fuller, Steve. (2011). *Humanity 2.0: What It Means to Be Human Past, Present, and Future.* Palgrave.

Fulvio, Mazzocchi. (2020). A Deeper Meaning of Sustainability: Insights from Indigenous Knowledge, *The Anthropocene Review*, January 13, https://doi-org.fgul.idm.oclc.org/10.1177/2053019619898888

Gaudelli, William. (2016). *Global Citizenship Education: Everyday Transcendence.* Routledge.

Goettner-Abendroth, Heidi (ed.). (2009). *Societies of Peace: Matriarchies Past, Present and Future.* Inanna Publications.

Goettner-Abendroth, Heidi. (2018). "Re-thinking 'Matriarchy' in Modern Matriarchal Studies Using Two Examples: The Khasi and the Mosuo, *Asian Journal of Women's Studies*, 24:1, 3-27.

Gupta, Shakti M. (1971). *Plant Myths and Traditions in India*. Brill.

Hayman, Eleanor, et. al. (2018). Future rivers of the Anthropocene or Whose Anthropocene is it?: Decolonising the Anthropocene! *Decolonisation: Indigeneity, Education, and Society.* 6, 2, 77-92.

Holzmer, David. (2013). Leadership in the Time of Liminality: A Framework for Leadership in an Era of Deep Transformation, in Melina, Loi Ruskai, Burgess, Gloria J., Falkman, Lena Lid, and Marturano, Antonio. (eds.). *The Embodiment of Leadership*, pp. 43-64. Jossey Bass.

Hyman, J. (2018). Why Humble Leaders Make the Best Leaders. *Forbes*. October 31. Retrieved from https://www.forbes.com/sites/jeffhyman/2018/10/31/humility/#31df9af51c80.

Kimmerer, Robin Wall. (2013). *Braiding Sweetgrass: Indigenous Wisdom, Scientific Knowledge and the Teachings of Plants*. Milkweed Editions.

Komatsu, Hikaru, Rappleye, Jeremy, and Silova, Iveta S. (2019). Culture and the Independent Self: Obstacles to Environmental Sustainability? *Anthropocene* 26, pp. 1-13.

LeGrand, Kevin J. (2015). Beyond Conservation: Exploring the Values and Norms of Environmental Activists, pp. 50-92, in Willis, David Bake, Steier, Fred, and Stillman, Paul, Eds. *Modern Strategies for Sustainability Leadership*. Fielding University Monographs, Volume 5. Fielding University Press.

Lovejoy, Arthur O. (1910, 1933). *The Great Chain of Being*. E-Version: https://books.google.com/books?id=ByHNG8GzUeAC&printsec=frontcover&source=gbs_ViewAPI#v=onepage&q&f=false

Maathai, Wangari. (2003). *The Green Belt Movement: Sharing the Approach and the Experience*. Lantern Books.

Mann, Barbara Alice. (2016). *Spirits of Blood, Spirits of Breath: The Twinned Cosmos of Indigenous America*. Oxford University Press. 2016.

Meyer, Robinson. (2018). Geology's Timekeepers are Feuding. *The Atlantic*. July 20. Retrieved from https://www.theatlantic.com/science/archive/2018/07/anthropocene-holocene-geology-drama/565628/.

Newland, Kathleen, and Soedjatmoko, Kamala Chandrakirana (Eds.). (1994). *Transforming Humanity: The Visionary Writings of Soedjatmoko*. Kumarian Press.

Obeyesekere, Gananath (2008). *Imagining Karma: Ethical Transformation in Amerindian, Buddhist and Greek Rebirth*. University of California Press. (See also http://www.ahandfulofleaves.org/documents/Imagining%20Karma_Obeyesekere.pdf).

Olson, Ronald. (1949). "Field notes taken at Rivers Inlet and Bella Bella, British Columbia." Bancroft Library, University of California at Berkeley. Referenced in Harkin, Michael (2013) "Person, Time and Being" (p. 208) in Mills, Antonia and Slobodin, Richard, *Amerindian Rebirth*. University of Toronto.

Preiser, Rika, Pereira, Laura M., and Biggs, Reinette (Oonise). (2017). Navigating alternative framings of human-environment interactions: Variations on the theme of 'Finding Nemo,' *Anthropocene*, Vol. 20, December, pp. 83-87, https://doi.org/10.1016/j.ancene.2017.10.003

Reddy, Jini. (2013). What Colombia's Kogi people can teach us about the environment: The Kogi people are warning society of destruction we face if we fail to embrace nature. *The Guardian*, 29 https://www.theguardian.com/sustainable-business/colombia-kogi-environment-destruction October.

Right Livelihood Award. (2020). See http://www.rightlivelihoodaward.org .

Satterwhite, Rian, Miller, Whitney McIntyre, and Sheridan, Kate. (2015). Leadership for Sustainability and Peace: Responding to the Wicked Challenges of the Future, pp. 59-74, in Sowcik, Matthew, Adenaro, Anthony C., McNutt, Mondy, and Murphy, Susan Elaine (Eds.). *Leadership 2050: Critical Challenges, Key Contexts, and Emerging Trends*. Emerald Group Publishing.

Schein, Steve. (2015). Cultivating an Eco-Psychological Foundation for Deep Sustainability Leadership, pp. 166-201, in Willis, David Bake, Steier, Fred, and Stillman, Paul, Eds. *Modern Strategies for Sustainability Leadership*. Fielding University Monographs, Volume 5. Fielding Graduate University Press.

Schuyler, Kathryn Goldman, Baugher, John Eric, and Jironet, Karin. (Eds). (2016). *Creative Social Change: Leadership for a Healthy World*. Emerald Group Publishing.

Schuyler, Kathryn Goldman, with Wheatley, Margaret, Scharmer, Otto, Schein, Ed, Quinn, Robert E., and Senge, Peter. (2016). Visions of a Healthy World: Views from Thought Leaders, pp. 23-90, in Schuyler, Kathryn Goldman, Baugher, John Eric, and Jironet, Karin. (Eds). (2016). *Creative Social Change: Leadership for a Healthy World*. Emerald Group Publishing.

Smith, Bonnie G. (2008). *The Oxford Encyclopedia of Women in World History, Vol. 1*. Oxford University Press.

Smylie, Janet, Olding, Michelle, & Ziegler, Caroline. (2014). *Sharing What We Know About Living a Good Life: Indigenous Approaches to Knowledge Translation*. JCHLA / JABSC 35: 16 23 doi: 10.5596/c14-009, Retrieved from http://www.wellivinghouse.com/wp-content/uploads/2014/04/sharing-what-we-know.pdf

Sowcik, Matthew, Adenaro, Anthony C., McNutt, Mondy, and Murphy, Susan Elaine (Eds.). (2015). *Leadership 2050: Critical Challenges, Key Contexts, and Emerging Trends*. Emerald Group Publishing.

Stillman, Paul. (2015). Sustainability as Organizational Culture: Uncovering Values, Practices, and Processes, pp. 13-49, in Willis, David Bake, Steier, Fred, and Stillman, Paul, Eds. *Modern Strategies for Sustainability Leadership*. Fielding University Monographs, Volume 5. Fielding Graduate University Press.

Toivanen, T., Lummaa, K., Majava, A., Järvensivu, P., Lähde, V, Vaden, T., and Eronen, J. T. (2017). The Many Anthropocenes: A Transdisciplinary Challenge for the Anthropocene Research, *The Anthropocene Review*, Vol. 4(3) 183–198.

Tomasello, Michael. (2019). *Becoming Human: A Theory of Ontogeny*. Harvard University Press.

Tudge, Colin. (2006). *The Secret Life of Trees: How They Live and Why They Matter*. Penguin.

U. S. Department of Education. (2018). *ED initiatives*. Retrieved from https://www2.ed.gov/about/inits/ed/index.html.

UNESCO. (2018). *Indigenous and Formal Education*. Retrieved from http://www.

unesco.org/education/tlsf/mods/theme_c/mod11.html?panel=5#top.

UNESCO. (2018). *Indigenous Knowledge and Sustainability*. Retrieved from http://www.unesco.org/education/tlsf/mods/theme_c/mod11.html.

Union of International Associations (UIA). (2020). Endangered Cultures. *Encyclopedia of World Problems and Human Potential*. Retrieved from http://encyclopdie.uia.org/en/problem/135023.

Villanueva, Edgar. (2018). *Decolonizing Wealth: Indigenous Wisdom to Heal Divides and Restore Balance*. Berrett-Koehler.

Webb, Hillary S. (2012). *Yanantin and Masintin in the Andean World: Complementary Dualism in Modern Peru*. University of New Mexico Press.

Welcome to the Anthropocene (2011). *The Economist*, (www.economist.com/node/18744401), May 26.

Welcome to the Anthropocene on Vimeo. (2012). A film about the state of the planet. Mar 23, (https://vimeo.com/39048998).

Welcome to the Anthropocene. (2013). (Welcome to the Anthropocene | Welcome) (*www.anthropocene.info/*).

Willis, David Bake, Steier, Fred, and Stillman, Paul (Eds.) (2015). *Modern Strategies for Sustainability Leadership*. Fielding University Monographs, Volume 5. Fielding University Press.

Wohlleben, Peter. (2016a). *The Hidden Life of Trees: What They Feel, How They Communicate—Discoveries from a Secret World*. Greystone Books.

Wohlleben, Peter. (2016b). *The Inner Life of Animals*. Vintage Books.

CHAPTER 4

Environmental, Social, and Governance (ESG) Goals and Global Supply Chain Management: *A Case Study of Leadership in Deckers Outdoor Corporation*

Katrina S. Rogers
Fielding Graduate University

Preamble

The subject of this chapter. This chapter examines actions that a socially and environmentally responsible company takes to advance sustainability in their business practices related to global supply chain management. The social and environmental performance of Deckers Outdoor Corporation offers an opportunity to examine how corporate performance is shaped within a large company that has global reach, both from operational and market standpoints. Focusing on the environmental, social, and governance (ESG) framework, often utilized by investors to guide socially responsible investing, provides a theoretical backdrop to evaluate specific actions that the company has undertaken in the last decade. Through examining global supply chain management, insights are offered for leaders across sectors. This study reveals findings for leaders seeking to improve their sustainability practices within an organizational setting as well as ideas for further research.

The nature of the study. This study based its analysis on three major sources of data: qualitative interviews with company employees; publicly available secondary materials produced by the company, such as annual reports and press releases; and third party written materials from industry observers and sustainable business scholars. For the most part, this research is situated with scholarly literature related to sustainability. Sustainability challenges for globally oriented companies are framed within the context of the rise of the Anthropocene. Relying on research about ESG and socially responsible investing provides additional conceptualization of Deckers practices in creating and improving their global supply chain.

The outcome of this chapter. This analysis offers the following findings that are useful for leaders in organizations, and for researchers in the field of sustainable business practices. The first finding is that the creation of environmental, social, and governance goals has been important to hold companies accountable for establishing and/or continuing to improve their sustainability business practices. Second, is that it is important for a company to publicly state the values that they are aspiring to in regards to sustainability. For Deckers, social and environmental practices are based on the three pillars of environmental sustainability, community engagement, and fair and safe factories. Third, a critical success factor focuses on building supplier capacity through training, development, assessment, and accountability practices. Finally, is the importance of a collaborative process—collaboration within the units across the company and between the corporate entity and vendors. As one of the top 50 socially and environmentally responsible companies in the world, these findings from this research on Deckers Outdoor Corporation offer specific action that leaders can take to improve corporate sustainable performance. These findings also point out useful future directions for researchers, including research on the usefulness of ESG for improving corporate sustainable practices.

Introduction: Corporate Responsibility in the Age of the Anthropocene

The global economy is driven by human activities, needs, and desires, and the corporation has become the vehicle for fulfilling these collective ingredients for modern living. It is increasingly evident that a small number of corporations control much of the world's commerce. Research has revealed this evidence through network analysis, demonstrating that just 737 companies control 80% of the world's commerce (Vitali, October 2011, p. 1). Therefore, any discussion of leadership for sustainability must take into consideration the actions of the for-profit sector. Indeed, it is critical to understand the extent to which individual leaders can be committed to improving corporate functioning through sustainable practices. Any scholarly understanding of leadership also needs to take into consideration the continuous learning and progress necessary for any company in mitigating their corporate impacts on the natural world.

In recent decades, there has been increased scrutiny of corporate performance related to their environmental and social records of accomplishment (Gillian et al., 2010). Companies, once judged primarily by their stock value, are now making commitments towards advancing their performance in environmental, social, and governance goals (ESG). The origins of ESG emerged in the 1990s with growing investor demands to invest in more socially responsible companies. This trend was concretized by the work of Robert Levering and Milton Moskowitz, who started the Best Companies to work for list, which argued that companies that were more socially responsible were more productive and effective (Anchor Perspectives, 2019). Corporate commitments to ESG have been researched as one component of overall corporate performance. In one study that examined stock valuation and operating performance of US listed companies, Peiris and Evans (2010) found a significant positive relationship between ESG rating and return of assets, and market-to-book-value measure. Their findings added evidence to the theory that social performance of a company has a positive impact on financial performance.

This abbreviated case study focuses on Deckers Outdoor Corporation, a large footwear company with a reputation that affirms the principles of corporate social responsibility (CSR). CSR is defined as the practice of incorporating environmental and social concerns into business practices (UNIDO, 2020). In 2019, Deckers garnered $2 billion of sales revenue, including revenue generated by several large brands such as Ugg, Teva, and Sanuk. They have operations in multiple countries (Deckers, Annual Report, 2019, p. 1). As an example of a company with global environmental impact, Deckers' scope makes their business a particularly interesting one in assessing their actions regarding progress towards ESG.

ESG refers to a set of measures for companies across environmental, social, and governance categories and is used to measure the sustainability and ethical impact a company has in their role as a participant in the global economy (Chen, 2020). ESG is the measure that is most often used by companies to track their progress in their desire to evidence CSR. Over the years, multiple firms have used ESG to categorize companies for investors who are interested in ethical or green investments. Using the ESG framework, this essay focuses on how Deckers analyzes and measures performance related to ethical supply chain management, which includes supplier code of conduct and supplier capacity building through training and development. Global supply chain management is a particularly useful aspect of corporate functioning to consider, as it encompasses many dimensions of ESG.

Through this case study, the connection between ESG and organizational functioning as a means of the enacting changes needed to confront the global environmental challenges we face as a species is explored. Conclusions are drawn about Deckers approach, as a company, that may be useful in thinking about strengthening sustainability leadership in a general sense in the for-profit sector.

The Rise of the Anthropocene

One striking feature in the breadth of history is the extent to which humans have manipulated the natural environment to serve our needs and desires. In the early written record, there are tales of deforestation and soil erosion (Plato, 360 B.C.E). As early as the seventeenth century, natural historians compared the grasslands around villages to inhabited areas and speculated on the consequences of human activity on natural systems (Goudie, 2009, p. 3). The onset of the Industrial Revolution combined with a growing understanding and knowledge of science have produced a circumstance of uncontrolled manipulation of the ecosystems and ever-fine ways to measure these consequences.

Within the last several decades, there has been a surge of scholarly and popular literature regarding global environmental change across a range of disciplines and issue areas. A quick browse of some of these titles demonstrates an ever-louder drumbeat of urgency and sense of pessimism. Consider some of the titles: *Silent Spring, The Limits to Growth, The Long Emergency, Our Plundered Planet, Scorched, Field Notes of A Catastrophe, Collapse, Spiritual Ecology—the Cry of the Earth, Blueprint for Survival, The End of Nature, The Population Bomb, The Carbon War,* and *The Last Chance to See*, to name a few. Regardless of scope and disciplinary background, the theme is similar; humans are on a runaway train when it comes to environmental degradation and we must slow this rush to oblivion if we are to survive as a species. Furthermore, we must create new economies that live within the natural means of the ecosystems, upon which all life depends. This daunting task is what lies before us.

Like many other species, humans have the ability to reason. Our capacity is better than all others and, with training, many of us have become competent analytical thinkers in the Modern age through education and practice. A common way to think about a problem that seems overwhelming is to break it down to its essential components, and then seek to solve each piece of that puzzle. There is, however, a danger in this way of thinking, as scholars are quick to point out, in that our compartmentalized approach to learning and problem solving is one aspect of the larger paradigm that got us into this fix. Common tools that are used tend to simplify the problem solving process when what is needed is a holistic, intrinsic, and qualitative understanding of ecological systems (Marchand, et al., 2020, preface).

There are innumerable cases of the unintended consequences of this way of thinking regarding the environment. As just one example, we introduced rabbits into Australia in the eighteenth century, initially for hunting; but, the species quickly overpopulated the continent because they had no natural predators. Rabbit overpopulation is considered the biggest single factor in species loss on the continent (Hillstrom & Hillstrom, 2003, p. 102). In another instance, the technological advance of drift nets in fishing was a primary cause of the collapse of the cod fishing industry off the Grand Banks of Newfoundland in the 1970s. Overfishing was compounded by flawed estimates of what constituted an allowable catch. As Pilkey and Pilkey-Jones have stated, "it is accurate to say that in the case of the codfish debacle [the Canadian Department of Fisheries and Oceans] made one of the most important and far-reaching scientific blunders of the age" (2003, p. 9). Compartmentalized thinking combined with ignorance is a dangerous combination.

If reducing problems to smaller parts in order to solve them is not the best strategy, given the complexity of integrated environmental systems in front of us, perhaps another approach would elicit stronger outcomes. If we are to reason this way, we could take a problem like climate change and address it at several levels, using a multilayered approach: these levels could be individual, national, societal, and global. The approaches would also be scientific, political, economic, and social. An example of an issue that was addressed in this way is the often-cited Montreal Protocol, concerning the protection of the ozone layer. The ozone layer is in the outermost layer of earth's atmosphere, called the stratosphere, and it protects the earth from damaging ultra-violet rays from the sun. Over time, human activities, such as the use of chlorofluorocarbons (CFCs), has damaged the ozone layer. In 1987, a multi-nation protocol was negotiated to end production of materials hazardous to the atmosphere. Current calculations predict that the ozone layer will be healed in 50 years (EPA, 2013, p. 1). This example reveals a concerted effort to address the issue at several levels through a multi-layered approach. The public (individual, societal) was made aware of the dangers of using CFC and other ozone-depleting chemicals. Nations agreed to cooperate to find new solutions, and to hammer other international agreements. In terms of approaches, scientists, politicians, and business leaders had to commit to seek a common solution. A problem so large required recognition of its complexity and a great degree of commitment to progress.

In contrast, global climate change seems unsolvable. This is partially due to multiple causes, not just simply ozone-depleting chemicals. Climate change is caused by a suite of human activities, some of which have created ecological processes that are now out of control and, perhaps, outside of limited understanding of the consequences. In the 2006 film *An Inconvenient Truth*, Former US Vice-President Al Gore made the case that climate change is the single most important environmental catastrophe facing us; yet, the call to action has fallen flat amidst disagreement over the scientific basis of our climate knowledge and a lack of political will amongst many nations. Recent research also suggests that people may be feeling a growing sense of helplessness about environmental issues, particularly climate change. In a study examining laypeople's knowledge about the causes and effects of global warming, scholars revealed that people had a poor understanding of the facts and were confused about differentiating between the causes and actions specific to climate (Read et al., 2006, p. 971). Other research has suggested that while people may become motivated to act, they do not have enough information on what action is possible to mitigate the effects of climate change (Lowe et al., 2006, p. 435). Additional research reveals that individuals take actions regarding sustainability based on a larger worldview that influences their approach and, likely outcomes, of the actions taken (Rogers, 2012).

Herein lies an interesting thread. We can motivate people to act, whether it is as individuals or as a collective, but it requires building knowledge and capacities to take action. In the case of global environmental change, it would seem to be the case that we could motivate groups of people, such as organizations, institutions, and states, if we can make a strong compelling case to do so and provide the tools for collective action. As Former US Vice-President Al Gore has written,

> the world's ecological balance depends on more than just our ability to restore a balance between civilization's ravenous appetite for resources and the fragile equilibrium of the earth's environment… we must restore a balance within ourselves between who we are and what we are doing. Each of us must stake a greater personal responsibility for this deteriorating global environment; each of us must take a hard look at the habits of mind and action that reflect—and have led to—this grave crisis (Gore, 1992, p. 12).

This case study now turns to Deckers Outdoor Corporation as having an opportunity to provide insight into the habits of mind of a global company with both operations and sales in many countries throughout the world. The leadership mindset and approach to improve a global supply chain requires integrated thinking that is congruent with ESG, in that leaders must take into consideration sustainability and labor practices throughout a complex chain of actors and product management cycles. By focusing on Deckers global supply chain, insights can be derived from their ongoing assessment and management for understanding leadership in sustainability.

Corporate Response to Environmental and Social Issues: Deckers Outdoor Corporation

In 2009, Bloomberg launched the ESG data service. Bloomberg collects ESG data for over 10,000 publicly listed companies (Huber and Comstock, 2017). This data covers 120 environmental, social, and governance indicators including: carbon emissions, climate change impact, pollution, waste disposal, renewable energy, resource depletion, supply chain, political contributions, discrimination, diversity, community relations, human rights, cumulative voting, executive compensation, shareholders' rights, takeover defense, staggered boards, and independent directors (ibid.). Companies are penalized for missing data. The data is derived from direct corporate interaction as well as published reports and other documents. In November 2019, *Investor's Business Daily* selected Deckers as one of the top 50 companies for ESG. In commenting on being ranked 20 on the list, CEO Dave Powers noted that, "performing well, while remaining socially and environmentally conscious is fundamental to our success and purpose as a company. . . As a leader in our industry, we have a responsibility to continue to advance sustainable business practices and do business in the right way (PR Newswire, 2019)."

In connecting their stated goals to the leadership within Deckers, I conducted a set of interviews with leaders who had been tasked with strengthening corporate sustainability practices. Additional data was collected from publicly available materials published by the company and by third party industry observers. This approach provided a comprehensive view of how Deckers is fulfilling their stated commitments. In this line of inquiry, global supply chain management reveals how Deckers organizes its' own understanding of both the ecological and labor impacts of their business. ESG defines supply chains as referring to the series of steps and processes involved in the production and/or distribution of goods and services. Supply chains have become increasingly complex, as they can include direct and indirect suppliers, manufacturers, distributors, and retailers, and may involve companies and individuals all over the world (Orr, et al., 2019).

In their written corporate documents, Deckers offers a definition of good business as "the kind that helps our community and our environment, and inspires the younger generation" (Deckers Corporate Responsibility Report, 2019, frontpage). For many years, Deckers has been a financially healthy company with a global reach. The company's total net sales for first quarter ending June 30, 3019 came to $276.8 million, compared to $250.6 million for the same period in 2018 (Fashion Network, 2019). They have 16 vendor partners, operating 23 factories: one in the United States, eight in China, one in the Philippines, two in Cambodia, and eleven in Vietnam (Deckers, Corporate responsibility report, 2019, p. 1).

The diversification of production has helped Deckers mitigate the impacts of the COVID-19 pandemic on their global supply chain. In their fourth quarter earnings report, the company noted that they had experienced certain disruptions to sourcing with its third-party manufacturers during the first quarter of fiscal year 2020, but by May 2020, these challenges were largely behind them. Deckers did note, however, that they may expect disruptions in the future to the supply chain. Specific to COVID-19, they reported that the company continues to modify and evolve its operations in response to COVID-19. To analyze ongoing operations in light of the pandemic, they review expert agency guidelines, as well as information from health officials and local authorities, while assessing the appropriate scope of operations and re-allocation of resources if necessary (Digital Supply Chain, May 21, 2020).

With over $2 billion dollars in global sales each year, Deckers has a stake in cultivating understanding and improving the movement of products and payments through the entire supply chain. According to one interviewee, this practice provides information to ensure that labor practices are safe and that waste is minimized through the manufacturing and transportation process (personal communication, 2013). Deckers has invested in these practices for many years. In 2013, then Senior Vice President of Supply Chair, Marg Fegley noted, "Our main objective is improving visibility across our extended supply chain. GT Nexus [a new cloud supply chain platform] replaces a number of disparate systems to help us closely track the flow of orders throughout the supply chain, from purchase order through settlement. We'll have consistent visibility into what is really occurring in the factory, at the packing station, and in transit (Chain Storage Age, May 24, 2013)."

Within this context of ethical supply chain management, Deckers' approach to corporate responsibility is based on three pillars: environmental sustainability, community engagement, and fair and safe factories, according to one interviewee (personal communication, 2013). The environmental component focuses on the impact of operations on the natural environment; the community aspect is mostly in encouraging volunteerism throughout the company; and the fair and safe factories initiative is focused on making sure that their factories are also following all international laws, as well as ethical standards, regarding workers.

An example of how this process works is through their Ethical Supply Chain (ESC) Program. The ESC strives to ensure that the factories, which manufacture their products, conform to fair labor standards. Those standards expressly preclude child labor, forced labor, and human trafficking. Every year, the company provides supply chain partners and employees with ESC training. In addition, an audit team regularly assesses partner compliance with Deckers fair labor standards. Results from the audit are tallied into a scorecard that is reviewed with each supplier. A section of this audit focuses on "zero tolerance" issues including child and forced labor. Any violation of "zero tolerance" issues will cause the supplier to automatically fail the audit and be asked to take immediate corrective action. Deckers includes their ESC Supplier Code of Conduct as part of their Manufacturing Agreement, which they have with each factory. Deckers designed its ESC program in 2008, to help ensure that workers in the factories that manufacture its products are treated ethically, and work in safe conditions. It also seeks to verify that its product supply chain, including the factories, conform to fair labor standards, which of course preclude slavery and human trafficking. They are also part of the Apparel and Footwork Brands Collaboration Forum (AFBCF), and third party networks such as HERproject, which is dedicated to gender equality in the workplace. Through these collaborations, it is clear that Deckers seeks to continue to make progress in maintaining an ethical global supply chain program.

Deckers Supplier Code of Conduct, which is their written document based on the ESC program, strives to ensure that their values are maintained throughout the entire supply chain. They monitor factory partners' adherence to the Supplier Code of Conduct on a regular basis by using the ESC audit to address human rights, environmental, health and safety, and management systems. The audit includes ensuring that materials used in their products comply with the laws of the country, or countries, in which their products are made. Deckers corporate representatives visit factories to conduct audits of facilities, factory records and to make sure they are following the Supplier Code of Conduct.

In the most recently published Supplier Code of Conduct, Deckers includes a section on assessment and monitoring. Key to ensuring ethical labor practices through the supply chain, Deckers employees conduct ongoing assessments and reviews of facilities (Deckers, Ethical Supply Chain, 2020). Using best practices of supply chain management, Deckers affirms that guidelines in local languages are to be produced and that there is a confidential process for reporting violations. Business partners are expected to maintain records that demonstrate and verify such compliance (ibid.). If a factory or supplier fails an audit, Deckers works with them to develop a corrective action plan. If the issue is resolved within an agreed-upon period, the partnership continues. If not, third-party remediation is engaged, and if the issue is still not resolved, the partnership is dissolved.

Regarding employee engagement, the task of the team is to conduct internal audits of factories and suppliers. When asked about enforcement related to labor and environmental practices, one interviewee noted the importance of management systems in finding poor practices or violations. She pointed out that, when a violation occurs, the company has a system to respond quickly. Initially, they work with the supplier to resolve the situation, and if that is not possible, they will move to terminate the contract. "Generally, it is not a challenge to terminate the contract — as long as we have clear, written expectations. The biggest challenge is good communication between the different parts of Deckers, overall, and the various supply chains. Coordination can be a challenge to make sure we all know that each part is conducting its business. Collaboration is key" (personal communication, 2013).

Using a checklist, the team evaluates everything pertaining to labor hours and safety conditions using a combination of sustainable development goals set forth by the United Nations and metrics derived from the International Labor Organization standards. These goals and their performance is publicly displayed on their website. They deploy teams in China and Vietnam that conduct internal audits and note where Deckers can improve. For example, in their 2019 report, they noted deficiencies in several areas, including issues with excessive overtime, insufficient personal protective equipment management, insufficient fire safety and machine safety management, and insufficient benefits (Deckers, Corporate responsibility report, 2019).

Supplier capacity building through training and development. Each year, representatives from Deckers' suppliers attend training sessions in Asia. Annual training sessions focus on adherence to the Deckers Supplier Code of Conduct. Additional training addresses topics like improving environmental programs, ensuring safe working conditions, and improving the treatment of workers. The training is accomplished through a combination of presentations and role playing activities.

When a significant issue arises, Deckers employees work with suppliers to gather feedback using a process called "root cause analysis" (RCA). This technique addresses the underlying cause of the problem, not just the symptoms. For example, in one case they performed a root cause analysis on a factory that had an excessive work hours issue. Based on the results of the RCA, the factory improved processes and adapted bonus structures. This led to a decrease in the number of continuous workdays and fewer overtime hours each week (Deckers, Corporate responsibility report, 2014, p. 13).

Deckers makes explicit their goal to drive continuous improvement in social and environmental standards in the footwear and apparel supply chain. On their website, they publicly post their list of factories and key suppliers, which represents approximately 90% of Deckers procurement expenditures. Deckers also uses its Supplier Code of Conduct to communicate its expectations about how factories and their suppliers should conduct themselves as related to fair labor standards, which includes ensuring that the materials used in the company's products comply with laws of the country, or countries, in which they are doing business. In the event that an employee or contractor fails to meet Deckers' internal accountability standards and procedures for fair labor standards, Deckers' corrective action process is used to develop a remediation plan. Deckers also provides ESC training to its supply chain partners at least once per year. Internally, Deckers employees are expected to be familiar with and be committed to the tenets of the ESC program and the Supplier Code of Conduct, both of which are sent to all employees on an annual basis.

In regards to advancing their own ethical behavior, Deckers has a robust program for continuing to seek sustainable alternatives for key materials, sourcing at least 90% from suppliers that are certified by third-party benchmarking organizations. In their 2019 report, Deckers reported that 97% of leathers used in their production cycles originate from Leather Working Group certified tanneries and that 90% of their sheepskin can be traced back to an appropriate processing facility. In addition, they have made a public declaration to evaluate land management and farming practices related to the sheep they use for a number of products. Deckers has also recently joined the Better Cotton Initiative (Deckers, Corporate responsibility report, 2019; Better Cotton Initiative, 2018).

Evidence of collaboration for collective action. An important component of continuous improvement and providing leadership in sustainability within any sector is being willing to work with other industry partners and competitors. In interviews, there was evidence that Decker's approach, in addition to the above, has a strong internal culture that is able to note successes and failures, and learn from others. As one interviewee noted,

> The industry does not yet have a common language in terms of figuring out environment impact. It depends on what you care about. Should we focus on water usage or greenhouse gases? From an industry wide perspective, do we emphasize chemical issues or find sustainable substitutes for parts of our products? How do improve

> some of our most difficult issues around socially responsible labor practices? So, while we focus on the ethical and environmental implications of our products, we spend a great deal of time also on industry collaboration. For example, our sustainability working group (SWG) is a place where we place a great deal of organizational energy on working with competitors and third parties to help us understand the multiple sustainability frameworks currently in use (personal communication, 2013).

The point made in the interview reflects the more general statement in Deckers' corporate documents, that the company is heavily invested in collaboration with other industry competitors (Deckers corporate responsibility report, 2019).

In the last several years, internal collaboration has become another element of driving sustainability innovation. For example, Deckers' use of 3D printing was one such innovation. One interviewee said, "Another way we activated a holistic approach to global supply chain management was a cross-collaboration of several units in implementing a program for 3D printing. So rather than sending pieces back and forth between the US and our vendors overseas, many pieces are now printed locally. It has had an enormous environmental benefit in terms of lowering our carbon use footprint" (personal communication, 2013). These two examples demonstrate that a mindset of collaboration is an important ingredient in sustainability leadership within companies.

Conclusion

Analysis of Deckers' approach to global supply chain management offers several findings for organizational leaders and sustainability scholars. This brief case study revealed the following discoveries:

1) The use of environmental, social, and governance (ESG) goals has been important to hold companies more accountable for establishing and/or continuing to improve their sustainability business practices.

2) It is important for a company to state publicly the values that they are aspiring to in regards to sustainability. For Deckers, their social and environmental practices are based on the three pillars of environmental sustainability, community engagement, and fair and safe factories.

3) A critical success factor is focusing on building supplier capacity through

training, development, assessment, and accountability practices.
4) Another finding is the importance of a collaborative process—collaboration within the units across the company, and between the corporate entity and its vendors.

As one of the top 50 socially and environmentally responsible companies in the world, findings from this research on Deckers Outdoor Corporation offer specific actions that leaders can take to improve corporate sustainable performance. These findings also point out useful future directions for researchers, including research on the usefulness of ESG for improving corporate sustainable practices.

Arguably, the second order effects of the Industrial Revolution and the choices made by humanity to exploit the planet's resources in an unsustainable way are now being visited upon twenty-first century inhabitants. Climate change, resulting in more severe and unpredictable weather, pandemics, and violent conflict over resources—both small and large—are likely to characterize the coming decades. Simultaneously, modernity is with us to stay in the sense that changing cultural habits and norms will occur incrementally over time. It is useful to look at companies that are striving to improve their own processes and continue to evolve their practices. With more than 9 billion people on earth, we have great needs for water, food, clothing, and safety. While Deckers is just one example of a company engaged in sustainable actions, its' practices are a foreshadowing of the large changes to come, in order for the needs of humanity to be fulfilled within the finite resource constraints of the planet. These practices include focusing on every step of the global supply chain with habits of mind that practice and transparency, holism, assessment and learning, all undertaken in an atmosphere of collaboration.

Questions for Discussion

1. How could leaders take these examples about sustainable practices related to global supply chains and incorporate these elements into their private and public sector organizations?
2. What are the strengths and weaknesses of using global Environmental, Social, and Governance (ESG) criteria to evaluate corporate practices?
3. How impactful can a socially responsible company be in light of a global economy predicated on extensive and expansive resource use?

4. What does the pandemic of 2020 reveal about global supply chains that could be useful for understanding socially responsible practices in times of disruption?
5. What other research questions could be raised based on the findings of this study?

About the Author

Katrina S. Rogers, PhD, is President of Fielding Graduate University in Santa Barbara, CA. As faculty, she has taught in her field in global environmental politics and policy, sustainability, social movements, research, and theory. In the course of her career, Rogers has served in many roles, including executive, board member, and teacher. She led the European campus for Thunderbird School of Global Management in Geneva, Switzerland for a decade, working with international organizations and corporations. Rogers also worked in the conversation movement with regional conservation organizations. She holds doctorates in political science and history. In addition to many articles focused on organizational leadership in sustainability, Rogers currently serves on the Boards of Prescott College, the Master's in Sustainability Advisory Council for Northern Arizona University, and the Toda Institute for Global Policy & Peace Research. She received a Presidential post-doctoral fellowship from the Humboldt Foundation and was a Fulbright scholar to Germany where she taught environmental politics and history.

References

Anchor Perspectives. (2019). *A brief history of ESG.* Retrieved 2020, June 3, from https://anchorcapital.com/the-value-of-values-esg-and-value-investing/.

Better Cotton Initiative, (2018). *Five brands and one civil society organization have joined BCI, showing their support to cotton farmers across the globe.* Retrieved 2020, April 18, from https://bettercotton.org/five-brands-and-one-civil-society-organisation-have-joined-bci-showing-their-support-to-cotton-farmers-around-the-globe/.

Chain Storage Age. (May 24, 2013). *Deckers Outdoor teams with GT Nexus on supply chain solution.* Retrieved 2020, May 3, from https://chainstoreage.com/news/deckers-outdoor-teams-gt-nexus-supply-chain-solution.

Chen, J. What are environmental, social, and governance criteria? (February 25, 2020) *Investopedia.* Retrieved 2020, April 18, from https://www.investopedia.com/terms/e/environmental-social-and-governance-esg-criteria.asp.

Deckers Outdoor Corporation. (2019). *Annual report.* Retrieved 2020, March 15, from http://ir.deckers.com/interactive/newlookandfeel/4391531/2019-Annual-Report.pdf.

Deckers Outdoor Corporation. (2020). *Deckers corporate responsibility report.* Retrieved 2020, January 18, from https://www.deckers.com/sites/default/files/images/responsibility/Deckers_CR_Report_2019a1.pdf.

Deckers Outdoor Corporation. (2014). *Deckers corporate responsibility report.* Retrieved 2020, March 15, from https://www.deckers.com/sites/default/files/images/responsibility/Deckers_CR_Report_2014.pdf.

Deckers Outdoor Corporation. (2020). *Ethical supply chain: Supplier code of conduct.* Retrieved 2020, April 19, from https://www.deckers.com/sites/default/files/pdf/Ethical%20Supply%20Chain%20Supplier%20Code%20of%20Conduct.pdf.

Digital Supply Chain. (May 21, 2020). *Deckers brands reports fourth quarter and fiscal 2020 finance.* Retrieved 2020, May 24, from https://www.supplychaindigital.com/press-release/10718542-2.

EPA, http://www.epa.gov/ozone/science/currentstate.html

Fashion Network. (July 26, 2019). *Deckers raises 2020 outlook on strong Q1.* Retrieved 2020, April 19, from https://us.fashionnetwork.com/news/Deckers-raises-2020-outlook-on-strong-q1,1123773.html.

Gillian, S. L., Hartzell, J.C., Koch, A., & Laura T. Starks. (November 10, 2010). *Firms environmental, social and governance (ESG) choices, performance, and managerial motivation.* Retrieved 2020, April 20, from https://www.researchgate.net/profile/Maretno_Harjoto/publication/265849879_Board_Diversity_and_Corporate_Social_Responsibility/links/56024b2e08aeb30ba7355cda.pdf

Gore, A. (1992). *Earth in the balance: Ecology and the human spirit.* NY: Houghton Mifflin.

Goudie, A. (2006). *The human impact on the natural environment: Past, present, and future.* Malden, MA: Blackwell.

Hillstrom, K. & L. Collier Hillstrom. (2003). *Australia, Oceania, and Antarctica: A continental overview of environmental issues.* Santa Barbara, CA: ABC-CLIO.

Huber, B. M., & M. Comstock. (2017). *ESG Reports and ratings: What they are, why they matter.* Retrieved 2020, March 30, from https://corpgov.law.harvard.edu/2017/07/27/esg-reports-and-ratings-what-they-are-why-they-matter/.

Lowe, T., Brown, K., Dessai, S., Doria de Franca, M., Haynes, K., & K. Vincent. (2006). Does tomorrow ever come? Disaster narrative and public perceptions of climate change. *Public Understanding of Science,* 15, 435-457.

Marchand, M.E., Vogt, K.A., Cawston, R., Tovey, J. D., McCoy, J., Maryboy, N., Mukumoto, C. T., Vogt, D. J. and M. S. Mobley. (2020). *The medicine wheel: Environmental decision-making process of indigenous peoples.* Michigan: Michigan State University Press.

Orr, S. K., Wyatt, K.S., & J. S. Waterhous. (September 10, 2019). *Companies should consider ESG supply chain issues.* Retrieved 2020, April 19, from https://www.globalelr.com/2019/09/companies-should-consider-esg-supply-chain-issues/

Peiris, D., & J. Evans. (2010). The relationship between environmental social and governance goals and U.S. stock performance. *The Journal of Investing,* 19 (3), 104-112.

Pilkey, O. H. & L. Pilkey-Jones. (2003). *Useless arithmetic: Why environmental scientists can't predict the future.* NY: Columbia University Press.

Plato. *Critias.* Retrieved 2013, May, 26, from http://classics.mit.edu/Plato/critias.html

PR Newswire. (November 26, 2019). *Deckers brands selected as one of 50 best ESG companies.* Retrieved 2020, April 4, from https://www.prnewswire.com/news-releases/deckers-brands-selected-as-one-of-50-best-esg-companies-300964974.html

Read, D., Bostrom, A, Morgan, M, Fischhoff, B., & T. Smuts. (2006). What do people know about global climate change? 2. Survey studies of educated laypeople. *Risk Analysis,* 6, 971-982. Retrieved 2013, May, 25, from http://onlinelibrary.wiley.com/doi/10.1111/j.1539-6924.1994.tb00066.x/abstract?deniedAccessCustomisedMessage=&userIsAuthenticated=false.

Rogers, K. (2012). Exploring our ecological selves within learning organizations. *The Learning Organization,* 19,1, 28-37.

UNIDO. (2020). *What is CSR?* Retrieved 2020, April 18, from https://www.unido.org/our-focus/advancing-economic-competitiveness/competitive-trade-capacities-and-corporate-responsibility/corporate-social-responsibility-market-integration/what-csr.

Vitali S, Glattfelder JB, Battiston S (2011). The network of global corporate control. *PLoS ONE,* 6, 10, 1-6.

CHAPTER 5

Creating an Organizational Culture of Sustainability: *A Practical Guide for Leaders*

Paul Stillman
Fielding Graduate University

Preamble

The subject of this chapter. Creating a sustainable organization is a question of fostering the right culture. For leaders striving to succeed in sustainable organizations, the challenge becomes a cultural one: How can I understand, embody, and engage others in a culture of sustainability across the enterprise? Many leaders, both experienced and emerging, are ill-equipped to help create this unique culture. They lack a practical understanding of what constitutes an organizational culture of sustainability and do not possess a framework from which to proceed and measure their efforts. The goal of this chapter is to provide sustainability leaders with both a conceptual framework and insights into the values, practices, and processes that have been used successfully at other organizations that are committed to embracing an all-encompassing culture of sustainability.

The nature of the study. This multi-site case study is based on 29 open-ended interviews, at all organizational levels, across four enterprises in different sectors: consumer retail, specialty foods, higher education, and eco-technology. The focus was to examine experiences across the four organizations to identify commonalities that could point towards a unified approach, rather than link the different contexts to different manifestations of sustainability. Thematic analysis was applied to the verbatim interviews to construct a roadmap for sustainability leaders, framed within the concepts of organizational culture, phronesis or practical wisdom, and systems theory. Findings include narrative richness, as captured in participant quotes, to help leaders develop a meaningful language of sustainability.

The outcome of this chapter. The research and analysis, guided by the three-part conceptual framework of culture, practical wisdom, and systems, yielded a synthesized model of sustainability that contains key values, practices, and processes. The model can help leaders formulate a personal vision of sustainability based on the three framing concepts. The themes, grouped into four major categories of (a) embedding the mission, (b) living the mission, (c) balancing ideals and practices, and (d) that relationships matter, provide guidance for leaders seeking to implement specific programs and initiatives. These action-oriented benchmarks can also offer a means to track progress, identify gaps, and build consensus among all stakeholders, both inside and outside of the organization. Moving forward, the outcomes of this research, with further validation and testing, could be utilized to develop assessment tools for measuring an organization's culture of sustainability. The model and themes could also be used to formulate, or refine, undergraduate and graduate education around sustainability culture and leadership. This practical guide for leaders, grounded in experience and prompted by the urgent need to create socially and ecologically responsible organizations, can be a valuable resource for constructing a new, more resonant sustainability narrative.

Introduction

A major challenge for leaders in forward-looking organizations is how to embrace concepts of sustainability in ways that are meaningful and authentic. The committed sustainability leader then faces the daunting task of communicating this vision and enlisting support to transform the organization, translating concepts into practice and embedding these new paradigms into the fabric of everyday organizational life. Few emerging leaders are equipped for this task; this research was designed to offer tangible support for this critical endeavor.

This multi-site case study focuses on four organizations committed to embracing sustainability in all aspects of governance and operations. The case study goal was not to concentrate on contextual differences among the organizations, but rather to distill common sustainability-related values, practices, and processes to develop a roadmap that other sustainability leaders could use. To guide the research and analysis, which involved uncovering themes from 29 open-ended interviews across the four organizations, a conceptual framework was developed based on (a) organizational culture, (b) phronesis or practical wisdom, and (c) systems theory. The framework, which will be described in more detail later in the chapter, helped organize and focus the inquiry to produce findings that would be holistic and culturally-derived, philosophically based on the powerful Aristotelian practical virtue of phronesis, and informed by both systems thinking and an appreciation for reciprocal relationships. Although conceptual, the framework has practical implications for sustainability leaders by privileging what is important. Creating the proper culture, valuing ethical wisdom, and encouraging positive relationships define the mission for leaders in sustainable organizations.

Sustainability is a topic of considerable current interest, but the concept has multiple meanings (Linnenluecke & Griffiths, 2013) and is contested and easily co-opted, as in the case of sustainable development and corporate greenwashing (Williams & Millington, 2004). Growing global threats, from climate change and the depletion of natural resources (United Nations, 1987) to the prospect of mass extinction (Barnosky et al., 2011), reinforce the need for clarity. Growing evidence of the impact of human activity on natural systems has led to the definition of a new era, the Anthropocene, and has sparked a reevaluation of traditional concepts of sustainability (Griggs et al., 2013). This critical reassessment has elevated ecological concerns by examining key planetary systems, moving away from the idea of a balanced approach that, by default, favors the perpetuation of corporate economic interests (Rockström et al., 2009). Simultaneously, key social and cultural aspects of sustainability are receiving heightened attention as the negative consequences on local people and supply chain participants of, supposedly, sustainable projects and practices become evident (Boström, 2012).

Sustainability as an organizational concept is rooted primarily in the realm of sustainable development as promulgated in the Brundtland Report of the World Commission on Environment and Development (United Nations, 1987). This historic report held that "humanity has the ability to make development sustainable to ensure that it meets the needs of the present without compromising the ability of future generations to meet their own needs" (p. 16). The commission report acknowledged environmental threats, recognized the need for equity for poorer nations, advocated limiting extreme population growth, and promoted food security and fair resource distribution. The commission also advocated continued economic expansion, viewed by critics as a bias toward growth and development at the expense of a true commitment to reducing environmental and social harm (Griggs et al., 2013). The foundation of sustainable development was defective, "substantially due to the conflation of the concepts of sustainability and development, which belong to essentially incommensurable worlds, thereby creating an oxymoron" (Kowalski, 2013, p. 76).

The growing realization that environmental concerns should have preeminence over economic development recognizes "the idea that there is always somewhere to absorb externalities is flawed, and it is a myth of progress that living systems will always recover from human demands" (Adams, 2006, p. 11). This reevaluation paralleled an evolution in ecological thinking, from a focus on homeostasis to an appreciation for non-linear dynamics and the limits of resilience. Emphasizing the social dimension of sustainable development also introduced the idea that equality, values, and aesthetics are relevant to sustainability and human wellbeing. From this perspective, true sustainable development would embrace new social and environmental goals of "thriving lives and livelihoods, sustainable food security, sustainable water security, universal clean energy, healthy and productive ecosystems, and governance for sustainable societies" (Griggs et al., 2013, p. 307).

Sustainability in organizations, particularly with regard to leadership, is an area that is receiving increased attention as more companies seek to adopt sustainable practices, often catalyzed by stakeholder demands (Kiron, Kruschwitz, Haanaes, & von Streng Velken, 2011). As discrete, self-governing entities, organizations have the ability to design and implement sustainability practices based on values, beliefs, and context. The challenge of how to lead a sustainable organization is a topic of keen interest in the business sector, with studies linking improved performance to cultural factors surrounding sustainability (Eccles, Perkins, & Serafeim, 2012). Mohrman and Worley (2010) observed, in their introduction to a special issue of Organizational Dynamics, that a sense of urgency is driving the change toward sustainable practices, yet how to achieve sustainability remains elusive, with a wide range of approaches offered.

Assessments of sustainable practices within organizations typically focus on the environment. Pfeffer (2010) advocated for the concept of social sustainability within organizations by noting, for example, the contradiction between applauding Walmart for sustainability while ignoring the company's oppressive human and community relations practices. An ethical assessment is vital when evaluating corporate claims of sustainability, particularly when examining intended or functional greenwashing of the concept. Walmart is a prime example of a company recognized for its sustainability efforts, but having a poor record on labor rights and being accused of disrupting local economies through the displacement of small businesses by predatory pricing (Cernansky, 2011). Walmart has sought to avoid outside regulation by developing proprietary standards for labeling and compliance, but, according to Cernansky (2011), its sustainability index has not resulted in any changes to supplier practices or alteration of the supply chain.

Sustainability has been the subject of research in organizational studies, but the focus has largely been on the role of leaders through interrogation of the chief executive or chief sustainability officer, and not the broad experience of organizational members (Doppelt, 2010). Organizational research that has looked at people in sustainability initiatives has frequently focused on the presence of active and engaged senior leadership as a precondition for developing a sustainable organization (Baumgartner, 2009; Doppelt, 2010). Another research thread has stressed the importance of leadership, but redefined and broadened the term. As Ferdig (2007) asserted, "Anyone who takes responsibility for understanding and acting on sustainability challenges qualifies as a 'sustainability leader,' whether or not they hold formal leadership positions" (p. 25). In addition, senior leaders, managers, and front-line employees within an organization have different perspectives on what constitutes sustainable practices, and assessing sustainability as a part of organizational culture requires an understanding of these distinctions (Stoughton & Ludema, 2012). As Rogers and Hudson (2011) observed, "Practitioners at every organizational level can have as great an impact as formally constituted leaders or outside mandates when it comes to transformation of organizational culture" (p. 3).

Developing a culture of sustainability entails profound changes in practices across the organization, from governance to management, to employee relations, to community and supplier relationships (Doppelt, 2010). A survey of the literature by Bertels, Papania, and Papania (2010) revealed that, while a portfolio of strategies and practices is often utilized in organizations, cultural embeddedness represents a clearer path towards organizational sustainability. This review also confirmed that research is needed to gain an understanding of how to embed sustainability in organizational culture, "for researchers to engage with and learn from those practitioners that are 'living' this every day in their own organizations" (p. 52).

The contradictions that permeated early conceptions of sustainable development continue to block acceptance of a holistic ethic of sustainability and prevent committed leaders, at all levels, from actualizing their values. As Rees (2010) maintained, "Most of the world today is in the thrall of a grand, socially constructed vision of global development and poverty alleviation centered on unlimited economic expansion fueled by open markets and more liberalized trade" (p. 17). Despite this, the challenges of embracing sustainability leadership offer an opportunity to transform the discourse. Human ingenuity can be just as compelling as human shortsightedness and "the (un)sustainability crisis thus provides the world community with the unique privilege of intentionally scripting a new, ecologically adaptive, economically viable, and socially equitable cultural narrative" (p. 21).

Framing the Case

The evolving model of sustainability outlined above, prompted by impending ecological disaster, global social disjunction, and destabilizing economic inequality, points toward adopting an action-oriented, holistic, and ethical perspective. In this context, the present study focused on organizations striving to embrace exemplary sustainable practices across multiple domains. A conceptual framework was formulated not to limit inquiry, but to enhance the theoretical sensitivity and focus of the research.

Mobilizing sustainability at the leading edge. A growing understanding of what constitutes exemplary practice in organizational sustainability is emerging from the literature. Mobilizing sustainability at the leading edge implies a commitment to ongoing, dynamic change, exemplary performance, and the embedding of meaningful sustainable practices throughout the organization. Mobilization also requires broad stakeholder participation as well as concerted action aimed at achieving organizational sustainability. A shift to privileging collaboration in organizational relationships has systemic implications for leadership in how boundaries of interactions are defined (Worley, Feyerherm, & Knudsen, 2010). Traditionally, companies looked at operations narrowly, assessing external relationships as necessary, though often problematic. Worley,

Feyerherm, and Knudsen (2010) found that Gap Inc. actively transformed relationships with non-governmental organizations and suppliers from competitive and adversarial to collaborative partnering. In the process, Gap Inc. drew larger and larger system boundaries and circles of collaboration, but also turned the effort inward to evaluate choices, rather than only managing the consequences of those choices.

Leading edge mobilization is complicated by the same factors that have made sustainability heavily contested and challenging to define. Despite the difficulty of the terrain, certain themes have emerged from the literature. To foster leading edge organizational sustainability, it is vital to (a) clarify meaning and acknowledge complexity, (b) value history and narrative, (c) distribute leadership and encourage innovation, (d) collaborate across boundaries, and (e) think critically, act wisely and ethically, and reflect constantly. Taken together, these factors imply a conceptual framework founded on (a) organizational culture, (b) phronesis or practical wisdom, and (c) systems theory. In a holistic and reciprocal sense, sustainability governs organizational life, defining how leaders act, how sustainable practices are expressed throughout the culture, how deliberation takes place, and how systemic relationships are conducted.

Sustainability and organizational culture. The concept of organizational culture was primarily influenced by the disciplines of anthropology, sociology, social psychology, and organizational behavior (Schein, 1990). Culture is deeper than climate or group norms. The evolution of the concept of organizational culture was also influenced by complex systems theory. As Schein (1990) said, "With a growing emphasis on work groups and whole organizations came a greater need for concepts such as 'system' that could describe what could be thought of as a pattern of norms and attitudes that cut across a whole social unit" (p. 109). Culture in organizations develops over time within groups sharing a common history and it may be passed on to new members of the society or organization.

Cultural observation involves the analysis of language, metaphor, story, and action to gain a full appreciation for the richness and subtlety of expression (Mouton, Just, & Gabrielsen, 2012). The transition to sustainability is exemplified by a shift from "a worldview that is linear, mechanistic, reductionist, expansionist, and consumerist to one that is cyclic, organic, complex, constrained and . . .

productive or self-generating" (Princen, 2010, p. 60). The hope is that "if the sustainability metaphors are at least as compelling as the modern industrial metaphors, then a broad swath of people may shift from the techno-commercial-militarist-exploitative discourse to a sustainability discourse" (p. 61). This has profound implications for leaders who seek to transform a traditional culture into a sustainability-oriented one.

Sustainability and phronesis. Phronesis, often described as practical wisdom or prudence, has a long tradition in Western philosophy, with Aristotle (2012) being its principal proponent. Phronesis provides a means for living a fulfilled life, governed by virtue arrived at through a series of practical choices and forming opinions about "what admits of being otherwise" (Aristotle, 2012, 1140b28–29). Phronesis is different than the other two intellectual virtues of episteme and techne. Episteme represents the purely theoretical knowledge of the laws of science that are not subject to deliberation. Techne is practical, as is phronesis, but its goal is the art and craft of production. Techne is seen in technological achievement and the imperative to make something because it is possible, regardless of consequence. Phronesis governs episteme and techne by imposing an ethical framework of practical wisdom on value-free theory and production, incorporating, but going beyond reason and contemplation, to determine conduct and action. It is an ideal leadership trait in a complex and uncertain world.

Phronesis has experienced a revival through contemporary interpretations of and applications to social science (Schram, 2012). Flyvbjerg (2001) held that phronesis was an example of expert learning based on experience; trial and error; and ethical, deliberative, and practical action. People use phronesis to guide action, from everyday acts to unexpected, contingent decisions. The ethical framework imposed by phronesis focuses on value rationality, a prospect that has implications for social science and sustainability. Lack of progress in addressing worldwide crises exemplifies the idea that "problems with both biosphere and sociosphere indicate that social and political development based on instrumental rationality alone is not sustainable" (Flyvbjerg, 2001, p. 53).

Phronesis is particularly relevant for sustainability leadership. Schwartz (2011) asserted that a person exercising practical wisdom is improvisational, perceptive, and empathetic; acts on experience; and makes emotion the ally of reason. For sustainability, its telos, the proper goal of a particular practice, is a sustainable world, arrived at through a phronetic appreciation for intuitive, ethical action unbounded by convention, but fundamentally practical. Phronesis is an ideal approach for examining the contested realm of sustainability, a concept that should represent the epitome of practical wisdom comprising judgment-in-context, ethical decision-making, and practical action. It is a key skill for sustainability leadership because phronesis serves "as a mode of critical reflection, not only on the reasons for events, but on the consequences of these events, both now and in the future" (Śliwa & Cairns, 2009, p. 238).

Sustainability and systems theory. Thinking systemically requires sensitivity to interactions, reciprocal interdependencies, and the dynamic, mutual relationship between stability and change (Meadows, 2008). System boundaries are often apparent, but may not represent real demarcations. The world is, in fact, a continuum and, at the highest level of punctuation, no separate systems exist (Meadows, 2008). Boundaries may be created to understand systems, but these boundaries are illusory and heuristic. As Mohrman and Worley (2010) noted, "In today's highly connected world, all boundaries are permeable" (p. 290). This is an important concept for leaders seeking to break down hierarchical structures and transcend traditional boundaries.

Systems thinking drew inspiration from processes in the natural world, including ecological relationships and evolution (Bateson, 2000). Bateson (2000) envisioned a cybernetic epistemology that, he believed, more accurately described the systemic relationship between the mind and the natural world. For Bateson (2002), systems were evident in the patterns that connect all living creatures. For Keeney (2002), a systemic worldview carries with it an aesthetic sensibility, "a type of respect, wonder, and appreciation of natural systems" (p. 8). Meadows (2008) held a systemic vision that recognized empowerment, goodness, moral judgment, and "expanding the horizons of caring" (p. 184). Resilience is another key ingredient of systems, derived from multiple feedback loops that bring a system back into a new state of dynamic balance, despite large perturbations far from equilibrium (Meadows, 2008).

The traditional model of sustainability based on balancing economic, environmental, and social dimensions is simplistic from a complex systems perspective (Fiksel, 2006). These domains interact dynamically and reciprocally, with change in one often producing unintended consequences in others, an ongoing challenge for organizational leadership. Achieving sustainability in a particular domain requires that leaders expand the boundaries of analysis to examine larger system implications. According to Fiksel (2006), "Sustainability is a systems problem requiring collaborative solutions. Only a coordinated global effort, with participation from public, private, and nongovernmental organizations, can achieve genuine systemic change" (p. 20).

A systems viewpoint applied to organizational leadership implies adaptive change rather than static balance. In this light, "organisational sustainability is not a continuation of the status quo but, seen from a complexity theory perspective, is a continuous dynamic process of co-evolution with a changing environment" (Mitleton-Kelly, 2011, p. 45). The recursive characteristics of interdependent systems imply that "the notion of 'sustainability' as a steady-state equilibrium is not realistic" (Fiksel, 2006, p. 16). Reciprocity suggests that "leadership and the creation of an enabling environment are necessary but not sufficient; the changes have to become embedded within the organisational culture, through a different way of working, relating and thinking" (p. 52).

Appreciating the wholeness of a system is a process of mind and leaders must struggle with this reality. It follows that "the massive aggregation of threats to man and his ecological systems arises out of errors in our habits of thought at deep and partly unconscious levels" (Bateson, 2000, p. 495). Doppelt (2010) echoed this prescient sentiment when he stated that climate change is not a scientific or environmental problem, but rather "the result of maladaptive beliefs, assumptions and thought patterns that have produced deeply entrenched, dysfunctional behavioural patterns as well as social and economic systems" (p. 14). This "massive crisis of thought," and failure to understand and embrace a cybernetic epistemology, challenges the sustainability of natural and human-made systems (Doppelt, 2010, p. 14). This pessimistic outlook can be contrasted with a vision of "ecological health" based on humility, flexibility, freedom, and creativity (Bateson, 2000, p. 502). In this way, systems thinking and sustainability become one, unified by a common worldview and practiced with ecological wisdom by emerging leaders.

Experience on the Front Lines

An initial screening identified twelve potential organizations that aspired to be sustainability leaders, and the following four agreed to participate: (a) a small, entrepreneurial, privately held solar energy company specializing in residential and small commercial; (b) a major, diversified, land grant state research university with significant academic and campus life involvement in sustainability; (c) an iconic, pioneering, leading brand producer and retailer of outdoor apparel; and (d) a long-established and unique image- and principle-driven specialty food company. The researcher conducted twenty-nine on-site, open-ended interviews, without a set protocol, prompted by an initial question: how is a culture of sustainability enacted within the organization? Participants representing many different organizational levels and roles, from frontline staff to senior leaders, were asked to describe their self-defined experiences of sustainability in the organization. Coding of the interview transcripts was done intuitively and iteratively, and thematic analysis was applied to the primary sustainability-related codes. Direct quotes preserved rich description and supported emergent themes across interviews. These verbatims convey the personal and emotional journeys of those discerning meaning out of sustainability. Primary codes were grouped inductively into thematic codes, themes, and, ultimately, major categories.

Lessons for Leaders

The outcome of the data collection and thematic analysis was a set of values, practices, and processes that reflected organizational life related to a broad culture of sustainability. These emergent qualities and characteristics can guide leaders who are striving to create such a culture in their organizations. They are, typically, expressed as gerunds, implying action and direction. The patterns that emerged tended to fall into four major categories: embedding the mission, living the mission, balancing ideals and practices, and that relationships matter.

Embedding the mission was a major undertaking across all organizations in the study. As the CEO of the solar energy company asserted, sustainability "was in the DNA of the organization." Another participant noted, "We have written sustainability into our mission statement, and we really try to walk the talk as much as we can." For others, the goal was still aspirational. As one person said, "We have these little piecemeal things, but no, there's not – we're all wearing sustainable accessories, but nobody has the overcoat on." Privileging values was central, as one leader stated, "The more we can build a mass shared value of a care for the commons in what we do, that's how we implement sustainability."

The elements of the first major category are shown in Table 1:

Table 1

Category 1 - Embedding the Mission: Themes and Thematic Codes

Embracing holism	Hardwiring social values	Leading with core values	Moving the culture
Changing course	Leveraging generational wisdom	Unlocking activism	Valuing stories
Broadening the conversation	Mainstreaming sustainability	Exercising power	Taking the long view
Connecting to nature	Privileging quality	Sustaining change	Empowering divergence
Thinking differently			Enacting values

Adapted from Stillman (2015) with permission.

Some participants took exception to the term sustainability, favoring more critical and precise language. As one manager stressed, "What's the right thing to do is about, again, to use the justice frame, how do we create justice here." Social commitment was palpable and preeminent. A manager remarked, "We're an activist company that happens to be good at making [what we make]." Work life was actively managed. As one person noted, "Culture development here is very deliberate." Taking the long view was in the fabric of all of these organizations. The founder of the outdoor apparel company, said one staff member, "talks about the concept of the business – we need to be making decisions based on 100 years."

Putting the mission into practice was paramount. One manager said, "I do a variety of stuff, internal and external, that's trying to bring social mission really to life. It's great work. It's fun work." The mission was made real in the workplace in a variety of ways. An employee at the outdoor apparel company observed, "You know, it's pretty much in your face when you come to campus." Commitment was also expressed at the emotional level. As a manager noted, "We have a lot of people who have a lot of passion around the issues."

An emphasis on practice was overarching. One leader remarked, "I think that sustainability's too big of a word to draw a box around. . . . It gets a little fuzzy when you get out of the tangibles." Highlighting the personal connection,

Table 2 describes the themes and thematic codes associated with the second major category:

Table 2
Category 2 - Living the Mission: Themes and Thematic Codes

Making it real	Grassrooting	Minimizing impact
Engaging passion	Activating social change	Evaluating consequences
Enlisting optimism	Bottoming up	Keeping it simple
Incentivizing action	Promoting progressive values	Reducing waste
Accommodating life		
Embracing the practical		
Bringing it home		

Adapted from Stillman (2015) with permission.

a participant noted that sustainability is "something that resonates not only in the company, but also with the people who work here." A strong commitment to bottom-up change was evident. As one manager said, "We really try to figure out a way to allow as much of this grassroots bubble-up as possible." Practical, incremental, and thoughtful efforts predominated. A staff member observed, "That's really what sustainability is for me – reducing my impact and improving the planet through this variety of practices."

The attributes of the third major category are depicted in Table 3:

Table 3
Category 3 - Balancing Ideals and Practices: Themes and Thematic Codes

Coping with commitment	Making it better	Making the case
Managing absolutism	Stepping forward	Measuring performance
Confronting reality	Being deliberate	Acting from data
Rationalizing growth	Hashing it out	Finding real solutions

Adapted from Stillman (2015) with permission.

Dynamic tension was often evident when trying to enact sustainability. As the CEO at the solar energy company lamented, "It's a failure of ours that we are still burning fossil fuels when we shouldn't be. I live with a tension between an absolutist view of sustainability and a one-step closer view." Some participants were frustrated with the balance between articulated belief and practice. One participant noted, "We have a commitment to sustainability that . . . leadership finally approved. . . . However . . . all of the justice-related bullet points that were in there were taken out before the final approval." Others were concerned about the apparent paradox between sustainability and growth. A supervisor wondered, "Why do you want us to grow 30%? Is that sustainable?"

Decision-making was very deliberate and mission driven. As one manager emphasized, "When you make a decision that has an economic impact, what are the social ramifications for that, as well?" Dialogue and participation were high priorities, as one participant noted, "There's different stakeholders, so different people are involved. It's a conversation." Conflict in the context of a common goal was often productive. A supervisor asserted, "I don't mind nonalignment, as long as we're all headed in the right direction and the vision is all the same. . . . I think those are the best fights to have." Balancing ideals and practice at work can be liberating, as one staff member remarked, "That was a revelation to me, that you could have ethically-focused income."

Interpersonal relations were highly valued as well. As a senior manager put it, "We have all these things that we talk about and toolkits and blah, blah, blah, and it actually comes down to relationships." Traditional boundaries often melted. As one person reported, "The questions people ask don't really have a lot of political boundary." Creativity and initiative typically trumped hierarchies, as a participant noted, "There's no gatekeeping about ideas." Positive relationships extended to supply chain partners. A leader noted, "I guess that's what sustainability means to me – our practices with them have to be sustainable for them as well, so we can have these long-term relationships."

A sense of closeness and inclusion prevailed, with the notion that "everybody's kind of wrapped together." Tolerance and empathy were also evident. As one participant said, "It's about building those relationships, where everybody ends up working together, warts and all. . . . Absolutely, it is a family." Leaders strove to make work life real, as a senior manager emphasized, "We want it to be an authentic experience for people." Appreciating people outside the organization

Table 4 presents the multiple values, practices, and processes of the fourth majority category:

Table 4
Category 4 - Relationships Matter: Themes and Thematic Codes

Melting boundaries	Engaging stakeholders	Partnering across the supply chain	Working like family	Valuing customers
Catalyzing partnerships	Getting people on board	Connecting on shared values	Being together	Connecting with people
Working the system	Voicing the message	Pricing sustainably	Fitting in	Sustaining engagement
Navigating complexity	Connecting to community	Partnering for the future	Feeling authentic	
Sustaining relationships	Leveraging social media	Maximizing influence		
	Making social issues commonplace	Looking deep		

Adapted from Stillman (2015) with permission.

was also a high priority. One supervisor expressed this sentiment, saying, "I read every single feedback that somebody leaves on our website. . . . Our customers are more passionate and amazing." Connections were based on much more than products or services. As a senior manager recounted, "When I think about communicating our values and connecting with consumers and people, there's education, emotion and activism."

The Path Forward for Sustainability Leadership

The picture that emerged from the findings was of sustainability as a rich, cultural phenomenon. The sustainable organization, facilitated by leaders at all levels, who embedded and lived the mission, balanced ideals and practices, and privileged relationships in every aspect of the enterprise. The organization evinced holism and leadership through hardwired core values, and close attention to culture. Organizational life valued real engagement, supported active and meaningful participation, and sought to minimize harmful impact. Grappling with dynamic tension was a constant endeavor for leaders within the organization, demonstrated by a realistic understanding of commitment, a dedication to deliberate progress, and a firm belief in practical action. Finally, relationships were preeminent across all boundaries, with engaged stakeholders, supply chain partners, employees, and customers. Taken together, these values, practices, and processes establish potential benchmarks for leaders to gauge an organization's progress toward sustainability. Translating these actionable, experientially-grounded elements into an organizational assessment is a key follow-up recommendation. The goal would be to help other leaders go beyond implementation and measure the key elements associated with a culture of sustainability.

The findings also support and refine a conceptual framework of sustainability based on organizational culture, phronesis, and systems theory. The various elements under each major category were evident in the literature, but the selection and emphasis emerged from the experiential findings. This synthesized model of sustainability could inform the development of new policy and analyses seeking to apply a holistic worldview to sustainability. In addition, the model could guide curriculum construction in undergraduate and graduate education aimed at teaching a contemporary, grounded vision of sustainability and sustainable leadership. Finally, certification programs for sustainability professionals could benefit from this integrated perspective to produce a new generation of knowledgeable and committed leaders dedicated to a cultural, ethical, and systems-oriented approach to creating authentic, socially-responsible organizations and a sustainable world.

Acting sustainably is the bottom line. Ethics must be at the heart of sustainability action to address inevitable conflicts at the intersection of economic, social, and environmental domains (Bañon Gomis, Guillén Parra, Hoffman, & McNulty, 2011). The recursive nature of the model, represented by intersecting domains, connotes the constant interplay between culture, practical wisdom, and systems thinking in the generation of a holistic, ecological, equity-driven, and actionable concept of sustainability. The model is intended to evolve to meet the needs of people striving to act in sustainable ways. Living with contradiction, the inevitable challenge of acting sustainably, was echoed repeatedly in the findings. For leaders, navigating those tensions is aided by prudential interaction with the world, sensitivity to system dynamics, and appreciation for cultural embeddedness (Bañon Gomis et al., 2011).

A recursive vision leads to an unending dialectical spiral of questions and answers, generating explanation and new questions (Harries-Jones, 1995). This vision prompts reflection on sustainability and ultimate survival. As Harris-Jones said, "In order to survive, we have to jump out of our predicament by the only means at our disposal. We must continue to weave our own metaphors – metaphors of the whole" (p. 234). The synthesized model of sustainability is envisioned in Figure 8:

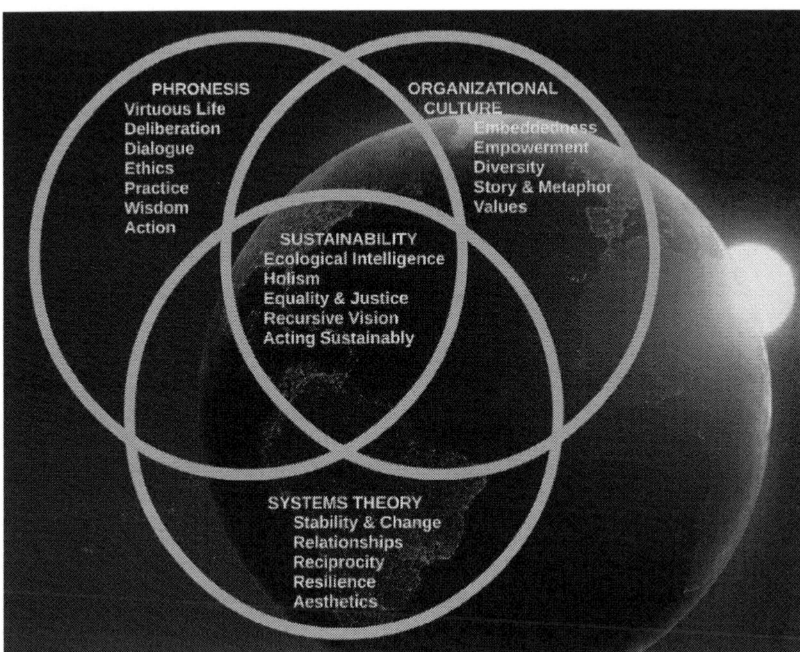

Fig. 8. Synthesizing sustainability: Integrating organizational culture, phronesis, and systems theory. Adapted from Stillman (2015) with permission.

Leaders committed to sustainability can mobilize this synthesized model and the practical elements outlined in each conceptual domain. These findings can guide initiatives at all organizational levels. For example, the importance of empowerment in a sustainability-oriented culture can prompt new forms of meaningful engagement, the preeminence of dialogue under phronesis can set the stage for critical and difficult discussions, and the dynamic of stability and change in systems theory can prioritize moving forward while preserving what is valuable in the past. The experiences described in this study, as expressed by verbatim quotes, give the committed leader a rich grounding in the language of sustainability, a dialogic syntax that can be used to foster open communication and create a common vocabulary.

For leaders seeking to act sustainably, the challenges are substantial, but the potential reward is great. Manifesting ecological intelligence, a commitment to equality and social justice, and dedication to action informed by reflection, the sustainability leader can engage vital stakeholders to transform the organization. In this way, new narratives will emerge that tell a story of caring, connection, and wholeness.

Questions for Discussion

1. What would you see if you looked at an organization that embraced the integrated vision of sustainability described in this chapter?
2. How would it feel to work in an organization with a culture of sustainability?
3. What qualities or characteristics would you like to exhibit as a sustainable leader?
4. What would your top three priorities be for moving forward if you were a leader striving to create a sustainable organization?
5. What further support and guidance would you like to have as an emerging sustainability leader

About the Author

Paul Stillman, Ph.D., has over 30 years of experience as a healthcare executive and consultant. He has held leadership positions in rural, suburban, and inner city hospitals, with responsibilities ranging from strategic planning to marketing to divisional operations. Paul was also a consultant with Planetree International, a pioneer in patient-centered care, conducting leadership retreats and focus groups to foster cultural transformation around an ethic of patient centeredness in a healing environment. Paul was formerly the Director of Organizational Vitality at Six Seconds, the global emotional intelligence network. He certified and supported coaches and consultants in Vital Signs, Six Seconds' organizational model and suite of assessment tools. Paul has a doctorate in human and organizational systems from Fielding Graduate University and a research interest in sustainability as organizational culture. He is a Life Fellow in the American College of Healthcare Executives.

References

Adams, W. M. (2006). The future of sustainability: Re-thinking environment and development in the twenty-first century. *Report of the IUCN Renowned Thinkers Meeting*. Retrieved from http://cmsdata.iucn.org/downloads/iucn_future_of_sustanability.pdf

Aristotle. (2012). *Nicomachean ethics*. (R. C. Bartlett & S. D. Collins, Trans.). Chicago, IL: University of Chicago Press.

Bañon Gomis, A. J., Guillén Parra, M., Hoffman, W. M., & McNulty, R. E. (2011). Rethinking the concept of sustainability. *Business and Society Review,* 116(2), 171–191.

Barnosky, A. D., Matzke, N., Tomiya, S., Wogan, G. O. U., Swartz, B., Quental, T. B., . . . Ferrer, E. A. (2011). Has the Earth's sixth mass extinction already arrived? *Nature,* 471(7336), 51–7.

Bateson, G. (2000). *Steps to an ecology of mind: Collected essays in anthropology, psychiatry, evolution, and epistemology.* Chicago, IL: University of Chicago Press.

Bateson, G. (2002). *Mind and nature: A necessary unity.* Cresskill, NJ: Hampton Press.

Baumgartner, R. J. (2009). Organizational culture and leadership: Preconditions for the development of a sustainable corporation. *Sustainable Development,* 17(2), 102–113.

Bertels, S., Papania, L., & Papania, D. (2010). Embedding sustainability in organizational culture: A systematic review of the body of knowledge. *Network for Business Sustainability.* Retrieved from http://nbs.net/knowledge/topic-culture/culture/systematic-review/

Boström, M. (2012). A missing pillar? Challenges in theorizing and practicing social sustainability: Introduction to the special issue. *Sustainability: Science, Practice, and Policy,* 8(1), 3–14.

Cernansky, R. (2011). Are Walmart's eco-efforts enough? Balancing sustainability & social responsibility at America's largest retailer. *TreeHugger.* Retrieved from http://www.treehugger.com/files/2011/01/walmarts-eco-efforts-enough-balancing-sustainability-social-responsibility.php

Doppelt, B. (2010). *Leading change toward sustainability: A change-management guide for business, government and civil society.* Sheffield, England: Greenleaf.

Eccles, R. G., Perkins, K. M., & Serafeim, G. (2012). How to become a sustainable company. *MIT Sloan Management Review,* 53(4), 43–50. Retrieved from http://sloanreview.mit.edu/article/how-to-become-a-sustainable-company/

Ferdig, M. A. (2007). Sustainability leadership: Co-creating a sustainable future. *Journal of Change Management,* 7(1), 25–35.

Fiksel, J. (2006). Sustainability and resilience: Toward a systems approach. *Sustainability: Science, Practice and Policy,* 2(2), 14–21.

Flyvbjerg, B. (2001). *Making social science matter: Why social inquiry fails and how it can succeed again.* (S. Sampson, Trans.). New York, NY: Cambridge University Press.

Griggs, D., Stafford-Smith, M., Gaffney, O., Rockström, J., Öhman, M. C., Shyamsundar,

P., . . . Noble, I. (2013). Sustainable development goals for people and planet. *Nature*, 495(7441), 305–307.

Harries-Jones, P. (1995). *A recursive vision: Ecological understanding and Gregory Bateson.* Toronto, Canada: University of Toronto Press.

Keeney, B. P. (2002). *Aesthetics of change.* New York, NY: Guilford Press.

Kiron, D., Kruschwitz, N., Haanaes, K., & von Streng Velken, I. (2011). Sustainability nears a tipping point. *MIT Sloan Management Review,* 53(2). Retrieved from http://sloanreview.mit.edu/article/sustainability-nears-a-tipping-point/

Kowalski, R. (2013). Sense and sustainability: The paradoxes that sustain. *World Futures: The Journal of Global Education,* 69(2), 75–88.

Linnenluecke, M. K., & Griffiths, A. (2013). Firms and sustainability: Mapping the intellectual origins and structure of the corporate sustainability field. *Global Environmental Change,* 23(1), 382–391.

Meadows, D. H. (2008). *Thinking in systems: A primer.* White River Junction, VT: Chelsea Green.

Mitleton-Kelly, E. (2011). A complexity theory approach to sustainability: A longitudinal study in two London NHS hospitals. *The Learning Organization,* 18(1), 45–53.

Mohrman, S. A., & Worley, C. G. (2010). The organizational sustainability journey: Introduction to the special issue. *Organizational Dynamics,* 39(4), 289–294.

Mouton, N., Just, S. N., & Gabrielsen, J. (2012). Creating organizational cultures. Journal of *Organizational Change Management*, 25(2), 315–331.

Pfeffer, J. (2010). Building sustainable organizations: The human factor. *Academy of Management Perspectives,* 24(1), 34–45.

Princen, T. (2010). Speaking of sustainability: The potential of metaphor. *Sustainability: Science, Practice, & Policy.* Retrieved from http://sspp.proquest.com/archives/vol6iss2/communityessay.princen.html

Rees, W. (2010). What's blocking sustainability? Human nature, cognition, and denial. *Sustainability: Science, Practice, & Policy.* Retrieved from http://sspp.proquest.com/archives/vol6iss2/1001-012.rees.html

Rockström, J., Steffen, W., Noone, K., Persson, A., Chapin, III, F. S., Lambin, E. F., . . . Foley, J. A. (2009). A safe operating space for humanity. *Nature*, 461(7263), 472–475.

Rogers, K., & Hudson, B. (2011). The triple bottom line: The synergies of transformative perceptions and practices for sustainability, *OD Practitioner,* 43(4), 3–9.

Schein, E. H. (1990). Organizational culture. *American Psychologist,* 45(2), 109–119.

Schram, S. (2012). Phronetic social science: An idea whose time has come. In B. Flyvbjerg, T. Landman, & S. Schram (Eds.), *Real social science: Applied phronesis* (pp. 15–26). New York, NY: Cambridge University Press.

Schwartz, B. (2011). Practical wisdom and organizations. *Research in Organizational Behavior,* 31, 3–23.

Śliwa, M., & Cairns, G. (2009). Towards a critical pedagogy of international business: The application of phronēsis. *Management Learning*, 40(3), 227–240.

Stillman, P. (2015). *Sustainability as organizational culture: Uncovering values, practices, and processes* (Doctoral dissertation). Available from ProQuest Dissertations and

Theses database. (UMI No. 3683401)

Stoughton, A. M., & Ludema, J. (2012). The driving forces of sustainability. *Journal of Organizational Change Management*, 25(4), 501–517.

United Nations. (1987). Our common future. *Report of the World Commission on Environment and Development.* Retrieved from http://www.un-documents.net/our-common-future.pdf

Williams, C. C., & Millington, A. C. (2004). The diverse and contested meanings of sustainable development. *Geographical Journal,* 170(2), 99–104.

Worley, C. G., Feyerherm, A. E., & Knudsen, D. (2010). Building a collaboration capability for sustainability: How Gap Inc. is creating and leveraging a strategic asset. *Organizational Dynamics,* 39(4), 325–334.

CHAPTER 6

Creating Shared Value through Aligned Corporate Leadership, Purpose, Strategy, and Governance

Karen Smith Bogart
Fielding Graduate University

Preamble

Subject of this chapter. This chapter assesses the changing interrelationship between the firm and society. It recognizes that human, ecological, economic, and social systems impact company strategies and practices, and, in turn, the systems are shaped by them. The study explores how a firm's corporate social responsibility (CSR) principles and stakeholder engagement bring to the surface risks and opportunities for the firm. It highlights diverse resolution opportunities through innovation, revised business and operational practices, and collaboration with external partners. This provides a basis for product and service innovation, market growth, and enhanced operating capabilities that create shared value (CSV) and benefit for the firm and its stakeholders. The chapter also considers the pressures that are broadly advancing corporate sustainability performance. These include the linkage of company purpose to long-term value creation, growth of sustainable investing, and recognition that sustainability is a critical corporate governance concern and responsibility.

Nature of this study. This chapter leverages scholarly literature that shapes corporate social responsibility, stakeholder theory, sustainable investing, shared value creation, and corporate governance. It identifies recent developments in business leadership, company purpose, environmental, social, and governance (ESG) performance, sustainable investing, ESG reporting, and company financial performance. This study draws upon qualitative research studies that assessed the board of directors' contributions to corporate social responsibility within US public companies that are recognized as CSR leaders, and acknowledges current sustainability achievements of leading firms. This evaluation integrates the findings of scholars that have assessed the effects of ESG commitments and business practices in enhancing financial returns and risk-reward management. It also considers the interrelationship of the firm and society, given growing social, environmental, and health system challenges and connectivity.

Outcome of this chapter. Sustainability is a significant corporate governance responsibility in an uncertain and connected world. Current and emerging conditions and needs remind us of our ecological, social, and human systems. Societal problems transcend the capabilities of any company and require broader transparency, investment, coordination, and accountability.

Commitment to sustainability has been shown to have diverse benefits for a firm's stakeholders including active engagement, product and service innovation, employment, capability development, environmental stewardship, and long-term value creation. This study identifies several factors that are advancing corporate sustainability performance. They include (1) an expanded definition of the firm's purpose, (2) the explosive growth of sustainable investing, and (3) recognition that sustainability is a critical concern and responsibility of corporate governance. The alignment of company purpose, business and ESG commitments, leadership, and governance practices enhances financial performance and risk management in corporations. It encourages increased transparency with investors regarding business directions, commitments, and achievements, enabling more informed decisions. This linkage fosters creative company partnerships and alliances to address emerging needs, manage risks, and advance opportunities that transcend the capability and impact of one firm. This also provides impetus for the firm to collaborate with other companies, universities, governmental entities, and non-government organizations in facing complex environmental, health, and social systems challenges.

Introduction

Dynamic connections intensify global opportunity and risk for firms in the flow of capital, innovation, market development, and resource usage. This chapter considers how company practices also have significant impact on local and broader human, ecological, economic, and social systems. Operational decisions can cause systems either to benefit or harm citizens, the environment, and other firms. Likewise, challenges such as climate change, epidemics, and resource scarcity require the collaboration of multiple firms. COVID-19 has demonstrated the need for coordinated responses from companies, non-profit organizations, governments, and citizens.

This chapter outlines a growing interrelationship between the firm and its leadership in society. This occurs through broader company purpose, business leadership, stakeholder engagement, and expectations of societal, constituent, and firm benefits. Use of CSR principles, ESG commitment, and sustainability practices yield these shared advantages.

Business leaders are visibly redefining "the firm's purpose in society. Their reinterpretations reflect broader responsibility, impact, and respect for the contributions of key stakeholders. They recognize that long-term company value creation requires both sustainability leadership and financial performance.

Firms have diverse stakeholders including customers, employees, suppliers, investors, and communities. These constituents have demanded greater corporate social responsibility in addressing societal challenges and in meeting their specific interests. Company-stakeholder engagement processes often promote new awareness of expectations, needs, and opportunities to address these challenges. Porter and Kramer (2011) observed that this provides a basis for product and service innovation, market growth, and enhanced operating capabilities that create shared value (CSV) and benefit for the firm and its stakeholders.

Institutions and individuals increasingly employ sustainable investing strategies. These investors desire superior financial performance and demonstrated corporate social responsibility. They desire transparent reporting and the tools to understand the firm's material risks as well as their actions to address them.

The US public board of directors has a fiduciary responsibility to maximize the firm's long-term company value and resilience, which requires an ongoing relationship with company stakeholders. CSR commitments must be integrated in strategy, operational plans, business and ESG commitments, risk management, and governance practices.

Company purpose, business leadership, and stakeholder engagement require continued commitment, investment, and performance. It requires a broader view of the firm's interrelationship with the world. This chapter considers related challenges and opportunities.

Corporate Social Responsibility Literature

Corporate social responsibility is founded in economic, legal, ethical, and philanthropic principles. It is shaped by stakeholder theory's assertion that the company exists in a dynamic web of internal and external stakeholders, to whom they have responsibility. Therefore, the firm continually engages with their constituents to comprehend and integrate their needs in marketing insights, strategy, and capability development. They also provide insights regarding ongoing improvements and investments.

CSR commitments outline company beliefs, values, and planned achievements. They address issues including stakeholder relationships, company and community capabilities, human resource practices, supply chain management, manufacturing processes, environmental impact, and health. Although voluntary, they influence company strategy, operating plans, and policies. Firms use these commitments to encourage new innovative approaches, value propositions, and business models to meet stakeholder needs.

Early accounting-based assessments of corporate social responsibility investments were unpersuasive. These evaluations often ignored contributions to strategy, customer satisfaction, market share, loyalty, brand, reputation, governance, and risk management. Furthermore, active constituent involvement encourages deeper understanding of market, value chain, and ESG opportunities and risks. That is why recent financial assessments disagree with the prior accounting-based reviews. Giese, Lee, Melas, Nagy, and Nishikawa (2019) found that ESG practices are associated with lower costs of capital and higher valuations, as well as higher profitability and lower exposure to risk volatility. This indicates that firms using sustainability commitments and processes have better and more predictable financial performance than those not employing these practices.

Company-stakeholder engagement processes have caused constituent needs, desires, and concerns to surface. This expands company awareness of product and service needs, including their availability, fit, usage, and benefit. These conversations often highlight specific conflicts between desired consumer usage and access to them. This could take the form of a health system not providing a specific drug needed to treat local patients. Engagement processes promote problem solution, strategy and policy changes, and operating practice changes.

Stakeholders benefit from break-through products and services and support, while firms realize competitive advantage through improved market understanding, business focusing, innovation, operational process efficiencies, and enhanced reputation. Both companies and constituents benefit from alignment of interests, trust building, and collaboration.

Companies have diverse stakeholders including customers, suppliers, employees, and communities. These constituents have demanded greater corporate social responsibility in addressing societal challenges and in meeting their specific interests. Company-stakeholder engagement processes often build knowledge of expectations, needs, and the means to address them. Porter and Kramer (2011) asserted that this provides a basis for product and service innovation, market growth, and enhanced operating capabilities that create shared value (CSV) and benefit for the firm and its stakeholders.

Some firms have chosen bolder paths; they have chosen to collaborate locally with other companies in the same industry as well as universities, vocational programs, suppliers, government leaders, non-governmental organizations, and venture capitalists, to foster the development of innovation clusters. Engel (2015) and Porter (1998) identified that these associations emerge as geographic concentrations of interconnected companies, capabilities, and entrepreneurial processes simultaneously compete and collaborate. They are shaped through formal and informal networks, venture capital, and governmental funding. Knowledge and skills developed in one firm are shared with others in the cluster; this spurs the development of expertise, new products and processes, and increased employment. This creates shared value (CSV) as company competitiveness is advanced, stakeholder needs are met, and the community benefits. Innovation cluster examples include the Silicon Valley (USA), Herzliya (Israel), and Zhongguancun (PRC) for software and Boston (USA) for biotechnology.

Corporate governance shapes how a company functions in its fiduciary duty, operations, relationships, and accountability. It seeks to protect constituent rights, balance firm and stakeholder interests, provide strategic and ethical guidance, and ensure transparency and accountability. The board of directors is the company's ultimate decision-making body. It is required to use independence, sound judgment, and critical questioning in its work to maximize firm value and strategic resilience. Primary board responsibilities include strategy review and resourcing, advisement, fiduciary accountability, governance, stakeholder engagement, and social responsibility. Sustainability is woven through all of these duties. Together, the board and management prioritize and invest in opportunities for realizing corporate purpose in brand differentiation, cost reductions, operational efficiencies, innovation, talent engagement, and risk mitigation. They develop strategic commitments that frame company priorities including multiyear operational improvements, employee diversity and inclusion, capability development, and expected value creation. Engagement in strategy encourages director knowledge of the impact of CSR on company performance, competitive advantage, and opportunities for shared value. This stimulates board support for CSR initiatives that enhance market opportunity, the value chains of the firm and their customers, and societal benefit. Examples of these strategic initiatives include Autodesk's development of machine learning-based software that improves worker safety and health in construction sites; Mohawk Industries, Inc.'s recycling of plastic bottles to produce residential and commercial carpeting; and Cisco's reduction of greenhouse gas emissions through the use of renewable energy.

Pressures Advancing Corporate Social Responsibility

Global connections have aided communications, innovation, supply chains, marketing, and access to capital. However, they have revealed inconsistencies and gaps in access, infrastructure, social systems, and resources. This has raised questions regarding the role and responsibility of the firm in society. Stakeholders have called for greater company leadership in mitigating and addressing both societal challenges and their specific interests. They have raised concerns regarding the company's impact on climate change and the subsequent risk to the company's future value. In response, companies have embraced corporate social responsibility, with specific pressures encouraging greater commitment, attention, and impact. These include business leadership defining a broader company purpose, investor expectations and funding, and corporate governance advancements.

Broader Company Purpose

Business leaders have long accepted the corporate responsibility for building financial value for their owners. However, they have recently recognized that long-term value must be created for all of their stakeholders. In 2019, The

Business Roundtable, comprising Chief Executive Officers of large American companies, outlined a new understanding of corporate purpose. It acknowledged that customers, employees, suppliers, communities, and shareholders are essential in the building of long-term value; therefore, they should benefit from it in employment, investments, capabilities, sustainable business practices, and fair and ethical relationships.

The Business Roundtable statement rejected longstanding shareholder primacy principles that dictated that the corporation existed primarily to serve shareholders through increased profits. That narrow business purpose had fostered short-term performance that met immediate financial goals, but sub-optimized longer-term value creation. Rather, The Business Roundtable statement described an expanded company purpose and leadership responsibility. It embraced the stakeholder theory perspective that all stakeholders should be respected, valued, engaged, and benefited.

Larry Fink, Chairman and CEO of BlackRock, one of the world's largest institutional investment firms, also identified the corporate purpose to be long-term profit creation and an "animating force" for realizing value through stronger strategy and culture. He acknowledged that achievement of long-term profit would require stakeholder engagement, alignment of interests, and related investments in innovation and capability development. He observed that firms must simultaneously deliver broad financial performance and demonstrate its contribution to society. Fink indicated that companies should disclose their strategic sustainability risks, and report their progress in addressing them. He also warned that BlackRock, as a major investor, would vote against management and director candidates in firms that failed to demonstrate progress in sustainability-related disclosures and operating practices and plans.

A broad corporate purpose reinforces the alignment between a company's ESG statements, claims, good behaviors, and positive outcomes. Simultaneously, it highlights inconsistencies between company claims and pursuant actions, as to encourage better practices. Conflicting examples could include a pharmaceutical firm's development and promotion of opioid drugs as a low risk means to manage chronic pain and a fossil fuel firm's denial of climate change. Public exposure of such divergences might also cause another firm's leadership to avoid the degradation of company reputation and legitimacy by meeting their stated purpose.

Investor Expectations and Funding

Institutional and individual investors are enthused about the impact of broader corporate purpose and corporate social responsibility outcomes. Their interest is reflected in the significant growth in assets using sustainable investing strategies. In 2006, when the United Nations Principles for Responsible Investment (PRI) was launched, 63 investment companies with $6.5 trillion in assets under management (AUM) signed a commitment to incorporate ESG issues into their investment decisions. By 2018, 1,715 companies had signed the agreement with $81.7 trillion assets under management. The US Sustainable Investment Forum (2018) reports that sustainable, responsible and impact investing assets now account for $12.0 trillion dollars in the United States. This would constitute 25% of total assets under professional management. This also reflects increasing investor demand for sustainable investment options, wider investment choices, and increased disclosure of company risk to guide investment decisions.

Industries have different sensitivities to risks including market fluctuations, natural disasters, environmental impact, technology obsolescence, competition, and regulation. A specific ESG issue may present significant risk to company performance in one industry, but provide little risk to firms in another industry. Company management facing these material risks must ensure prevention-related investments, positive actions, and contingency plans. Khan, Serafeim, and Yoon (2015) empirically showed that company financial performance is higher when it is rated well on material sustainability issues than same-industry companies with poor ratings on those critical issues. However, they observed that firms with good ratings on immaterial issues did not perform better than same-industry companies that received poor ratings on those less critical factors. This suggests that effectively addressing material industry issues is fundamental to a firm's financial performance. This suggests that a paper company that is rated well for addressing material issues including deforestation, air pollution, greenhouse gas emissions, water pollution, and solid waste would realize higher financial performance than another paper firm that did not effectively deal with those critical issues. Investors have demanded greater insight from companies regarding their significant ESG risks but firms have varied in their disclosure. Additionally, some companies have not addressed critical shared risks such as climate change. Given this resistance, investors have sought more transparency regarding the expected impact of all material ESG risks and planned company actions to mitigate these risks.

Some investors have also suggested that CSR "commitments" are more intentional than tangible. They have questioned whether ESG investments yield significant business or social benefits. They have sought transparency regarding company strategy, sustainability-related Key Performance Indicators (KPIs), and outcomes. In response, companies increasingly express their commitments as objectives against material issues with measurable environmental, social, and governance performance goals. To assist investors, firms often contextualize their ESG commitments against industry problems, risks, and initiatives.

The United States Security and Exchange Commission does not require ESG reporting in corporate disclosures; however, firms report their performance through multiple channels. Companies report directly to stakeholders, through industry organizations, non-governmental organizations (NGOs), and voluntary sustainability disclosure frameworks to reveal progress, impact, and gaps. The sustainability disclosure frameworks include the Global Reporting Initiative (GRI), International Integrated Council (IIRC), Sustainability Accounting Standards Board (SASB), and the Task Force on Climate Related Financial Disclosures (FCFD) and they address material sustainability areas including climate change, human rights, governance, and social well-being. Large institutional investment firms including BlackRock, Vanguard, and State Street Global Advisors require company disclosure and perform associated risk analysis, data testing, and monitoring as they invest funds on behalf of their clients. Glass Lewis and Institutional Shareholder Services evaluate and report company ESG performance to investors in proxy advisory reports. Finally, environmental, social, and governance related concerns are reflected in corporate shareholder proposals. Currently, over half of these shareholder proposals relate to ESG issues including climate change, other environmental issues, human rights, human capital management, and diversity.

Disclosing companies and investors have both raised concerns regarding ESG reporting. Companies have struggled with the volume, complexity, and burden of reporting to multiple frameworks with unique requirements. Investors have highlighted differing framework standards, and conflicting rating definitions and criteria. They have also questioned the intention of company public relations stories that celebrate corporate social responsibility successes rather than actual impact. Improvement opportunities clearly exist in the alignment of voluntary frameworks and ratings, simplification of disclosure processes, usability of content, improved linkage to financial performance information, and provision of absolute ratings, enabling comparability across industries and companies.

Corporate Governance

Constituent demands for societal impact, corporate governance accountability, and transparency have encouraged broader director attention to corporate social responsibility. The board considers and shapes business and ESG commitments during strategy reviews and related funding approvals, business performance assessments, risk management reviews, management compensation decisions, succession planning, and board practices. They use these sustainability commitments and expectations as a lens through which they assess strategic business opportunity and risks. This attention has increased due to investor interest, shareholder activism, rating organizations, political pressures, and the media.

The board of directors also assists in stakeholder engagement. This demonstrates a commitment to gaining diverse constituent perspectives, and it also provides directors with direct, unfiltered input, which shapes their awareness of stakeholder interests, needs, grievances, and actions. These learnings assist in their assessment of company attentiveness, innovation, and value chain effectiveness. It also enables directors to serve as boundary spanners sharing company directions, accessing resources, and recognizing alignment opportunities.

The board and management contribute to CSR through complementary roles and experience. Management uses industry and company knowledge, and specific business expertise in strategy and operational direction. Directors provide diverse industry experience in identifying needs, risks, and strategic alternatives. They establish the company's appetite for maximum acceptable risk given the expectations of strategic rewards. Together, they determine the firm's strategies, business and ESG commitments, corporate ethical standards, and governance practices to maximize stakeholder access, inclusion and impact.

Implications

Shared value can be created through aligned company purpose, strategy, and governance. However, it requires leadership accountability, stakeholder engagement, strategic and operational investment, capability development, and organizational resilience.

The company statement of purpose explains the reason why the company exists in society. It frames the broader problems that it intends to address through knowledge of stakeholder needs and its differentiating capabilities. It identifies its key internal and external stakeholders and their contributions to the firm. Long-term value creation is acknowledged both as the outcome of the firm, its capabilities, and performance, as well as the renewing source of company investment. The purpose can also highlight the firm's values and expected behaviors.

Stakeholder engagement provides a source of discovery, interest matching, opportunity identification, and resolution of conflicts. Some stakeholder needs may be discerned and addressed by the company through product and service innovation, new market approaches, and business practices. Others may require the firm to creatively ally with other organizations to understand gaps and to develop integrated solutions. This is particularly true when a firm is addressing a stakeholder need for a product or service within a complex social system with unaligned missions, motivations, and capabilities.

Environmental, social, and governance leadership, capabilities, and accountabilities are critical elements of strategy, business leadership, and operating systems. ESG practices encourage continuous improvement in issues important to key stakeholders. Therefore, ESG commitments and investments must be integrated in business strategies and the associated actions must be measured as key business performance deliverables. A leader's success in achieving business and sustainability commitments and expected benefits should be reflected in performance assessment, compensation, leadership development, and succession planning decisions.

Company management and the board of directors should promote the firm's attainment of ESG commitments. They must select and resource strategies with business and ESG commitments that indicate priorities, constituent relationships, investments, and tradeoffs. Their processes should include the identification and assessment of current and emerging risks including those specific to the firm, shared risks with other firms, and broader societal risks. Regular reviews of strategic and operational planning progress and impact would reinforce the criticality of achievement.

Finally, both institutional and private investors need clear and meaningful information to guide their sustainability investing decisions. The company should provide details regarding specific firm and shared ESG commitments, risks, related progress, and impact. It should avoid public relations positioning and should, rather, factually inform their investors. They should also advocate for the alignment of voluntary frameworks, criteria, and ratings to aid in investment decision-making.

Conclusions

Commitment to sustainability has been shown to have diverse benefits for a firm's stakeholders including active engagement, product and service innovation, employment, capability development, environmental stewardship, and long-term value creation. The alignment of company purpose, integrated business and ESG commitments, leadership, and governance results in higher company financial performance and enhanced risk management. It encourages increased transparency with investors regarding business directions, commitments, actual achievements, and behaviors that enable more informed decisions. The linkage fosters creative company partnerships and alliances that address emerging needs, manage risks, and advance opportunities that transcend the capability and impact of one firm. This also provides motivation to collaborate with other firms, universities, governmental entities, and non-government organizations to meet environmental, health, and social systems challenges.

Questions for Discussion

1. How can company management and board of directors use a broader "business purpose" to address specific company and broader sustainability opportunities and challenges?
2. How can CSR principles, stakeholder engagement, and ESG commitments improve the content, execution, and impact of a company's strategy?
3. The creation of innovation clusters is one example of shared value. Can you identify companies and communities that have worked together to build an innovation cluster? What benefits and costs have been experienced by them?
4. How should company governance practices encourage consistency between a firm's stated business purpose, positioning, and its actual behaviors?

5. The focus of this chapter has primarily been on the company and its stakeholders. Government is a critical stakeholder and potential partner too. How can companies and government organizations (national, state, local) work together to proactively address larger, complex, sustainability risks and opportunities?

About the author:

Dr. Karen Smith Bogart is the President of Smith Bogart Consulting. She has founded and led start-up firms, and taught at the University of California at Santa Barbara. Previously, she was a Senior Vice President of Eastman Kodak Company and managed global consumer, health, and commercial businesses. She also was the Chairman and President of Greater Asia, located in Shanghai, China. She currently is a director of Mohawk Industries (MHK), a NYSE listed floor covering firm, and Michelman, Inc, a private specialty chemicals company. She also chairs the Fielding Graduate University Board of Trustees. She holds a PhD and Masters of Arts in Human and Organizational Systems from Fielding Graduate University, a Masters of Business Administration from the University of Rochester, a Masters in Industrial and Labor Relations from Cornell University, and a BA, Political Science, from the State University of New York at Geneseo.

References

Autodesk. (2020). Autodesk FY2020 Sustainability Report. Retrieved from https://damassets.autodesk.net/content/dam/autodesk/www/pdfs/autodesk-fy2020-sustainability-report-Edit-Final.pdf

Business Roundtable. (2019). Statement on the purpose of a corporation. Retrieved from https://opportunity.businessroundtable.org/wp-content/uploads/2019/08/BRT-Statement-on-the-Purpose-of-a-Corporation-with-Signatures.pdf

Cisco. (2020) Cisco Corporate Social Responsibility Report. Retrieved from https://www.cisco.com/c/en/us/about/csr/csr-report.html

Eccles, R., Ioannou, I., & Serafeim, G. (2014). The impact of a corporate culture of sustainability on corporate behavior and performance. *Management Science*, Vol. 60, No. 11, 2835-2857.

Eccles, R. & Klimenko, S. (2019). Investor revolution. *Harvard Business Review,* Reprint R1903G.

Engel, J. (2015). Global Cluster of Innovation from Silicon Valley. *California Management Review,* Vol. 57, No. 2, 36-65.

Fink, L. (2019). A letter to CEOs: A sense of purpose. BlackRock. Retrieved from https://www.blackrock.com/americas-offshore/2019-larry-fink-ceo-letter

Fink, L. (2020). A letter to CEOs: A fundamental reshaping of finance. BlackRock. Retrieved from https://www.blackrock.com/corporate/investor-relations/larry-fink-ceo-letter

Freeman, R.E. (1984). *Strategic management: A stakeholder approach.* Pitman, Boston, MA.

Freeman, R.E., Harrison, J., Wicks, A.C., Parmar, B., & de Colle, S. (2010). *Stakeholder theory: The state of the art.* Cambridge University Press, Cambridge, UK.

Giese, G., Lee, L., Melas, D., Nagy, Z., & Nishikawa, L. (2019). Foundations of ESG investing: How ESG affects equity valuation, risk, and performance. *The Journal of Portfolio Management,* Vol.45, No. 5.

Hart, S.L. & Prahalad, C.K. (2013). *New age of sustainable capitalism: The business models to drive Growth and Social Change.* Pearson Education, Upper Saddle River, NJ.

Khan, M., Serafeim, G., & Yoon, A. (2015). "Corporate Sustainability: First Evidence on Materiality." *Harvard Business School Working Paper,* No. 15-073.

Mohawk Industries. (2020). Continuum. Retrieved from https://www.mohawkflooring.com/continuum

Porter, M. (1998). Clusters and the new economics of competition. *Harvard Business Review,* Reprint 98609.

Porter, M. & Kramer, M. (2006). Strategy and society: The link between competitive advantage and corporate social responsibility. *Harvard Business Review,* December, Vol. 84, No. 12, 78–92.

Porter, M. & Kramer, M. (2011). Creating shared value. *Harvard Business Review,* January–February, Vol. 89, Nos. 1–2, 62–77.

Winston, A. (2019). Is the Business Roundtable Statement just empty rhetoric? *Harvard Business Review,* Reprint H054YQ.

CHAPTER 7

Leadership as an Ecosystem for Sustainability

Alice E. MacGillivray
Fielding Graduate University, Institute for Social Innovation

Preamble:

The subject of this chapter. Leadership as an ecosystem for sustainability argues that people are thinking of leadership in new ways. It explores increasing complexity and how complex natural systems can help to describe and shape these new directions. This chapter focuses on an illustrative case study in which an organization's leadership was transformed from a rigid hierarchy to a vibrant and inclusive model of shared leadership reminiscent of healthy biodiversity. Van Manen writes about working in ways that emulate goals by drawing on concepts from natural systems, leadership for sustainability may become more agogical and effective.

The nature of the study. Leadership as an ecosystem is explored in two, related ways. Concepts are discussed in relation to complex natural systems and sustainability challenges. Each major concept is then related to a public sector study site (Broken Arrow, Oklahoma). When the organization started to focus on interactions rather than hierarchies, it benefited in many ways including morale, innovation, services, problem-solving and measurable skills. Data were gathered through day-to-day observation and five interviews. Complex system scholars such as Gerald Midgley and Kurt Richardson, as well as sustainability resources such as Canada's changing climate report, informed this chapter.

The outcome of this chapter. The natural world operates very differently than most organizations, especially hierarchical organizations. Even in unlikely contexts, ecosystem-like approaches to leadership have been successful. Specific ecosystem elements used in this case study are the result of firm, but permeable, boundaries (think of wildlife moving across the boundary between forest and grassland), valuing diversity (a healthy tropical forest is more resilient than a simpler arctic ecosystem) and aiming for healthy emergence (Darwin's finches are a well-known example) rather than simply following detailed plans. Benefits for the organization that are described in this chapter include innovations related to workplace wellness, an innovative program to serve the public, and unanticipated successes. If leadership that is implicitly based on natural system principles can help in the context of this case study, it has the broader potential, especially when used agogically, to be sustainable leadership.

This chapter explores a case study related to nature as a complex system. We use leadership, which we learn through school and life, to support sustainability and nature. How might leadership evolve if it were shaped by concepts from nature? Could that inform enhanced approaches to sustainability leadership? And these concepts, including complex systems, boundaries, diversity, research ecosystems and indicators of success, illuminate the case study. These are topics that interest me deeply as a human being, community member, faculty member, and researcher. I am bringing myself to this chapter as a whole person. Some disciplines discourage this, wherein authors and researchers strive to be objective outsiders. In qualitative research, especially research that spans fields and disciplines, first person writing is often accepted or encouraged.

The case study I reference in this chapter is from a medium-sized police department in Broken Arrow, Oklahoma, U.S.A. The content of their work does not focus on ecological sustainability, but the chapter does illustrate an ecosystem-like approach to leadership in a very unlikely context. Use your critical thinking skills to envision how these concepts and approaches might be applied in your workplaces, learning spaces or lives.

Complexity

It seems everyone talks about complex problems, but what does that really mean? Systems scientist Gerald Midgley (2014) outlined five elements of complex problems: interlinked issues, multiple agencies, varied views of the problem, conflict over desired outcomes, and uncertainty about the effects of actions. Richardson (2008) emphasized that only complex systems exhibit emergence. For example, a "complicated" system, such as electrical wiring of an office building, is predictable. Good planning is needed, and regulations and best practices for design and installation exist; if you follow codes, the wiring is safe. You plug in your computer and current flows reliably from the plug to the machine. In contrast, "complex" system elements interact and often produce surprises or emergence. If the office building manager told renters that all electricity would be generated by solar and wind within a year, it is likely that there would be conflicting opinions, technical concerns, and unintended consequences. In other words, in a complex system the future cannot be predicted in detail. As Richardson (2008) noted, "It is the existence of nonlinear feedback in complex systems that allows for emergence, self-organization, adaptation, learning and many other key concepts that have become synonymous with complexity thinking and all the things that make management such a challenge."

Four examples of complexity include:

Plastics and Pollution: Many products that were made of, or packaged with, glass, metal, cloth, leather or paper are now made with plastic. Plastics can take hundreds of years to break down, and can damage habitats and wildlife. It is estimated that 91% of plastics are not recycled (Parker, 2018). This is not sustainable, and we do not know how it will be resolved.

Climate change: Many think of climate change as temperature change, but the boundaries are much broader. Fresh water is essential for human and planetary health, and "seasonal availability of freshwater is changing, with an increased risk of water supply shortages in summer" (CCCR 2019) when parts of the western world are increasing water consumption for agriculture, swimming pools, and lawn and garden watering. On the rural island where I live in Western Canada, we explain to newcomers that in this small system it is normal, and important, for grass to be brown in the summers and green in the rainy winters. When advocates are trying to shift big systems, they face big challenges. For example, rules about language often emerge. Politicians and media outlets can marginalize terms (e.g., "do not use tar sands; use oil sands" or "avoid climate change and use severe weather").

Political unrest and terrorism: We draw boundaries around nation-states, religions, races, genders, sports teams, communities, and assign them values. We are implicitly encouraged to fight for those that are like us, and to stereotype others based on anecdotal information. During periods of resource constraints or stress, collaboration can become very challenging. It is difficult to predict how tensions will de-escalate or increase, and what will emerge.

Impacts of "the single story": Humans crave and create simple, single stories to avoid being overwhelmed. We draw boundaries and promote stories based on what we think we have learned. Single stories from recent years show how their simplicity gives them longevity: "Boomers don't understand technology." "Muslims are potential terrorists; white Americans are not." "Canadians are nice but boring." "Anyone can make it in America." "Women don't commit to becoming leaders." "Nature needs taming." "Innovations from Europe don't work here." "Bottled water is better than tap water." "It isn't worth the time to consult with Indigenous groups." "Immigrants take our jobs." "We must plan better, so we won't have surprises."

How did complexity play into the police department case study? We will begin with the "single story." Many think of police culture as enforcement rather than service-focused, and very hierarchical, and some are. Orders come down from the top to deal with issues at hand, and subordinates obey. Promotions are not solely based on merit; one has to spend a set period of time at a given rank before having the opportunity to advance. Stereotypes include black and white thinking: "black and white" is actually a slang term for police vehicles. The culture and work sound complicated, rather than complex.

Fig. 9. Pre-Case Study Poster in Broken Arrow Police Station

Context and "initial conditions" are important in complex systems. As context for this case study, the previous Chief of Police had risen through the ranks and had consistently behaved as the head of a strictly hierarchical organization. The culture suffered, as her successor, Todd Wuestewald, put it: "That shut me down after a time. When you get slapped down enough, you stop offering objections to things that are bad ideas. And what happens when that occurs is the organization blunders into a blind alley that it didn't need to go in, at all. Because somebody knew; somebody saw the freight train coming but either they weren't listened to, or they were so accustomed to not being listened to that they didn't say 'Hey there's a train coming.'" Hierarchies have the potential to make organizations rigid, even brittle. These initial conditions set the stage for a change in leadership approach.

When Wuestewald became chief, he essentially gave away the leadership power he had worked for decades to win. He experimented with the creation of a leadership team with rotating membership from all elements of the department: sworn members, civilians, senior and junior levels, and members from three unions. The team made the tough decisions. When I asked him about command and control with critical incidents, he agreed it was important, adding that perhaps 1% of the time they were involved in critical incidents, so they had 99% of the time to be collaborative. More about that team later.

Success Indicators

Gross domestic product (GDP) is central to our culture's measures of success. Readers of this chapter probably live in countries where GDP is glorified and is considered the measure of economic health. A constantly growing economy is seen as a good thing, regardless of whether citizens are happy or the ecosystems on which they rely are healthy. GDP has become a standard metric, embedded in larger systems such as capitalism, and practiced in a huge network of interconnected financial and political interests. It encourages practices such as ownership of cars, more paving of roads and bottling of drinking water for convenience. GDP is relatively simple and measurable. It tells a single story. Its simplicity and familiarity can be placed in stark contrast to the complex goals of human wellbeing and planetary health. Around the world, in places including New Zealand, Canada and, especially, Bhutan, there is interest in broader national indexes for wellbeing. Such indexes increase focus on social and environmental systems such as robust health and good living standards (e.g., University of Waterloo, n.d.). Another important element is that GDP is often thought of as a private sector and political tool, whereas broader indexes can foreground public and not-for-profit sectors.

How does wellbeing relate to the case study? Let me share an illustrative story from Chief Wuestewald. One day, the local Fire Chief came up to him on the street and said, "'Hey, that's a great program you guys are doing.'

I said, 'What program's that?'

The Fire Chief replied, 'You know: the one where the fire prevention officer goes out with a police officer to the elderly person's home. And they check all the smoke alarms and their safety systems, and the officers checking them on their security procedures and all their property is marked and all that kind of stuff. That's a great program!'

And I went, 'Oh. Okay, good' and immediately I called the Deputy and said, 'What's this?' He knew about it; I didn't know about it." (MacGillivray, 2009, p. 192). This story sheds light on several things. By this time, the leadership team had been operating for a while and they had embodied the idea of leading change. I spoke with several of them one-to-one and observed the team in action. Without exception, they were passionate about serving and protecting their community, and this creative new program emerged from their passion. I am sure the seniors felt heard and cared for by the department, the fire chief was convinced that fires had been prevented, and there may have been other spin-off benefits for the community as well. The story also shows that if you support a more ecosystem-like leadership approach in your organization, you cannot micromanage. I commented to Chief Wuestewald that very few public sector leaders would react positively to hearing of a program they didn't know about. He replied with a smile that they now know to keep him better informed. Under the previous chief, the department risked being fragile, something like an arctic ecosystem where one impact could cascade into a series of disasters. The new leadership approach was more like a robust, tropical ecosystem or a healthy estuary, where diversity and redundancy make the system vibrant and resilient.

Boundaries

I first "met" systems scientist Gerald Midgley when he was peer-reviewing a paper I had submitted. He wrote to me with his comments, saying that he does not like the double-blind review process, a common practice in the social sciences, where you do not know who is reviewing your work and vice versa. He introduced himself and shared his thoughts in a more collaborative way, which was very helpful. Midgley claims that the concept of boundary is the most important concept for systems work. The concept of boundary is critical for leadership, but often ignored in leadership approaches that aren't systems-oriented. Nature is full of boundaries such as community edges, different ecosystems at different altitudes, territorial boundaries, and fragmentation from human-introduced boundaries. The boundaries between ecosystems are called ecotones.

Ecotones include elements of both ecosystems or communities and can be very diverse, rich and productive spaces. Human beings make choices about boundaries every day. We will invite certain groups to the consultation, but not other groups. We will work closely with biologists, but not with the economists. The road will go through the agricultural land, not the forest. Sometimes boundary choices involve binary thinking; alternative energy is good, petroleum

Fig. 10. Ecotone in Nova Scotia, showing transition from ocean to forest

is bad. Boundary choices are ethical choices, and sometimes we are not even conscious of that. The following three examples show links between boundaries and ethics:

1. "A child died right outside a Chicago area hospital because his young friends were unable to drag him through the door and the health care providers refused to go out to help him....Where do services begin and end? What is the doctor's work and responsibility? The nurse's? The patient's or patient's family's? Boundaries are often uncertain, and the cracks between them can be large" Harte (2002, as cited in MacGillivray 2009, p. 39).
2. Waterfront property is often well-marketed and in high demand. Underwater, a study from the Union of Concerned Scientists estimates a steep $1.07 trillion worth of property is currently at risk from its exposure to the encroaching coastline. It also predicts 300,000 residential and commercial properties will face chronic and disruptive flooding by 2045, meaning flooding occurs 26 times per year or more, amounting to $135 billion in property damage and forcing 280,000 Americans to adapt or relocate (Penn, A.R., 2019).
3. "...Intelligence and law enforcement agencies had pieces of information before the September 11, 2001, terrorist attacks that, had they been shared, might have led to the unraveling of Al Qaeda's plot" (The Center for Public Integrity, 2014).

Boundaries are social constructs. In each of the examples above, humans decided where they would be drawn, and, probably, made assumptions about how beneficial their choices would be. In several of his publications and presentations, Midgley highlights his Theory of Boundary Critique (2015) and the importance of boundaries as the central concept in systems thinking. Think about the idea of improvement; this concept was important to C.W. Churchman who had a strong influence on Midgley's work. Churchman wrote about this idea of sweeping in as many perspectives as possible for decision-making in order to make the decisions as ethical as possible. As an example, you may be living in a city where there are "big box" stores and large shopping malls. These outlets require people to travel sometimes-long distances to shop, or to get the best bargains, or to find the latest fashions. Malls thrive, in part, because most families have one or more automobiles with easy access to fuel and paved roads. Advertising makes it easy to know what is available or discounted. However, nearby small stores selling local items may go out of business. Residents may spend less time getting to know each other in cafés, parks, or on almost obsolete front porches. There is nothing inherently good or bad about these choices; your values and choices of boundaries will shape your preferences and actions, but only if you think consciously about inclusion and ethics. Think more about boundaries. Who made the decisions? Who profits? How does each choice influence ecological, social, or financial sustainability? One of Midgley's systemic principles for work with complex problems is to "explore boundaries (stakeholders and issues), values and processes of marginalization *up front,* and revisit the boundaries of your work when new aspects of a wicked problem present themselves" (2014). This guidance foregrounds questions of privilege and power, which are central to both sustainability and leadership.

Boundary work is important in this case study. A few examples follow: When Chief Wuestewald realized the department could not function well with "business as usual," he was willing to explore any alternatives. Not surprisingly, other police departments were not rich sources of leadership innovations. He explained to me that the seed of his idea came from reading about private sector experiments; his exploration crossed boundaries. When he set up the first leadership team, there was a firm, but permeable, boundary around it. People communicated throughout the organization, but when it came to making an important policy decision, you were either on the team or you were not. Midgley's work focuses on the dynamics of this in/out boundary. In nature, you've seen it at play in relation to territorial boundaries during bird nesting seasons, and at a different time scale, when an introduced species moves into a new, natural ecosystem. Sometimes humans deliberately disrupt an ecosystem with good intentions, the Cane Toad introduction to Australia is a good example, and the introduction does not go as planned. As ecosystems are disrupted, there are tensions, some adaptive and some destructive. Similarly, there were tensions when the Broken Arrow leadership team was first established as illustrated by the following stories.

A leadership team member told me about the first time the group reached consensus on a very difficult issue that plagues many police departments. And, because the team was new, they were aware that the Chief had a very different opinion on how to deal with that issue. They invited him into the room and prepared for the "inevitable." However, the Chief simply told them it was their decision. As the officer told me this story, you could see him reliving the moment and the group's realization that this new approach was real. The dynamics across boundaries changed during that short conversation, and the Chief later acknowledged that the team's decision was the right one. After hearing this story, I said to the Chief something like, "But there must have been resistance, too; this was pretty radical." He suggested I go down the hall and talk with Major Carole Newell.

Major Newell did not seem at all disturbed by my unexpected arrival, and invited me in. I explained why I was there and we followed the steps to allow me to record our conversation. She had worked extremely hard to achieve her rank and she felt undermined when she had not been placed on the inaugural leadership team. After working her way up the ladder, seemingly less competent people were making the decisions she was supposed to make. As she said, "I was the first female to ever promote on the department: the very first one." This idea of more horizontal or collaborative leadership did not appeal to her at all. By now, I had the sense that she now supported the new leadership approach. I asked her what changed her mind, and she spoke about three things. I believe these three things are worth remembering for all leadership efforts.

First, she respected the chief and had a degree of faith that he was trying to accomplish something worthwhile. Second, was her own reflection and learning through writing a paper on shared leadership as part of the process of advancing to Major. She spoke with passion about the third: experiential learning through a novel and distributed approach to solving a difficult murder investigation in her detective squad. She thought the case might never be solved, and she was very impressed when it was. The new approach was helping her to do her job better. She was now firmly on board.

Research Ecosystems

Many think of sustainability research as quantitative and following the scientific method. Other forms of research are also critical if we are to effect positive change. In qualitative research, we are immersed as humans with histories in the systems we are studying. We should be visible to some degree. So, who am I as the author? In my 20s, I worked as an "interpreter" in a Canadian oceanfront park, where we led programs to help the public learn about and appreciate natural world. My favorite place was by an estuary: an ecotone-rich area where Black Creek flowed into the ocean. After work, I'd sit on the beach with the forest to my left, ocean to my right, and creek and salt water mixing ahead of me. From this vantage point, I would see intertidal, ocean, forest and fresh water plants and animals. It was inherently diverse, but more importantly, there were unusual species that travelled to the estuary because of that rich diversity. You never knew exactly what would be there or what activities would emerge. It reminded me of my human community: a rural settlement with third generation residents, Mennonite farmers, back-to-the-landers, loggers, commuters and retirees, all contributing in different ways.

Most estuaries are impacted by human development. Estuaries in good health are the richest and most productive places on the planet. The value of diversity is showcased in these special places. The most productive places on the planet must hold some wisdom for our human communities and our relationships with nature.

Wanting to span the boundary of academic and practical work, I became the first in my family to go to university, studying undergraduate biology and ecology. I later branched out into other fields, but continued to understand humans as embedded in ecological systems. I mention this because our society holds "the scientific method" in high regard. Emerging scholars may feel they have to stand outside of their research and be invisible in their work. For many forms of research it is helpful and ethical to acknowledge that the researcher sits in the middle of a research ecosystem. Our lenses and filters influence our work, even if we don't explore or acknowledge this fact. My love of nature, time in nature and education in biology and ecology all influence the ways in which I understand the world, including leadership. I acknowledge that. When I watched the leadership approach in Broken Arrow, I saw its estuary characteristics. Members with very different backgrounds were able to explore with a richness and depth that benefited the department and citizens. My lens can be framed both as a bias, and as a way of diversifying our approaches to important sustainability challenges.

Shifts in Leadership Thinking and Practice

There are many ways, including language, theory and practice, in which themes from natural. and other complex systems are showing up in organizational leadership. This section gives a brief overview of these shifts and their implications.

Language shifts and varies across sectors, disciplines and geography. As one example, I now hear "leadership" used as a process or practice (e.g., "we are working to develop leadership throughout the organization") more than I hear it used to describe a group of executives (as in "the leadership of our organization decided…".

The term "complex" is used frequently: Business leaders often report through surveys that their work is increasingly complex. On the positive side, this shows growing awareness that leadership in complex systems is not 'business as usual,' and that new approaches are needed. A down side is that the term may become a fad, and may be used frequently, but not necessarily, accurately or thoughtfully. The word "organic" is often used in a similar way, to comment on challenges that are not mechanical and futures that are less predictable. "Cross-pollination" has been adopted from botany and is used as a term to describe ideas being moved across boundaries from one group to another.

Theories are evolving. A boom occurred in leadership theory work after WWII, and for decades the dominant focus was on individual, formal leaders influencing followers. Those approaches continue to have merit. Since the 1990s, new theories are emphasizing leadership approaches that incorporate more diversity. MacGillivray (2018) lists a sample of these theories and frameworks, with several focusing on process and relationships. Researchers have characterized leadership as complex (Uhl-Bien, Marion & McKelvey, 2007), relational (Uhl-Bien, 2006), shared (Pearce & Conger, 2002), emergent (Plowman & Duchon, 2007) distributed (Gronn, 2002), generative (Hazy & Uhl-Bien, 2015), and pluralized (White, Currie & Lockett, 2016). Goldstein, Hazy and Lichtenstein (2010) researched leadership as interwoven with events that emerge from interactions. Raelin (2016) developed a theory focused on leadership interwoven with practice. These recent leadership frameworks are more ecosystem-like and more estuary-like than they are mechanical. In practice, unless you are in the sustainability leadership field, it does not necessarily matter whether these links to nature are explicit. What is more important is the recognition that diversity, fluidity, agility and humility are important in working with complex problems.

These ecosystem-like theories often emphasize how shared-leadership entities interact more than individual entities. There is recognition of complexity and the related need for agility and novel approaches. Emergence is acknowledged. Yet, is there "leadership" in nature? Some species are indicators of the health of an ecosystem. But is that leadership? Some individual animals are enforcers in their groups, maintaining order. Does that qualify? How about groups of wild horses, or elephants, where an older, experienced female often makes decisions for the health of the herd? If an invertebrate evolves to live in a polluted area and that evolution takes hold, is that a form of species leadership? If you have quick answers to any of these questions, try adjusting the examples to human communities. Are your answers the same?

Conclusion

This leadership case study is one of several I have explored as a scholar-practitioner. It is an unlikely story for policing, yet a real one with the potential to encourage those leading change, by providing insights that might make leadership more effective. By using concepts from complex natural systems in our work with sustainability leadership, we are creating a diverse, yet coherent, ecosystem of thinking and practice. In his work with the phenomenology of practice, Van Manen (2014) uses the term agogical, from the same root as pedagogy and androgogy. He describes an agogical approach as one that tries to be an example of what it is showing. Why do we assume that leadership rules or laws or checklists from business schools and training programs are well-suited to enhance sustainability?

In using concepts from complex natural systems in a leadership context, some success elements are, arguably, restricted to humans: trust, for example. Is trust really restricted to humans?

Others exemplify the ways in which healthy ecosystems thrive: (1) emphasize the importance of diversity for overarching goals (bigger than GDP), rich engagement, and exploration of leadership perceptions and assumptions; (2) deliberately plan "lightly," as sustainability is complex, which means careful planning will not predict the future in detail and may even be counter-productive; (3) develop and encourage a more integrated systems view in a culture where simple stories and binary thinking are often respected; (4) understand that boundaries are rarely real and almost never permanent, and if they result in damage or inequities, they can be changed; (5) know that resistors may become the most important collaborators; (6) instead of creating efficient teams, make space for intellectual estuaries; (7) consider becoming an authentic researcher who cares about impacts in the real world; (8) and realize that controversial leadership approaches can be better: people may just need time to observe and experience the benefits. I mentioned Major Newell's change in perspective when her group was able to solve a very challenging murder case, and I will end with one other success story.

Police departments around the world have international competitions, made up of tasks that require everything from strength to innovation. After the new leadership approach had been implemented, Broken Arrow sent a team to compete in Germany. Broken Arrow competitors had never attended such a competition before and were up against very large police departments from around the world with considerable competition experience. Much to almost everyone's surprise, Broken Arrow won. As you advance in your careers, watch for opportunities to show how re-designed leadership and collaborations can exemplify wellness and measurable success.

Questions:

1. Which sustainability issues have been highlighted in the mainstream press in the past month? Do you see differences between mainstream media in North America and Europe, especially around what or who are included or marginalized? Do mainstream press coverage differ from coverage in social media and alternative press sources? Why or why not?
2. Can you recall any news items or personal experiences where something went wrong because a junior person was afraid to speak up to someone more senior? When might that happen in an environmental protection field?
3. What challenges are you seeing in your life (community, workplace, college or university...)? Write down two challenges (one per post-it note or virtual equivalent,) and work in teams to decide whether each should be approached as complicated or complex.
4. Choose one of those challenges in your team and brainstorm ways of effecting change, with attention to the nature of the challenge and ethical boundaries for

your work.
5. Listen to Chimamanda Ngozi Adichie's TED talk on the "single story." What single stories are you hearing about sustainability, and how might leaders disrupt those stories?
6. Is there leadership in natural systems?

About the Author

Alice MacGillivray works with graduate students in the Schools of Leadership Studies, and Environment and Sustainability at Royal Roads University. She is also an ongoing fellow with the Institute for Social Innovation at Fielding Graduate University. She spent several years working with major park and protected area organizations as an internal and external consultant. Her papers have been published in several peer-reviewed journals and she has presented at international conferences on three continents. Alice always works to span practical, applied work and scholarly research in the hope each can improve the other.

References

Adichie, C.N. (Nov. 20, 2019). *The Danger of a Single Story* [Video file]. TED. https://www.ted.com/talks/chimamanda_ngozi_adichie_the_danger_of_a_single_story?language=en

The Center for Public Integrity (Updated May 19, 2014). *Agencies failed to share intelligence on 9/11 terrorists.* https://publicintegrity.org/politics/agencies-failed-to-share-intelligence-on-9-11-terrorists/

CCCR. (2019). Canada's changing climate report. Retrieved from https://changingclimate.ca/CCCR2019/chapter/executive-summary/

MacGillivray, A. (2018). Leadership as practice meets knowledge as flow: Emerging perspectives for leaders in knowledge-intensive organizations. *Journal of Public Affairs.* 18(1), https://doi.org/10.1002/pa.1699

MacGillivray (2009). *Perceptions and uses of boundaries by respected leaders: A transdisciplinary inquiry.* (3399314) Doctoral dissertation, Fielding Graduate University. Proquest Dissertations and Theses.

Midgley, G. (2014). An Introduction to Systems Thinking. Retrieved from https://www.youtube.com/watch?v=yYyTUs9ipmc

Midgley, G. (2015). Systemic Intervention. U of Hull Business School. Retrieved from https://hull-repository.worktribe.com/preview/385236/memorandum-95-insert.pdf

Parker, L. (2018). Planet or plastic: A whopping 91% of plastic isn't recycled. Retrieved fromhttps://www.nationalgeographic.com/news/2017/07/plastic-produced-recycling-waste-ocean-trash-debris-environment/

Penn, A.R. (2019). What Climate Change Means for Coastal Real Estate Values and Property Investors. Retrieved from https://www.allpropertymanagement.com/blog/post/what-climate-change-means-for-coastal-real-estate-values/

Raelin, J. (2016). *Leadership-as-practice: Theory and application.* Routledge.

Richardson, K. (2008). Managing Complex Organizations: Complexity Thinking and the Science and Art of Management. *E:CO* Issue Vol. 10 No. 2 2008 pp. 13-26.

University of Waterloo. (n.d.). Canadian Index of Wellbeing. https://uwaterloo.ca/canadian-index-wellbeing/

Van Manen, M. (2016). *Phenomenology of practice: Meaning-giving methods in phenomenological research and writing*. Routledge.

CHAPTER 8

Using the Sustainability Mindset Model to Develop Leadership Capacity

Kerul Kassel
Fielding Graduate University
Shelley Mitchell
Hult International Business School
Isabel Rimanoczy
Convenor Sustainability Mindset Working Group

Preamble

The subject of this chapter. This chapter delves into two of the central tensions that future managers will face in the context of their organizations as they endeavor to be responsible leaders in their firms. These tensions include achieving short-term financial profit and growth, while attending to longer-term social, environmental, and economic impacts, the time tension; while attending to the organization's interests while integrating the concerns of a wider stakeholder universe, the inclusion tension. These tensions are examined through the lens of a holistic model to develop a sustainability mindset, within the context of three dimensions: being (values), thinking (knowledge), and doing (competencies). We briefly review literature relevant to management tensions using the lens of the Sustainability Mindset Model. We look at the time and inclusion tensions through the model's four content areas of ecological worldview, systems perspective, emotional intelligence, and spiritual intelligence, and their respective developmental goals. We finish by discussing how the Sustainability Mindset Model can be used for leadership development, training and coaching.

The nature of the study. In this chapter we introduce the Sustainability Mindset Model (SMM) as a framework to navigate two central, responsible management tensions and to develop more advanced leadership skills for future managers in workplace environments. The SMM breaks away from traditional management disciplinary silos by integrating management ethics, environmental studies, systems thinking, self-awareness and spirituality within the dimensional contexts of being (values), thinking (knowledge) and doing (competency). As such, it aligns with the tenets of responsible management (Laasch & Moosmayer, 2015). The SMM provides practitioners, such as internal and external development professionals and change agents, (Caldwell, 2003) with a way to understand and balance managerial tensions relating to sustainability, responsibility and ethics. These tensions can serve as sources of organizational learning, leading to innovation such as new practices, products, services, structures, business models, and organizational forms, responding to stakeholder needs at local and global levels.

Outcomes of this chapter. This chapter offers a Sustainability Mindset Model for students to use as future managers and leaders. The SMM includes the three dimensions: being (values), thinking (knowledge) and doing (competencies) for responsible management. These dimensions help students to explore decision-making in a way that is more respectful of society and the environment. As we examine the time and inclusion tensions through the model's four content areas of ecological worldview, systems perspective, emotional intelligence and spiritual intelligence, the Sustainability Mindset Model can be applied in leadership development, training, and coaching. Thus, students can learn how to address sustainability and leadership issues through a set of ideas that, hopefully, will be useful in training future managers in ways that incorporate extensive experience with critical thinking, systems thinking and problem-solving skills.

Introduction

In this chapter, we explore two central tensions that students will eventually encounter as managers. The tension of time originates in the goal of achieving short-term financial profit and growth, while attending to longer-term social, environmental, and economic impacts. The tension of inclusion stems from prioritizing an organization's interests while integrating the concerns of a wider stakeholder universe, including shareholders, employees, suppliers, customers, communities, and the natural environment. We explore these tensions through the lens of the Sustainability Mindset Model's four content areas of ecological worldview, systems perspective, emotional intelligence and spiritual intelligence. In presenting the Sustainability Mindset Model, we introduce the dimensions of being (values), thinking (knowledge), and doing (competency) in each of the four content areas as a type of phoropter to understand and address these tensions. The SMM dimensions and content areas propose a more deeply ethical stance, a broader human, biospheric, and chronological scope, and a balanced approach to responsible management and leadership development. We conclude by discussing utilizing the SMM for the development of responsible management.

Overview on Tensions and Responsible Management

Managers at all levels and in all industries face a range of tensions when dealing with matters of sustainability, corporate responsibility and ethical practices. Scholars examining management tensions have recognized that they can be caused by institutional complexity and scarcity of resources, and that they can be especially challenging due to new regulations. When this occurs, a re-evaluation of organizational priorities is triggered, causing debate and realignment. When managers are faced with tensions triggered by environmental turbulence, such as climate change-related events—droughts, floods, fires, severe weather events, for example— there is an opportunity for collaboration and implementation of risk management strategies, allowing organizations to reconcile conflicting demands. Tensions may stem from various organizational, professional and political structures, such as hierarchies and their power differentials – an aspect of what we label the inclusion dimension. Managers experience time and inclusion tensions when they toned to balance the implementation of socially and environmentally responsible programs with the viability and profitability of their organizations, as opposed to only supporting profitability.

A study examining the qualities that define responsible management (Nonet, Kassel, & Meijs, 2016) utilized terms such as self-awareness, intuition, emotions, values, and ethics in relating the importance of time (short vs. long-term) and a higher purpose as connected to responsible management (p. 729). These terms complement the qualities that define responsible management and demonstrate a strong application of the SMM in understanding the tensions between short and long-term decisions and strategies, and between organizational entity and biosphere.

Time scales are viewed as salient, as well as short-term financial metrics, quarterly performance, annual gains, and exponential growth as among the most prioritized management values. The emphasis on rapid and explosive growth in the near term has frequently resulted in "negative externalities," or damaging impacts on stakeholders, in the longer span of time, with these impacts occurring both within the organization, and among stakeholders. Damage to the long-term viability of the organization, its employees, vendors, resource base, and customers occurs due to the pressure for immediate results. This speaks to the tension managers may face on a day-to-day basis: balancing short-term goals with long-term impacts.

Organizations do not exist in a vacuum; their success is linked to the well-being and engagement of their employees, the strength of the communities within which they operate, the financial ability of their customers to afford the products, and the health of the biosphere in enhancing security to their operations. This forms the inclusion tension between the primacy of the organizational entity and the health of the society and of the biosphere.

Using an either/or logic generates these tensions: either short term or long term; either profit or the environment. Yet these are false options, since the economic system and its subsystem of industry, depend on the social and biospheric systems. Businesses cannot survive unless they are financially viable. The biosphere is the living planetary envelope within which all social and economic activity occurs, and investors are typically used to a rapid return on their investments. The current and next generation of managers must be prepared to address this reality, and this includes examining the underlying assumptions and values motivating our behaviors at the personal level, to create a paradigmatic shift toward a sustainability mindset for more responsible management.

As demand expands for responsible management expertise and leadership within organizations across sectors of business, government and society, the question of the most significant skills and competencies that managers should possess has become a core topic in sustainability education research. In the next section we describe how the SMM considers the skills and competencies needed for meaningful and responsible careers.

Sustainability Mindset Model

In this section, we start by offering a definition of the sustainability mindset and then describe a model through which we will further explore these workaday tensions that are experienced by managers in their organizational contexts. We define sustainability mindset as a way of thinking and being that results from a broad understanding of the ecosystem's manifestations, from social sensitivity to an introspective focus on one's personal values and higher self, and finds its expression in innovative actions for the greater good of the whole.

By 'broad understanding of the ecosystem's manifestations,' we refer to an appreciation of the interconnections between different components of our ecosystems, and the complexity of impacts our human behaviors have on those systems (Capra, 1997). 'Social sensitivity' means an empathetic understanding of human interactions and interconnectedness. An 'introspective focus on the personal values' implies self-awareness of one's espoused values and any concordance or dissonance with one's values in action (Argyris, 1987, p. 93) as they relate to our sustainable or unsustainable behaviors. The spiritual dimension forms the 'focus on the higher self' and the consideration of purpose or meaning (Delbecq, 2008; Neal, 2008), and one-ness (Krishnan, 2008). Finally, 'innovative actions for the greater good of the whole' includes not only altruistic or philanthropic actions, but entrepreneurial or business actions that integrate a wider diversity of stakeholder interests, including interest in the planet and future generations (Mackey & Sisodia, 2014; Porter & Kramer, 2011).

This definition points to the complexity of the challenges, at differing levels: the individual, the social, and the ecosystem, and also within the cognitive, emotional, psychological and spiritual realms. Attitudes and mental inclinations are formed by many factors: experiences, information, values, emotions, and beliefs, which exist beyond a rational or "thinking" sphere. Yeager and Dweck (2012) suggest that mindset is an implicit theory, that core assumptions are rarely made explicit, but they "create a framework for making predictions and judging the meaning of events in one's world" (p. 303). Mindset has a socially-constructed root, and it is also shaped by personal experiences, purpose and one's character (Wong, 2012).

Disorienting situations or crises can cause individuals to experience cognitive dissonance, which undermines their basic underlying beliefs (Fang, Kang, & Liu, 2004; Mezirow, 1994) thus prompting an opportunity for a mindset shift. As society undergoes fundamental changes, these trigger shifts in organizational paradigms as well.

The Sustainability Mindset Model: Dimensions, Content Areas, and Elements

The Sustainability Mindset Model includes four content areas, which are enacted through collaborative and innovative action, via projects or initiatives that nurture the development of the four areas, and become the "mindset in action".

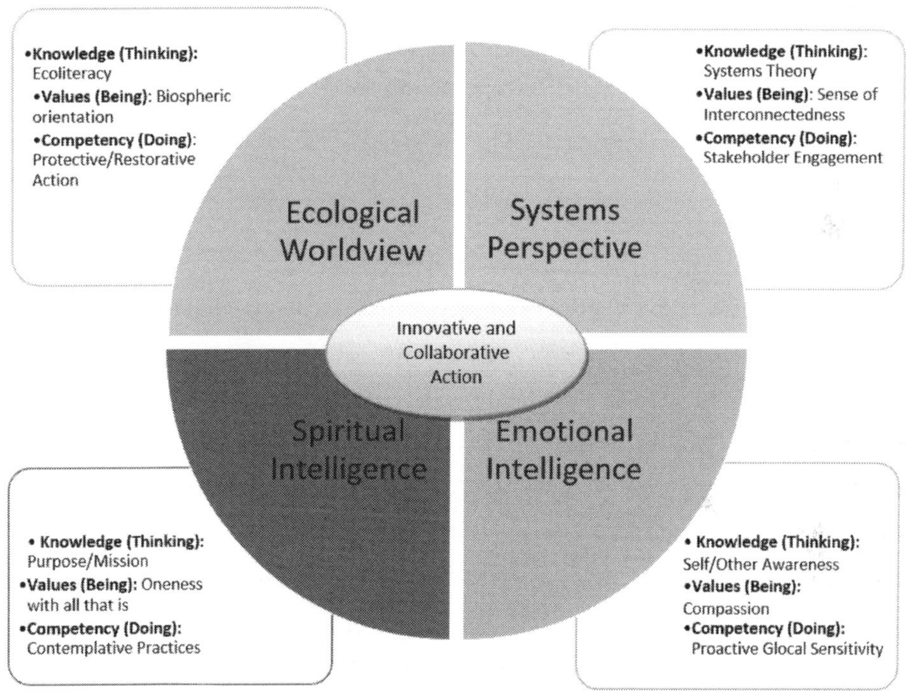

Fig. 11. Sustainability Mindset Model (from Kassel, K. & Rimanoczy, I (2018). Printed with permission.

The first content area, ecological worldview, incorporates local, regional and biospheric environmental conditions; trends and challenges; values and acts to preserve and restore resources while mitigating harm and adapting to new conditions. Ecological worldview considers interactions and impact between the natural world and human action, and also between individuals, organizations, and nations, taking into account the sense of place within an ecological system

(Goleman, 2009; Hawken, 1993; Kegan, 1982; Kohlberg, 1984).

Leaders that feel the pressure to attend to nature or social factors, while still making good business decisions, experience both of the central tensions: inclusion and time. Yet, it is difficult to relate to facts and numbers. The more we understand the impacts of our personal actions, our habits and our lifestyles, the more likely we are to care and feel the urge to find solutions. The tension that causes stress in leaders is related to the realization that behind statistics of social or environmental problems is a deeper discovery; managers are prompted to ask themselves how they may be contributing to this problem or how their firms might be making things worse. Becoming conscious of a personal contribution makes it possible to act in new ways, which then reduces the tension.

The second content area is systems perspective, which recognizes that every individual, organization, and industry is a subsystem of the larger biosphere, in interdependence with a host of environmental, social, and economic subsystems. As such, the needs and interests of these deeply intertwined subsystems, or stakeholders, influence research, analysis of data, strategy, and decision making (Elkington, 1998; Hawken, Lovins & Lovins, 2013; Senge, 2008). Although individuals experience the interrelationship of different systems in their day-to-day decision-making, leaders may not be fully conscious of the importance of considering the systemic interconnections as they analyze information, and make decisions. Thus, the inclusion tension emerges, as managers have the awkward sense that they must select one option over another, from within an either/or logic.

The third content area of emotional intelligence addresses the importance of introspection, self-scrutiny, the anchors of our identity; and resilience in maintaining equanimity, persistence, and concerted action on individual, team, organizational, and community levels (Goleman, Boyatzis & McKee, 2002; Senge, 2006). This content area provides a guide to conversations or exercises that can help leaders explore their motivations, what are the values with which they sustain their self-image and are there any inconsistencies with their actions? These inconsistencies create tensions and stress when managers are asked to balance demands from various stakeholders. Managers can be invited to explore their feelings in a confidential conversation, expanding, for example, their self-awareness and pondering different solutions.

The fourth content area is spiritual intelligence which refers to purpose, principles, values, and sense of one-ness (Doppelt, 2012; Rimanoczy, 2010; Scharmer & Kaufer, 2013; Zohar, 2012). It addresses meaning and purpose, and how we consider our actions in a deeper and wider meaning-giving context, as well as the internal judgment to assess the wisdom of one course of action versus another. When leaders sense cognitive dissonance between their values and their actions, they experience a stressful tension. Inclusion tensions arise between caring about the damage to the environment versus prioritizing short-term returns; decisions to cut costs may benefit the bottom line, but may also hurt other stakeholders. Recognizing and acknowledging this tension becomes the gateway to innovative solutions that can bring peace of mind, and align with purpose.

Connecting the four content areas is collaborative and innovative action, which integrates thinking, doing, and being, as a goal and a learning process. When developing a sustainability mindset with managers, the inclusion of collaborative projects requiring innovation provides an experiential learning opportunity that feeds back into the four content areas, providing insights and opportunities to develop social sensitivity, ecoliteracy, self-awareness, and to discover the satisfaction of meaningful work.

Based on the model, the authors developed a grid of specific, developmental elements that could provide guidance for leadership and management development in cultivating a sustainability mindset (See Table 5).

	DIMENSIONS		
CONTENT AREAS	**Knowledge (knowing, thinking)**	**Values (being)**	**Competencies (doing)**
Ecological Worldview	Ecoliteracy	Biospheric	Protective/Restorative Action
Systemic Perspective	Systems theory	Sense of interconnectedness	Stakeholder engagement
Emotional Intelligence	Self/Other-awareness	Compassion	Proactive glocal sensitivity
Spiritual Intelligence	Purpose, Mission	Oneness with all that is	Contemplative Practices

Table 5. Dimensions, Content Areas and Themes

This grid further elucidates the four content areas, as viewed through the lens of the thinking/being/doing dimensions, and those developmental elements on which management development practitioners might focus in nurturing a sustainability mindset in managers and leaders.

The Sustainability Mindset Model for Developing Responsible Management and Leadership Practices

We live in a world where leaders are experiencing daily social and environmental pressures in making their business decisions including diminishing natural resources, extreme transparency about which stakeholders are included and which ones are left out, more educated consumers with higher expectations, and the threat of fast damages to reputation. The tensions of time and inclusion, which represent a failing economic model, which is focused only on the short-term profits of shareholders, are requiring a paradigm shift toward a new mindset, where businesses are equally responsible for the social and natural environment in which they operate.

The authors suggest that the tensions can be addressed with a more holistic approach, that includes the thinking/knowing, but also the being/values dimensions, in addition to action. Building on the work of Dweck on the role of mindsets in motivation and impact on achievement (2006), we see the potential for high leverage in developing a new leadership mindset (Meadows, 2008, p. 194). The Sustainability Mindset Model offers a framework for developing such a mindset, covering four content areas that can be integrated into management learning and development. By questioning our way of thinking through a systemic lens, managers can develop solutions that are innovative and transcend an either/or thinking constraint. The exploration of personal contributions to the problems seen as "outside" the organization provides a path to a larger awareness and a greater introspective understanding of a manager's own personal values, in addition to organizational culture and values. Opening a dialogue about purpose and ethical approaches brings new perspectives to what managers do, and why and how they do it. Finally, it is important to create opportunities where individuals can explore their values, and their feelings about them, as they align, or conflict, with the organization's expressed values. Their tensions can be a powerful fuel to action. The SMM offers multiple possibilities to integrate social and environmental aspects, to develop self-awareness, make connection with purpose, and enact social sensitivity, leading to an internal call to action.

When managers adopt a sustainability mindset, they find new ways of problem solving, embedding systems thinking, managing risks, spurring innovation and transforming environmental and social pressures into competitive advantages. In this process, the sustainability mindset is translated into action, converting the stressful tensions into creative challenges to tackle with a purposeful, enriching multi-stakeholder perspective.

How the Sustainability Mindset Model Might be Applied in the Real World

The Sustainability Mindset Model is presented as a scaffolding to organize contents and facilitate the development learning goals of responsible management. Sustainability is, in itself, a systemic concept, which implies a certain transdisciplinary "messiness". Within the values dimension, for example, are inclinations such as a sense of interconnectedness, oneness with all that is, and biospheric orientation, which may seem to overlap, as might systems theory and ecoliteracy. These terms are used within specific definitions, and as such, they posit opportunities for future research. Additional research could explore the transformative impact of a leadership development program to develop a sustainability mindset using this model, and the lasting impact in a longitudinal study. Additional research could further investigate the use of the Sustainability Mindset Model in decision-making, and how the model is applied across different cultures.

In many ways, additional research would add to a body of literature that aligns with responsible management and management education studies. The Sustainability Mindset Model crosses multiple dimensions, as well as disciplines, and holds both potential and promise for a new generation of globally responsible leaders.

SMM can be used by individuals, firms, and leadership development professionals to understand two central tensions experienced by managers striving to be responsible leaders in their organizations. The tensions of time and inclusion are viewed through the lens of a holistic model to develop a sustainability mindset, within the context of three dimensions: being (values), thinking (knowledge) and doing (competencies). The tensions are also grounded in the model's four content areas of systems perspective, ecological worldview, emotional intelligence and spiritual intelligence .

The time and inclusion tensions that leaders face call for new competencies and skills— systems thinking and ecoliteracy, but also deeper self-awareness and spiritual and emotional intelligence— in order to be successful (Laszlo & Brown, 2014). Management and business leaders will benefit from using the SMM in creating learning hubs and work environments where people can experience a deeper sense of connection to and caring for others and the planet. The SMM has been developed for the purpose of educational training and facilitation of responsible management programs for students, managers and business leaders to cultivate this mindset.

The SMM can be applied to different cultures and contexts as demonstrated by members of LEAP, the PRME Working Group, the Sustainability Mindset, and at professional development conferences worldwide on. Adopted and adapted in over 43 countries in Europe, Africa, Asia, and the Americas, the applications of the SMM are facilitating dialogue among multiple stakeholders, use by management decision-makers, spurring innovation, story-telling, executive coaching and leadership development as a tool to develop globally responsible leaders for the world. The SMM provides a path for managers to experience interconnectedness, caring, and values alignment to sustainability from an innovative perspective leading to meaningful responsible management.

Questions for Discussion

1. In developing a Sustainability Mindset, what type of activities and practices would you engage in or explore in order to apply the model's three dimensions of being (values), thinking (knowledge) and doing (competencies).
2. Describe how utilizing a Sustainability Mindset can balance the tensions managers face? Tensions can include: short-term vs. long-term decision-making, local vs. global impacts, taking control vs. risk taking for innovation, or taking a reactive vs. creative approach in problem solving. Conduct a short literature review (5-7 references) of other mindset models (i.e. leadership or growth) to compare and contrast their elements and approaches to the Sustainability Mindset model.
3. Discuss how the Sustainability Mindset model can be a source of innovation within an organization.
4. In the Sustainability Mindset model, explain how 'systems thinking' can be applied. Give specific examples that demonstrate your ability to apply the model.

5. Think of a decision you recently made, and explore it from the perspective of time tension: did you consider the long-term impact? and from the perspective of inclusion: which stakeholders will be impacted? Did you consider any of them? Are there some you didn't think of and should be considered? In view of that reflection, would your decision have changed? In what ways?
6. What aspects of the SMM speak more personally to you, because you find them very different to how you think and make decisions. What are the implications for you in this? Are there any unwanted consequences that you think you could avoid by developing new ways of thinking?
7. Go to aim2flourish.com and select one featured initiative, and analyze if from the perspective of the time and inclusion tensions. How do you think that enterprise addressed the tensions? Did they consider them sufficiently? If not, why not?
8. In the recent news cycle, find some real-world examples in which management tensions (short-term versus long -term decision-making; local versus global impacts, taking control versus risk taking for innovation, or taking a reactive versus creative approach in problem-solving) have been apparent or driven behavior in organizations. What impacts have those organizations experienced as a result?
9. In developing a Sustainability Mindset, which of the model's four content areas of ecological worldview, systemic perspective, emotional intelligence and spiritual intelligence do you find most appealing, and why? Which are most challenging for you…and why?
10.Compose a 250-word essay that describes the Sustainability Mindset Model; the essay should include the model's merits and how it would apply inside an organization.
11. The authors of this chapter believe the Sustainability Mindset Model can apply inside for-profit, non-profit, governmental, and even military and religious organizations. Make an argument for why you believe the model is not appropriate for any one or more of these types of organizations.

About the Authors

Dr. Kerul Kassel is the author of several books, including The Thinking Executive's Guide to Sustainability (Business Expert Press, 2014), and lead editor of Developing Sustainability Mindset in Management Education (Routledge,

2018). She serves as adjunct faculty at Fielding Graduate University and holds a PhD in Human and Organizational Systems. Her work has appeared in peer-reviewed journals and in conferences around the world and she has been awarded year-on-year fellowships at Fielding's Institute for Social Innovation. Dr. Kassel is the president of First Nature Foundation, a non-profit leadership development organization, which partners with nature and animals to enhance crucial 21st century leadership capacities: www.FirstNatureFoundation.org.

Shelley F. Mitchell, Ph.D., is Professor of Management & Sustainability and a Research Fellow at Hult International Business School in Cambridge, MA. Prior to that she taught at the University of New Hampshire for 8 years. Her most recent publications include: Handbook of Sustainability in Management Education (SiME) (2017), A Sustainability Mindset for Management Education Chapter (2018), A Comparative Analysis of USA Enterprise Support Organizations for Conscious Capitalism and Conventional Capitalism Chapter (2020), and is a Guest Editor for the Journal of Management Education Special Issue on SiME: Advances and Future Directions (December, 2020). Dr. Mitchell has received awards from the AOM MED Division for Junior Faculty Best Paper Award (2016) & Best Professional Development Workshop (2018).

Isabel Rimanoczy is the convener of the UN Principles of Responsible Management Education (PRME) Working Group on the Sustainability Mindset, a global network of academics promoting a mindset shift. Her research and teaching are focused on developing educators who can accelerate much needed change by working with the values, assumptions and paradigms of their students. She published several books on the Sustainability Mindset, on the new pedagogical approaches this century calls for, and also poetry. In 2018 she was awarded the Women Servant Leadership Award, Hong Kong, and the First Prize (Gold) for the Sustainability Mindset Indicator Project, at the Reimagine Education event, organized by Wharton and QS, UK.

References

Argyris, C. (1987). Reasoning, action strategies, and defensive routines: The case of OD practitioners, in Woodman, R.A. & Pasmore, A. A. (Eds.), *Research in Organizational Change and Development.* Vol. 1: 89-128. Greenwich: JAI Press.

Caldwell, R. (2003). Models of change agency: a fourfold classification. *British Journal of Management*, 14 (2), pp. 131-142.

Capra, F. (1997). *The web of life: A new scientific understanding of living systems* (1st Anchor Books trade paperback ed.). New York, N.Y.: Anchor Books.

Delbecq, A. L. (2008). Spirituality and leadership effectiveness: Inner growth matters. In J. Gallos, (Ed.), *Business leadership,* A Jossey-Bass reader (2nd ed.): 485–503. New York: John Wiley and Sons.

Doppelt, B. (2012). *The Power of Sustainable Thinking: " How to Create a Positive Future for the Climate, the Planet, Your Organization and Your Life".* London: Routledge.

Dweck, C. (2006). *Mindset: The New Psychology of Success.* New York: Random House Publishers.

Edersheim, E. H. (2007). *The definitive Drucker.* New York, NY: McGraw-Hill Professional Publishers. pp. 83

Elkington, J. (1998). *Cannibals with forks: The triple bottom line of 21st century business.* Gabriola Island, BC; Stony Creek, CT: New Society Publishers.

Ericksen, N. J. (2004). *Plan-making for sustainability: The New Zealand experience.* Burlington, VT: Ashgate.

Fang, F., Kang, S.-P., & Liu, S. (2004). Measuring mindset change in the systemic transformation of education. Paper presented at the The National Convention of the Association for Educational Communications and Technology, Chicago, IL.

Francis, C. (2011). Critical pedagogy, ecoliteracy & planetary crisis: the ecopedagogy movement. *Environmental Education Research,* 17(6), 851-851. doi:10.1080/1350 4622.2011.626972.

Goleman, D. (2009). *Ecological intelligence: How knowing the hidden impacts of what we buy can change everything.* N.Y., N.Y.: Crown Business.

Goleman, D., Boyatzis, R. E., & McKee, A. (2002). The new leaders: Transforming the art of leadership into the science of results. London: Little, Brown.

Gupta, A. K., & Govindarajan, V. (2002). Cultivating a global mindset. *The Academy of Management Executive,* 16(1): 116-126. doi: 10.5465/ame.2002.6640211 <http://www.accenture.com/Microsites/ungc-ceo-study/Pages/home.aspx>

Hawken, P. (1993). *The ecology of commerce: A declaration of sustainability.* New York: Harper-Collins.

Hawken, P., Lovins, A. B., & Lovins, L. H. (2013). *Natural capitalism: The next industrial revolution.* London: Routledge.

Kegan, R. (1982). *The evolving self.* Cambridge: Harvard University Press,

Kohlberg, L. (1984). *Essays on moral development.* Vol. II: The psychology of moral development. San Francisco: Harper & Row.

Krishnan, V. R. (2008). Does management education make students better actors? A longitudinal study of change in values and self monitoring. *Great Lakes Herald*, 2: 35-48.

Laasch, O., & Moosmayer, D. (2015). Competences for responsible management: A structured literature review. CRME Working Papers, 1(2).

Laszlo, C., & Brown, J. (2014). *Flourishing enterprise: The new spirit of business.* Stanford, CA: Stanford University Press.

Mackey, J., & Sisodia, R. (2014). *Conscious capitalism: Liberating the heroic spirit of business.* Cambridge, MA: Harvard Business School Publishing Corporation.

Meadows, D. H. (2008). *Thinking in systems: A primer.* White River Junction, Vt.: Chelsea Green Pub.

Mezirow, J. (1994). Understanding Transformation Theory. *Adult Education Quarterly,* 44(4), 222-232. doi: 10.1177/074171369404400403.

Neal, J. A. (2008). Leadership and spirituality in the workplace. Retrieved July 15, 2009. http://www.judineal.com/pages/pubs/leadership.htm

Nonet, G., Kassel, K., & Meijs, L. (2016). Understanding responsible management: Emerging themes and variations from European business school programs. *Journal of Business Ethics,* 139 (4), 717.

Porter, M. E., & Kramer, M. R. (2011). Creating shared value. *Harvard Business Review,* 89(1/2): 62-77.

Rieckmann, M. (2012). Future-oriented higher education: which key competencies should be fostered through university teaching and learning? *Futures,* 44 (2012), pp. 127-135.

Rimanoczy, I. B. (2010). *Business leaders committing to and fostering sustainability initiatives.* Teachers College, Columbia University.

Scharmer, O., & Kaufer, K. (2013). *Leading from the emerging future from ego-system to eco-system economies.* San Francisco: Berrett-Koehler Publishers.

Senge, P. M. (2006). *The fifth discipline.* London: Random House Business.

Senge, P. M. (2008). *The necessary revolution: How individuals and organizations are working together to create a sustainable world.* New York, NY: Doubleday.

Wong, P. T. P. (2012). The Meaning Mindset: Measurement and Implications. *International Journal of Existential Psychology and Psychotherapy*, Vol 4-1, July 2012.

Yeager, D. S., & Dweck, C. S. (2012). Mindsets That Promote Resilience: When Students Believe That Personal Characteristics Can Be Developed. *Educational Psychologist,* 47(4): 302-314. doi: 10.1080/00461520.2012.722805

Zohar, D. (2012). *Spiritual intelligence: The ultimate intelligence.* Bloomsbury Publishing.

CHAPTER 9

Environmental Activists: *Self-Directed Leaders of Societal Change*

Kevin J. LeGrand, PhD
Fielding Graduate University

Preamble

The subject of this chapter. Humanity faces an existential question: Can societies provoke the significant changes in human lifestyles and economic systems that are needed to avert ecological collapse? Prior research suggests social contexts supportive of pro-environmental choices may reduce future environmental damage. Other research has demonstrated activism's role in changing engrained societal systems. This chapter provides insights about the types of people whose sustainability leadership work aims to change social contexts and bring about institutional change (LeGrand, 2014). What do individual values and perceived social norms, as moderators of relationships between environmental concern and select environmental attitudes, tell us about the leadership needed for societal change? In this chapter, we explore the interplay of values, norms, and attitudes and assert that sustainability leaders at the forefront of societal change are more likely to be self-directed individuals. We also point to the importance of social contexts in which pro-environmental choices are readily accessible and viewed as norms.

The nature of the study. In order to understand how a sustainability leader's attitudes and values may influence decisions about engaging in environmental activism, this chapter incorporates existing research into behavior antecedents, individual values, and activism propensity. The study also employs a new Environmental Activism Propensity (EAP) scale developed through the chapter author's research. The research reported here employed a survey that collected data on respondents' individual values. The new EAP scale, as well as scales for commitment to environmental sustainability, perceived social norms of environmental activism and attitudes toward personal conservation were also included.

The outcome of this chapter. This chapter provides insight into the importance environmental activists, a group viewed by the author as society's sustainability leaders, place on independence over conformity. It also makes the case that the context in which an environmentally significant decision is made may have greater sway than the attitudes or values of the decision maker. The author argues that these factors—valuing independence and the influence of context—should be considered when encouraging future sustainability leaders, when promoting environmental actions or causes, and when determining environmental priorities. Examples in both public and private spheres are provided.

Values and Environmental Activism

The earth faces a climate emergency due to human transmutation of natural resources. Not only have we burned fossil fuels at a rate that chokes the atmosphere with greenhouse gases, but we have destroyed forests that have sequestered carbon dioxide. We have mined our planetary home of its mineral deposits, over-farmed the continents, over-fished the oceans, and upset natural ecosystems. Along the way, we have generated harmful toxins, pollutants, and non-biodegradable waste that will remain for millennia as signs of our misjudgment. Worldwide, humans would need an additional half of a planet to keep up with our current demand for natural resources; that demand would increase to over four additional planets if everyone, worldwide, lived like a U.S. citizen (Ehrlich & Ehrlich, 2013). Our overconsumption and misuse of Earth's resources threatens our very existence and that of countless other species.

Attempting to counter this destructive path, climate activists continued to advocate for the environment in bold and noteworthy ways in 2019 and 2020. The group Extinction Rebellion stopped traffic in major international cities. Climate strikes initiated by Greta Thunberg mobilized millions of students and others around the globe, including on September 20 and 27, 2019, to take to the streets in protest. In Washington DC, Jane Fonda led climate change protests called "Fire Drill Fridays." She and others were arrested on successive Fridays in the Fall of 2019. Over 11,000 scientists representing more than 150 countries and a wide span of disciplines have declared a "Climate Emergency."

Persons participating in and leading environmental activism efforts aim to sustain earth's ability to support life and are, therefore, society's sustainability leaders. This chapter provides insights into environmental activists from an individual values perspective. It explores how differences in independence – defined as prioritizing self-direction values over conformity values – correlate to individuals' attitudes toward environmental activism. This insight is particularly important because prior studies have shown that social context often has a greater impact on an individual's environmental choices than that individual's attitude toward environmental sustainability; thus, survival of the human species may depend upon provoking changes in social context that will encourage pro-environmental behavior. Environmental activists provoke such change.

Taking a values perspective. The theory of individual values advanced by Shalom Schwartz (Schwartz, 1992; Schwartz, Cieciuch, Vecchione, Davidov, Fischer, Beierlein, … Konty, 2012) provides a meaningful lens and organizing construct to help make sense of individual and social responses to climate change. Self-transcendental values of universalism and benevolence are associated with environmental concern. Recognizing that, and given that scientific evidence increasingly points to human activity as a major cause of environmental damage, it would seem logical for the human species to adopt self-transcendent values and pro-environmental behavior as a means of survival. Yet, in the public sphere, citizens' demands for government action have not produced sufficient policy changes (Crompton & Kasser, 2009). In the private sphere, too few people make the lifestyle changes that would lessen human exploitation of the natural world.

Provoking change in order to survive. Behaviors that have an impact on the environment, whether that impact is intended or not, are called environmentally significant behaviors (ESBs). While values influence ESB choices, social context often holds greater sway (Guagnano, Stern, & Dietz, 1995; Stern, 2000, 2011). The strong influence of social context suggests that survival of the human species may depend upon provoking changes in social context that will encourage pro-environmental behavior.

How does change in social context come about? Oftentimes, activists play a key role. For example, activists focused on lesbian, gay, bi-sexual, and transgender (LGBT) equality have brought about significant changes in the attitudes, laws, and policies that affect LGBT persons. Similarly, environmental activists endeavor to change society's institutions and norms in ways that promote environmental sustainability.

As they become aware of human causes of environmental change and the non-sustainable demands current human activity places on the earth, some people choose to engage in environmental activism while others, who may be as concerned about the environment, choose personal conservation. The phenomenon of different ESB choices by persons with similar levels of environmental concern provided the impetus for the dissertation study (LeGrand, 2014) that is the subject of this chapter.

Though prior research reveals some antecedents of activism, there are few direct studies of the relationships between values and environmental activism. Given the extensive use of values theory in studies of other pro-environmental attitudes and behaviors, this dearth of research presents an opportunity for interested scholars. The current study is situated in this opportunity space. To provide a comparison, it also explores relationships between values and personal conservation.

Conformity versus Self-Direction: A Study of Environmental Attitudes

To address these issues, I conducted a study to investigate whether the relative importance people place on conformity versus self-direction values makes a difference in their environmental attitudes; specifically, attitudes about going beyond personal conservation to engage in activism. It also explored the role of context. The conceptual frame for this research finds its roots in three areas of existing research. First, behavior antecedent theories provided perspectives on factors that influence behavior choices and the processes through which these factors have their effect. Second, the theory of individual values (Schwartz, 1992; Schwartz et al., 2012) provided the structure of opposing values that was used in the study as a potential moderator. Third, activism propensity theories undergirded the development of the Environmental Activism Propensity (EAP) scale and informed hypotheses about relationships between values and environmental attitudes.[1]

The 219 people responding to the survey varied in their commitment to environmental sustainability, from those who were strongly committed to those with little or no commitment. Independence (IND) scores were positive on average indicating participants overall placed greater importance on self-direction than on conformity. This is consistent with other researchers' findings across cultures (Schwartz et al., 2012). Participants perceived personal conservation as a social norm to a greater degree than environmental activism. Similarly, study participants expressed more positive attitudes toward personal conservation than toward environmental activism.

Among study participants, women were more committed to environmental sustainability, were more likely to view environmental activism as a social norm, and had more positive attitudes toward personal conservation than men. Men had higher independence scores on average than did women.

Insights for Sustainability Leaders

• ***Environmental concern plays a larger role in personal conservation than environmental activism.*** Does greater concern for the environment correlate with more highly positive attitudes toward personal conservation? The answer among the study's participants is a resounding "yes" with 42% of attitude variance explained. Environmental concern also predicted attitudes toward environmental activism, but here the amount of variance explained was lower at 29%. The difference in explained variance is logical because activism requires that a person not only care about the underlying issue, in this case the environment, but is also willing to reveal beliefs and to embrace efforts to change societal institutions, policies, or laws. These environmental activism impediments (self-revelation and intent to change the status quo) are much less prevalent for personal conservation.

• ***Independence helps predict environmental activism propensity.*** How does independence moderate the relationship between environmental concern and the study's dependent variables? Independence did not predict attitudes toward personal conservation but did predict attitudes toward environmental activism among study participants committed to environmental sustainability. Self-directed environmentalists have greater propensity to engage in environmental activism than conforming environmentalists.

These results are logical. High independence means a person prioritizes self-direction, which relates positively to self-expression and willingness to advocate change. Conversely, low independence, i.e., giving greater weight than others to conformity, implies anxiety about self-revelation and attachment to the social and institutional status quo. Because environmental activism generally requires some self-revelation (as it takes place in the public sphere) as well as willingness to advocate change, it follows that greater independence correlates with a higher propensity toward environmental activism. In contrast, because personal conservation takes place in the private sphere, independence might not be a significant predictor.

• ***Social norm perceptions greatly influenced attitudes.*** Among the study's participants, norm perceptions had a main effect more so than interacting with environmental concern. In other words, increased perception of personal conservation as a social norm raised positive attitudes toward such conservation fairly evenly across different levels of environmental concern. The same was true for the relationship between perceptions of environmental activism as a social norm and attitudes toward such activism.

Practical Implications for Sustainability Leadership in Society

The study results have implications for environmental advocates, society's sustainability leaders, whether their focus is public-sphere or private-sphere decision-making. In the public sphere, the challenge is to encourage people to become active in their outwardly visible, environmentally significant behaviors. Convincing people to lend such active support presents a struggle for environmental organizations. In the private sphere, the challenge is to increase the number of people who consider the environmental impact of their decisions and to increase the breadth of decisions that people recognize as environmentally significant.

• ***Public-sphere implications.*** The finding that environmental activism propensity (EAP) is correlated with independence offers useful insights to sustainability leaders and environmental activists as they work to recruit individuals to public-sphere pro-environmental actions. As calculated in the study, independence rises with increased self-direction and falls with increased conformity. Thus, messages intended to increase environmental activism should seek to stimulate self-direction values and not provoke conformity or related values. Self-direction has two parts: thought and action. To stimulate self-direction of thought, environmental campaigns should convey the importance of thinking for oneself and critically assessing ads or political rhetoric that deny or ignore climate change. Effective environmental campaigns may ask audience members to question the motivations and sponsorship behind ads and rhetoric that promote continued reliance on carbon-based fuels or that oppose action to move toward clean energy sources.

To stimulate self-direction of action, environmental campaigns may need to address contextual challenges people face as they endeavor to take pro-environmental public-sphere action. As an example, organizers of the People's Climate March on September 21, 2014, in New York reserved buses to transport people from distant cities and encouraged same-day marches around the world (Brody, 2014). Recent mass environmental protests, such as the Global Climate Strike, September 20-27, 2019, have also encouraged activists to participate in same-day local protests around the world. Such efforts expand the number of people participating and, consequently, the sense among each participant that he or she was part of a high-impact action. Additionally, because internal locus of control—having a sense that one's actions make a difference—has similarities to self-direction of action, it is wise for climate campaigns to trumpet environmental activism success stories far and wide.

Campaigns promoting environmental activism that promote conformity or related values may be counterproductive because conformity values are opposed to the self-direction values that are associated with activism. For example, ads intending to increase support for clean energy advocacy may be counterproductive if they place strong emphasis on America as world leader, and thus, stimulate nationalism and the value of tradition, which is opposed to self-direction.

The study's finding of a strong relationship between perceived social norms and EAP suggests advocates may wish to characterize environmental activism as a social norm among persons whom the intended audiences view as relevant. For example, conveying that a higher percentage of residents in most other wealthy countries, as compared to the United States, place importance on global warming may raise perceptions among U.S. residents that environmental advocacy is a global social norm. Efforts to bring out entire affinity groups or communities to protest on behalf of the environment can also increase the perception that such activism is a social norm. Social media and the Internet have the potential to accelerate social movements (Melville, Dedrick, & Gish, 2014) and should therefore be employed by advocates who seek to encourage environmental activism.

• ***Private-sphere implications.*** How can environmental advocates make use of the study's finding of a strong relationship between perceived social norms and personal conservation to prompt more people to consider the environment across a broader range of their private-sphere decisions? They can raise the perception that such environmental consideration is a social norm. One way to do this is to encourage people to publicize the decisions they make on behalf of the environment through social media or in conversations. For example, an organization that sells carbon offsets could make it easy for their customers to post news of their purchases. Similarly, blogs that cater to people who compost, grow vegetable gardens, voluntarily simplify, or otherwise reduce their carbon footprint could encourage their readers to post their actions on social media and to engage their friends in conversations about environmentally benevolent choices.

Advocates of personal conservation may want to link these conscious behaviors to long-standing American norms and values, and also portray widespread conspicuous consumption as a more recent anomaly in human development—one that cannot become the norm if humanity is to survive. They may also wish to publicize evidence that success in attaining extrinsic aspirations for money, fame, and image does not result in happiness or psychological health. Conversely, attainment of intrinsic aspirations for personal growth, relatedness, and community involvement—aspirations associated with lower carbon footprints—does relate positively to psychological health (Niemiec, Ryan, & Deci, 2009).

• ***Shaping perceptions.*** Local government leaders should consider the role their policies play in shaping perceptions of societal norms related to the environment. For example, while decisions to use single stream refuse receptacles rather than dedicated recyclables containers may simplify collection and reduce space requirements, the absence of recycling containers represents a lost opportunity to convey how important it is to recycle, and the remaining undifferentiated trash receptacles promote the view that putting recyclable materials into regular trash containers is acceptable behavior. Environmental advocates can ask government leaders to consider both the direct and the indirect (e.g., norm shaping) effects of community refuse collection. This small step can help transition societies to a new normal, in which ecological consciousness is the social norm (De Young, 2013) and partnering with our planet's ecology displaces the currently entrenched economic logic based on limitless growth and ever-increasing consumption (Meadows, Randers, & Meadows, 2004).

The perception that an action is both widely practiced in society (a descriptive norm) and is sanctioned by society (an injunctive norm) is strongly related to the adoption of that action (Cialdini, 2003). Showing the acceptance of pro-environmental actions and the positive outcomes (social belonging and sense of contributing) for those engaged will help convey that such actions are social norms (both descriptive and injunctive). Consistent with the study findings (LeGrand, 2014), Cialdini (2003) found that portraying an environment-damaging action as the social norm increased its occurrence. The implication is that messages portraying pro-environment actions as social norms may be more effective in achieving lifestyle change than messages conveying a desperate need for lifestyle change due to the prevalence of environment-damaging actions in society.

Further Explorations in Societal Sustainability Leadership

Environmentally-concerned advocates of social change can build upon the research reported in this chapter and make use of the newly developed EAP scale. An area that is ripe for further exploration is the relationship between particular social contexts and environmental attitudes. The study used perceptions of social norms as proxies for context. Future studies could assess the impact that interventions in actual, physical contexts may have on environmental attitudes, as well as on perceptions of social norms. The innumerable contexts in which ESB choices may be made offer limitless contexts to investigate. For example, schools provide opportunities to explore context interventions in areas such as composting, water bottle refill stations, and recycling. A study conducted on a university campus found that removing waste bins from classrooms and locating waste bins only next to recycling bins greatly reduced the number of recyclables going to landfill (Binder, 2012).

On another track, activists working to lead society toward sustainability can venture beyond individual decision-making to explore how changes in context affect decisions made by organizations and governments. For example, Henry Paulson (2014), former Secretary of the U.S. Treasury, advocates a carbon tax as a fair and effective approach to encouraging businesses to reduce their carbon footprints. More recently, the U.S. Green Building Council encouraged LEED certification of buildings, noting that employees working in LEED-certified green buildings have higher levels of health, happiness, and productivity than employees in other buildings.

Conclusions

Human societies have made inadequate changes to their collective environmentally significant behaviors in the face of increasing awareness that Earth's regenerative capacity has limits. Its resources cannot be endlessly plundered, and its atmosphere, waters, and surface cannot continue to be heaped with toxic waste without consequence, yet extraction and greenhouse gas emissions continue to rise. The current study affirmed the important role of context on decision-making that affects the environment. Context affects decision-making about pro-environmental actions in both the private sphere, such as consuming less and recycling, and in the public sphere, as in environmental activism expressed through protest, boycotts, letter writing, and other means. Because social context often outweighs values and attitudes as predictors of behavior, human societies must foster pro-environmental changes in social contexts.

Changing society's institutions and norms so that they give higher priority to ecological sustainability is the domain of environmental activists working to lead society to a sustainable future. The study found that a propensity toward environmental activism was higher, even among highly independent persons, when perceived to be a social norm. Similarly, attitudes toward personal conservation were more positive when perceived to be a social norm.

Therefore, to increase pro-environmental behavior in both the private and public spheres, societies must promote perceptions of such behavior as social norms and change contexts to support pro-environmental choices. The resulting encouragement of individual action in both spheres may alter humanity's collective behavior on the grand scale needed to avert the greatest climate emergency risks. This is the work of environmental activists, society's sustainability leaders.

Questions for Discussion

1. Find printed or electronic materials encouraging people to participate in a climate protest or march. What messages were used? How do these messages align with or differ from the guidance offered in this chapter?
2. Imagine two non-profit organizations that each seek to combat global warming. One prompts people to change their own behavior and resist consumerism, and the other organizes climate marches aimed at changing policy at state and national levels. How might the messaging of the two organizations differ? How might it be the same?
3. In the wake of the coronavirus pandemic, is it still important for environmental activists to advocate for the environment? Why or why not?
4. How might catastrophic worldwide events, such as the outbreak of the coronavirus, affect the capacity of people to hear and act upon the messages of environmental activists?
5. Name 3 - 5 consumption patterns that have significant impacts on global warming. For each, identify entities that would oppose environmental activists' efforts to reduce such consumption. For example, the pattern of consuming beef has been identified as contributing to global warming. Who would oppose efforts to reduce beef consumption? How might reduced consumption of beef be promoted as a norm in society?
5. What steps can environmental activists take to be responsive to the need to practice "social distancing" yet continue their work?

End Notes

[1] For more information about the theoretical framework of the study, including the various scales used to determine the study's environmental activism construct, please see Kevin J. Legrand. (2015). "Beyond Conservation: Exploring the Values and Norms of Environmental Activists." *Sustainability Leadership: Integrating Values, Meaning and Action.* Fielding University Press, pp. 52-92.

About the Author

Dr. Kevin LeGrand consults to corporations, nonprofits, and government agencies on matters of governance, executive leadership, succession planning, strategy development, and organizational alignment. He has led numerous governance improvement efforts, primarily in the health care and education sectors, guided succession planning and executive evaluation efforts, and planned system-wide leadership development programs. As examples of his work, Kevin devised the 18-month multi-phase, multi-track approach to prevent leadership gaps as the head and top executives of a 200,000 employee U.S. Government Department departed in conjunction with a Presidential administration change. He also helped regional healthcare providers affiliate across systems and cultures to form partnerships focused on improving population health. His scholarly interests include adult development stages, individual values, climate-focused social psychology, executive and board member competency models, and organizational development. Kevin resides in Washington DC where he is active in board leadership and volunteers regularly with nonprofit organizations.

References

Binder, K. J. (2012). The effects of replacing dispersed trash and recycling bins with integrated waste receptacles on the accuracy of waste sorting. Western Michigan University, Kalamazoo, MI. Retrieved from www.wmich.edu/sites/default/files/attachments/Kate%20Binder%20Thesis.pdf

Brody, R. (2014, September 22). Marching for a Cleaner Earth. *US News & World Report.* Retrieved from http://www.usnews.com/opinion/articles/2014/09/22/new-yorks-peoples-climate-march-urges-against-oil-gas-and-global-warming

Cialdini, R. B. (2003). Crafting normative messages to protect the environment. *Current Directions in Psychological Science, 12*(4), 105–109. doi:10.1111/1467-8721.01242

Crompton, T., & Kasser, T. (2009). *Meeting environmental challenges: The role of human identity.* Dartington, UK: Green Books.

De Young, R. (2013). Transitioning to a new normal: How ecopsychology can help society prepare for the harder times ahead. *Ecopsychology*, *5*(4), 237–239. doi:10.1089/eco.2013.0065

Ehrlich, P. R., & Ehrlich, A. H. (2013). Can a collapse of global civilization be avoided? *Proceedings of the Royal Society B: Biological Sciences, 280*(1754), 1–9. doi:10.1098/rspb.2012.2845

Guagnano, G. A., Stern, P. C., & Dietz, T. (1995). Influences on attitude-behavior relationships: A natural experiment with curbside recycling. *Environment and Behavior, 27,* 699–718.

LeGrand, K. J. (2014). *Attitudes toward environmental activism and conservation: Independence and norms as moderators of commitment to environmental sustainability* (Doctoral dissertation). Available from ProQuest Dissertations and Theses database. (UMI No. 3645745)

Meadows, D., Randers, J., & Meadows, D. (2004). *Limits to growth: The 30-year update.* White River Junction, VT: Chelsea Green.

Melville, K., Dedrick, J., & Gish, E. (2014). *The democracy project.* Unpublished manuscript.

Niemiec, C. P., Ryan, R. M., & Deci, E. L. (2009). The path taken: Consequences of attaining intrinsic and extrinsic aspirations in post-college life. *Journal of Research in Personality, 43*(3), 291–306. doi:10.1016/j.jrp.2008.09.001

Paulson, H. M. (2014, June 21). Lessons for climate change in the 2008 recession. *The New York Times.* Retrieved from http://www.nytimes.com/2014/06/22/opinion/sunday/ lessons-for-climate-change-in-the-2008-recession.html

Schwartz, S. H. (1992). Universals in the content and structure of values: Theoretical advances and empirical tests in 20 countries. In M. P. Zanna (Ed.), *Advances in experimental social psychology* (Vol. 25, pp. 1–65). New York, NY: Academic Press.

Schwartz, S. H., Cieciuch, J., Vecchione, M., Davidov, E., Fischer, R., Beierlein, C., … Konty, M. (2012). Refining the theory of basic individual values. *Journal of Personality and Social Psychology, 103*(4), 663–688. doi:10.1037/a0029393

Stern, P. C. (2000). Toward a coherent theory of environmentally significant behavior. *Journal of Social Issues, 56*(3), 407–424. doi:10.1111/0022-4537.00175

Stern, P. C. (2011). Contributions of psychology to limiting climate change. *American Psychologist, 66*(4), 303–314. doi:10.1037/a0023235

CHAPTER 10

Is "Greening the Curricula" for "Sustainable Development" an Oxymoron? *Without an Indigenous Worldview - YES!*

Four Arrows
Fielding Graduate University

Preamble

The subject of this chapter. This chapter will argue that a vital missing link in sustainable development education relates to metacognitive worldview reflection, as relates to the problematic aspects of our dominant, Eurocentric worldview and that our original, Indigenous worldview is still practiced by relatively few societies today.

The nature of the study. This chapter will draw on literature from eco-psychology, sustainability education, worldview studies, curricula analysis and my personal experience and research as relates to Indigeneity.

The outcome of this chapter. This chapter will offer a strong argument for the importance of re-embracing an Indigenous worldview as a vital solution to our existential ecological crises and conclude with seven specific Indigenous worldview precept descriptions that educators and students can use immediately.

The 2003 United Nations Decade of Education for Sustainable Development Resolution significantly influenced the international "greening the curriculum for sustainable development" movement. However, it may be that connecting ecological health to economic development may be a contradictory endeavor (Brown, 2015). Of course, this problem has been considered by many others over the years. Search the keywords "capitalism and ecological sustainability," and you will get about ten million hits debating various positions about what Wim Carton refers to as "The Nature and Myth of a Sustainable Capitalism"

(2009)in his Master's Thesis. Harmful effects of capitalism, however, stem from a worldly, rather than a Nature-based, consciousness. Use the words "Indigenous worldview and ecological sustainability," and you get only 400,000 hits, most of which have appeared relatively recently. However, this is promising, if we seriously consider the most comprehensive and recent study on sustainability and extinction (Four Arrows, 2019). The UN study concludes with the worldview that if "green development" is an oxymoron, it is because of how we have come to understand our connection to Nature. As such, even with the most state-of-the-art, environmentally friendly innovations, we must reconsider what greening the curricular means from a much deeper level of awareness.

Note that the Association for the Advancement of Sustainability in Higher Education (AASHE) does not specifically refer to development it in its mission statement, which is "to empower higher education to lead the sustainability transformation" (Rowland & Nolet, 2012, p. 240). However, it does emphasize structure and technology much more than philosophy, psychology or worldview concepts, the latter of which I submit are more crucial. AASHE has almost 900 universities signed up with the organization's STAR program. The goal of the program is for institutions to score themselves according to certain criteria. With the exception of only two curricular items about social justice, the rest relate to building design and maintenance, clean and renewable energy, sustainable dining, janitorial purchasing, water use, investments and other innovative practices that promote sustainable campuses. This over-emphasis on technological, scientific, economic and structural solutions, while neglecting the promotion of a pro-nature psychological consciousness, is not likely to bring us back from the edge of mass extinction (Four Arrows, 2019). Classroom work that brings forth a very different consciousness is the most important goal for a green curriculum.

There is evidence that higher education's focus on sustainability curricula focuses almost exclusively on a structural or technological approach. In 2013 the *Princeton Review's Guide to 322 Green Colleges* chose 322 top scoring universities out of 2000 schools in terms of sustainability education. It was based on ten criteria that included:

- Percent of environmental preferable food expenditures
- Alternatives to single-passenger transportation
- Whether new buildings are certified according to certain standards

- Waste diversion rates
- Whether the school has climate action plan
- Percentage of energy derived from renewable sources
- If school has full-time sustainability officer
- Whether school has an environmental studies concentration or major
- If school has formal student committee on advancing sustainability
- If school has environmental literacy requirement.

These goals are important, but are insufficient in producing graduates with a deep and dedicated passion for a more holistic approach to sustainability leadership, and enacting a change of consciousness and/or worldview. Nor may it have intended to do so, considering that the list is produced, not by Princeton University, but by the U.S. Green Building Council that is sponsored by United Technologies Corporation. *The Princeton Review* is published by IP Holdings, manufacturers of apparel and lifestyle products, and specifically focuses on its business of test preparation and college admissions services. This commercial affiliation may or may not be intentional, but in any case, it still keeps the focus on economic development rather than a genuine relationship with nature.

Eco-psychology scholars have, of course, studied such relationships to a degree for decades. One study looked for students with "pro-sustainability orientations" (PSO) who exhibited behavioral predispositions toward sustainability and also engaged in pro-social and pro-environmental activities. The study included 360 students in their freshman and senior years, at four universities with sustainability visions and missions (Tapia-Fonllem et al, 2017). The authors conclude that the university programs and courses they investigated did not produce statistically significant differences between freshmen and senior students, because the focus was on reduction of environmental degradation, per se, as opposed to a focus on a more holistic interaction of social, philosophical and bio-physical dimensions of sustainability. In other words, a more dynamic contextual interconnectedness between personal and societal contexts within the other-than-human world is missing. Higher education, like businesses and communities in general, seem unable to bring about this deeper relational context between humans and the rest of the natural world.

Carter (2016) refers to such research as "social emotional and environmental education development" (SEED). In their edited text, *Integrating Sustainability*

Thinking in Science and Engineering Curricula, Filho et al, address, SEE, and write that, "Although most students at the higher education may have autonomy, objectiveness and pro-activity, teachers limit their role focusing only on professional knowledge and skills. Attention to attitude needs to be part of their development to help professionals to work in and maintain a sustainable world" (2014, p.4). Thus, in spite of growing attention to greening the curriculum and the increased urgency to do so, we are barking up the wrong tree. Of course, there are the usual barriers to transformational curriculum development, including funding priorities, bureaucracy, academic territorialism, fear of innovation that might threaten established reputation, lack of interdisciplinarity across curricula, concerns about alienating conservative students who see such an ecological curriculum as political, personal alienation from nature, and, what Haigh refers to as "persistence of the obsolete mind-sets of the industrial age" (2007). However, virtually untouched is the solution to all of these challenges—worldview reflection between dominant and Indigenous worldviews.

Worldview studies, including metacognitive reflection about human and other-than-human relationships and priorities, that are relevant to each student's life must become a major topic across the curricula. To put it more bluntly, the ecological problems we face today signify a worldview problem and curricular solutions must engage in worldview reflection. Moreover, I propose that there are only two worldviews to consider. One is the Indigenous worldview that guided us for most of human history, with proven success in terms of maintaining ecological balance. The other is our dominant worldview that I assert has been responsible for ecological destruction.

Annick Hedlund-deWitt thought it important for her doctoral studies to research the influence of worldviews on our ecological crises and its possible solutions. She writes in her 2013 dissertation, *Worldviews and the Transformation to Sustainable Societies*, "Worldview is a concept 'whose time has come," and its increasing appearance in the contemporary climate change and global sustainability debates can be understood as both a response to, and a reflection of, the challenges of our time and the solutions they demand. One of the main arguments and premises of this dissertation is, consequently, that an understanding of worldviews has a major role to play in addressing our highly complex, multifaceted, interwoven, planetary sustainability issues" (p. 3).

Unfortunately, worldview understanding has been stifled in recent years by beliefs among many that there are countless numbers of them. People use "worldview" to describe religious, cultural and moral beliefs. Some academics and psychologists have viewed humanism, post-modernism, nihilism, existentialism and many other "isms" as worldviews as well. Hedlund-deWitt supports a deeper view, defining the concept as the foundational assumptions about the nature of reality and our place in it. The concept of worldview may appear to be similar, or even interchangeable, with concepts such as ideology, paradigm, religion, and discourse, and they do indeed possess some degree of referential overlap. However, worldviews can, nonetheless, be clearly distinguished from these concepts (p.19).

For a green curriculum to investigate the source of our western beliefs is counter-hegemonic, and thus, will face resistance. Our current K-12 curricula socializes us to the tenets of Eurocentric philosophy and our colonial assumptions, but worldview reflection is not a topic that only applies to philosophy courses and it may be a matter of survival. It is not enough to prepare New York City's buildings to withstand floods, or planting trees in parks to provide shade for the elderly, which was part of the city's response to the White House's long-delayed warnings about climate change. Our technologies alone will not save us unless we come to remember a morality fostered by our ancestors' worldview. Craven (2014), a member of the Blackfoot Nation and a professor of economics and geography, concisely captures the difference between the dominant and Indigenous worldviews as relates to sustainability and morality when he describes the contrast between their different core values, such as (1) competition vs. harmony, (2) materialism vs. prudence, (3) acquisition vs. reciprocity (4) accumulation vs. distribution, (5) ownership vs. kinship, (6) growth vs. sustainability and (7) immediacy vs. caring for future generations. Note, in the worldview chart that expands on Craven's list below, the moral implications in the general comparisons between those common beliefs on the left and those on the right. It may reveal how immoral, and even stupid, our dominant culture has become, in spite of our remarkable technological accomplishments.

With worldview reflection and proper academic research, critical thinking, metacognitive work and courageous conversations, we might come to realize that population growth and economic development on a finite Earth are biophysically impossible. Steve Latouche, a professor of economics at the University of Paris, writes that, within the developmentalism paradigm "there is room neither for the ecologists' care for nature nor for the humanists' respect for man" (2003). Yet this is the language of sustainable development and "greening the curriculum." It is past time for us to come to the conclusion of the famous MIT scholar, Noam Chomsky, who writes, "The grim prognosis for life on this planet is the consequence of a few centuries of forgetting what traditional societies knew, and the surviving ones still recognize" (2014).

"Traditional Ecological Knowledge" (TEK), which is a term that describes Indigenous ways of understanding and managing the sustainability of local resources was supposed to be incorporated when developers come into Indigenous territory, but it has not been sufficiently respected. TEK is known only by specific, unique First Nations and cannot be generalized from Indigenous worldview precepts that various traditional cultures share. However, without an appreciation for the broader worldview perspective, I propose that development efforts reject and ignore the part of TEK that relates to how specific Indigenous cultures sees land, water, and bio-diversity not as natural resources, but rather as relations. Such a spiritual perspective gets in the way of goals that are driven by our dominant worldview.

Studying value differences and looking for complementarity with a values approach is what Pappas endorses in a piece published in the *Journal of Sustainability Education.* "The university needs to develop values-based sustainability content for classes across disciplines...We have come to understand that the greatest and most immediate sustainability problems humans face are related to our relationship with the natural world" (2012). Similarly, in "What is 'Greening the Curriculum?" Amber Katherine writes, "The way to increase ecological literacy involves enabling students to understand humans, the earth and the relationship between humans and the earth from a variety of disciplinary perspectives" (ND). Such literature refers to alternative worldview consciousness in questioning dominant notions, such as anthropocentrism, material wealth and hierarchy, as they relate to the very survival of our species. Such conversations are largely missing across curricula, though they can apply to, and be addressed in, almost any academic course offered in a university.

Indigenous Ways

To bring forth such conversations across the curricula, I recommend starting by targeting the following concepts and weaving them into existing sustainability subjects. I have selected these from decades of my own work bringing generalized Indigenous ways of understanding and Indigenous perspectives into sustainability and wellness instruction and dialogue.

Comprehensiveness. It is important that all ten of the items on this list be covered in a green curriculum for development or survival with attention to how they interconnect. The typical fragmentation of coursework will not serve. Greening the curriculum— whether specifically for sustainability majors or "across the curriculum" for all majors— as has been suggested earlier, is essential if any of the topics on this list are to help students understand and work toward authentic sustainable futures.

Holistic education. Coursework must attend to the body, mind, social, spiritual aspects of each student as both receiver and creator of relevant learning. Such teaching/learning assures that sustainability issues connect student identity and purpose in life to human and non-human communities via authentic engagement with both.

Critical consciousness. Educational hegemony continues to stifle authentic challenges to status-quo thinking about curricula and requires students pay attention to the oppression and colonization that results. "Who benefits?" is the key question when considering state sanctioned curricula. Additionally, "ecocriticism" literature can be utilized in classrooms, "a field of enquiry that analyzes and promotes works of art which raise moral questions about human interactions with nature, while also motivating audiences to live within a limit that will be binding over generations is or should be" (Gomides, 2006, p.16).

Spiritual acknowledgement. It is important to recognize the interplay of energies that connect all of us and all of life, from discussing synchronicities to exercises involving communicating, at some level, with other-than-human life forms.

Place-based field study. The best way to make the curriculum relevant to students is to emphasize a basic tenet of Indigenous worldview that emphasizes place-based knowledge. What we know or can learn about our particular environment is crucial for creating the deeper connections required for sustainability to be realized.

Questioning anthropocentrism. At every juncture, a solid sustainability curriculum reflects upon how human-centered a decision may be. Our economic system and Western-based philosophy tends to see all of life in terms of how it benefits our species, with rivers, oceans, birds, animals, etc., as utilitarian, and at the disposal of human beings. As mentioned previously, until we can truly think of "natural resources" as relatives, our priorities will always be susceptible to selfishness, greed or imbalance.

Challenging hierarchical authoritarianism. The highest source for authorizing decisions and actions, according to the alternative Indigenous worldview, is one's own honest reflections on lived experience along with critical, creative, intuitive research done, in light of remembering the need for complementarity among interconnected relations.

Ceremony and Alternative Consciousness. Most of our anti-sustainability habits come from a kind of hypnosis that has worked against our best interests and the best interests of others. Any reasoning behind the pollution of our world can be understood accordingly. Such misguided beliefs can be reversed or prevented via ceremonies that give us opportunity for concentration-activated transformation (Four Arrows 1998) and can help override such automatic and destructive behaviors, and lead us into transformation.

Courage. In Indigenous Worldview, the highest expression of courage is generosity. Courage that leads to actions in which we trust the universe as we go forward in the face of risks will undoubtedly be required if we are to face the many forces standing in the way of social/ecological justice and sustainability curricular implementation. Courage is also important as it relates to confronting the field of "ecophobia" which is generally defined as a fear of one's environment and a feeling of powerlessness to prevent the cataclysmic events being foretold. In his paper about pathways to the eco-fear problem and ecophobia, R. Michael Fisher writes the it is important "not to focus on the anxiety *per se* (e.g., fears) in confronting environmental catastrophes but to focus on seeing the fear(ism) underneath it, that is, the subtle, that which is systemic pathology (if not insanity) that is not reducible to individual psychology but is more a toxic worldview, a toxic ideology, a toxic politics and ultimately an insidious "culture of fear" itself that is producing individuals who act out the fear(ism)" (2017, p. 19).

Playfulness. There are scores of articles, chapters and books on how playing in nature benefits very young children and begins the formation of a positive ecological consciousness, but too little is done in formal schooling to implement this wisdom for children, or even adults, of all ages. Beyond scientific understanding and empathy with other-than-human life, we must engage with our other-than-human surroundings with unmitigated joyfulness, breathing it into our very souls.

In addition to the above Indigenous perspectives, I offer the following list that contrasts how the two worldviews generally manifest in the world. I created this list for my book, *The Red Road: Linking Diversity and Inclusion Initiatives to Indigenous Worldview* (in press with Information Age Publishing).

Questions for Discussion

1. Which items on the worldview contrast list do you think are generally applicable to one worldview or the other?
2. Which precepts would obviously lead toward a more ecologically sustainable living that you might be willing to adopt that you do not currently hold?
3. Because organized religions generally reflect worldview, how discussions about Indigenous worldview, inseparable from spirituality, avoid sensitive problematics?
4. Some individuals believe individuals who do not speak an Indigenous language and who were not raised in a traditional culture can "teach" Indigenous worldview precepts as recommended in this article. Do you agree or disagree?
5. How would you bring a non-anthropocentric perspective into a social studies course? A physics course? A biology course? Or any other courses?

Appendix

Common Dominant Worldview Manifestations	Common Indigenous Worldview Manifestations
1. Rigid hierarchy	Non-hierarchical
2. Fear-based thoughts and behaviors	Courage and fearless trust in the universe
3. Living without strong social purpose	Socially purposeful life
4. Focus on self and personal gain	Emphasis on community welfare
5. Rigid and discriminatory gender stereotypes	Respect for various gender roles and fluidity
6. Materialistic	Non-materialistic
7. Earth as an unloving "it"	Earth and all systems as living and loving
8. More head than	Inseparability of head and heart
9. Competition to feel superior	Competition to develop positive potential
10. Lacking empathy	Empathetic
11. Anthropocentric	Animistic and biocentric
12. Words used to deceive self or others	Words as sacred, truthfulness as essential
13. Truth claims as absolute	Truth seen as multifaceted, accepting mystery
14. Rigid boundaries and fragmented systems	Flexible boundaries and interconnected systems
15. Unfamiliarity with alternative consciousness	Regular use of alternative consciousness
16. Disbelief in spiritual energies	Recognition of spiritual energies
17. Disregard for holistic interconnectedness	Emphasis on holistic interconnectedness
18. Minimal contact with others	High interpersonal engagement, touching
19. Emphasis on theory and rhetoric	Inseparability of knowledge and action
20. Acceptance of authoritarianism	Resistance to authoritarianism
21. Time as linear	Time as cyclical
22. Dualistic thinking	Complementary duality
23. Acceptance of injustice	Intolerance of injustice
24. Emphasis on rights	Emphasis on responsibility
25. Fighting as highest expression of courage	Generosity as highest expression of courage
26. Ceremony as rote formality	Ceremony as life-sustaining
27. Learning as didactic	Learning as experiential and collaborative
28. Trance as dangerous or stemming from evil	Trance-based learning as natural and essential
29. Human nature as corrupt or evil	Human nature as good but malleable
30. Humor as entertainment	Humor as essential tool for coping
31. Conflict mitigated via revenge, punishment	Conflict resolution as return to community
32. Learning is fragmented and theoretical	Learning is holistic and place based
33. Personal vitality minimalized	Personal vitality is essential
34. Social laws of society are primary	Laws of Nature are primary
35. Self-knowledge not prioritized	Holistic Self-knowledge is most important
36. Autonomy for self	Autonomy for group and future generations
37. Nature as dangerous	Nature as benevolent
38. Other-than-human beings are not sentient	All lifeforms are sentient
39. Low respect for women	High respect for women
40. Linear thinking	Non-linear thinking

About the Author

Wahinkpe Topa (Four Arrows), aka Donald Trent Jacobs, Ph.D., Ed.D. is the former Dean of Education at Oglala Lakota College and currently a professor with Fielding Graduate University. Selected by AERO as one of 27 "Visionaries in Education" for their text, Turning Points. Author of forthcoming book 21 books, including, *The Red Road: Linking Diversity and Inclusion Initiatives to Indigenous Worldview* (A UNESCO Counter-Hegemonic Democracy Project). His text, *Teaching Truly: A Curriculum to Indigenize Mainstream Education,* was selected by the Chicago Wisdom Project as one of the top 20 progressive education books of the century along with books by Neil Postman, Paulo Freire and John Dewey. Awarded the 2004 Moral Courage Award by the Martin Springer Institute for Holocaust Studies for Indigenous activism. He lives and plays in Mexico and Canada with artist wife, Beatrice.

References

Brown, J.H. (2015). "The oxymoron of sustainable development" in *BioScience,* Vol.65, Issue 10, pp 1027-1029. https://doi.org/10.1093/biosci/biv117.

Carter, D. "A Nature-based social-emotional approach to supporting young children's holistic development in classrooms with and without walls" (2016) in *International journal of early childhood environmental education.* Vol. 4 , p. 10.

Carton, W. (2009) "The nature and myth of sustainable capitalism." Master's Thesis at Aalborg University. https://projekter.aau.dk/projekter/files/17802828/Thesis_Final.pdf

Craven, J.M. (2014) "Indigenous approaches to economic development and sustainability." http://sttpml.org/indigenous-approaches-to-economic-development-and-sustainability/

de Witt, A.H. (2013) *Worldviews and the transformation to sustainable societies* (Doctoral dissertation) dare.ubvu.vu.nl/bitstream/handle/1871/48104/dissertation.pdf

Filho, W.L., Azeiteiro, U.M., Ceiro, S., Alves, F. (2014). *Integrating sustainability thinking in science and engineering curricula.* San Francisco: Springer

Fisher, R.M. (2017). "Why ecocriticism now? Pathways to the eco-fear problem and ecophobia" Calgary: In Search of Fearlessness Research Institute.

Four Arrows (1998). *Primal awareness: A true story of survival, awakening and transformation with the Raramuri shamans of Mexico.* Rochester, VT: Inner Traditions International

Four Arrows (2014) *Teaching truly: A curriculum to indigenize mainstream education.* New York: Peter Lang Publishers

Four Arrows (2016) *Point of departure: Returning to our more authentic worldview for education and survival.* New York: Information Age Publishing

Four Arrows (2019) "The media have missed a crucial message of the United Nations biodiversity report. *The Nation.* https://www.thenation.com/article/archive/biodiversity-un-report-indigenous-worldview/

Gomides, Camilo. 'Putting a new definition of ecocriticism to the test: The case of the burning season, a film (mal)adaptation". ISLE 13.1 (2006): 13-23.

Haigh, M. (Jan 22, 2005). "Greening the university curriculum: Appraising an international movement" in *Journal of geography in higher education.* Vol. 29, Issue 1, p. 42.

Katherine, A. (2009) "What is 'greening the curriculum?' https://www.smc.edu/ACG/AcademicSenate/Documents/Environmental_Affairs_Committee/GreeningtheCurriculum9-09.pdf

Latouche, S. (2003) "Sustainable development as a paradox" http://rsesymposia.org/themedia/File/1151679499-Plenary2_Latouche.pdf

McKeown, R. & Nolet, V. (2012). *Schooling for sustainable development in Canada and the United States*. New York: Springer

Pappas, E. (2012) "A new systems approach to sustainability: University responsibility for teaching sustainability in contexts" in *Journal of sustainability education*, Vol. 3, March 2012. Available at http://www.jsedimensions.org/wordpress/wpcontent/uploads/2012/03/PappasJSE2012

Princeton Review (2013). https://sustainability.gwu.edu/sites/sustainability.gwu.edu/files/downloads/PrinRevGdGreenCols_2013Edn-2_1.pdf. Accessed Nov 14, 2017).

Tapia-Fonllem, C., Fraijo-Sing, B., Corral-Verdugo, V. Valdez, O. (2017) "Education for sustainable development in higher education institutions: Its influence on the pro-sustainability orientation of Mexican students. *Sage Open Journal.* http://journals.sagepub.com/doi/full/10.1177/2158244016676295. Accessed Sept. 27, 2017.

CHAPTER 11

Radical Gandhian Strategies for Sustainability Leadership: *Building Inclusion, Spirituality, and Socio-Ecological Transformation*

David Blake Willis
Fielding Graduate University

Preamble

The subject of this chapter. Whatever was happening in early 2020, of one thing we could be certain: *It was an Emergent New World.* What we are experiencing today, as the coronavirus pandemic spreads around the world, is a call for extraordinary and transformative leadership, a call that mixes urgency and agency. The chapters in this book reflect the transformational leadership of key figures in Sustainability Leadership and their exemplary paths in the 20th and 21st centuries. At the same time, the dramatic reach of Covid-19, the movement for social justice represented by the powerful Black Lives Matter movement, and the increasing impact of the climate crisis thrust us into new realities. The drumbeat is more urgent, and we now know that we must take into account the social, as well as ecological, dimensions of environmental depredations and destruction. We need tools, and we need examples. That is the subject of this chapter.

The nature of the study. Effective Sustainability Leadership during challenging times requires new exemplars of courage from whom we can learn. The research reported here on Gandhian activists, some of them Dalits, some Muslims, Hindus, Christians, or Atheists, reveals humble heroes of severe struggles against an ancient system of oppression, who inspire and lead us to action. This chapter reports on research carried out in South India from 1977 to the present, with a special focus on 2004-2020, during which time I interviewed literally hundreds of activists, workers, and revolutionaries, many at the Workers

Home in Gandhigram, South India, where activists, including Martin Luther King Jr. (the 'American Gandhi') have experienced leadership training. My case studies are thus about contemporary Gandhian social activists in India who could be considered Sustainability Leaders.

The outcome of this chapter. Outcomes from this chapter include reflections on leadership for sustainability, organizational, and institutional reflections as well as notes on the changing nature of castes and outcastes. Some of the major questions for the research have included: "What are the major issues facing marginalized communities in India, including Dalits, Dalit leaders, Muslims and their leaders?," "Whose voices have the most resonance and are most representative of resilience for these communities today?," "What aspects of Gandhian philosophy and social action still have relevance for Dalits, Scheduled or Backward Castes, or Adivasis?," "How are the actions of Dalits and Gandhian-inspired organizations like LAFTI reflective of larger human issues of social change and social justice?," and "What can we learn from Dalit and Gandhian philosophy and social action that might inform broader questions of human development and organization in the context of social transformation?"

Introduction: What Does Sustainability Leadership Mean in Traditional Indian Contexts and Philosophy?

"Looking ahead by looking back" is a key precept of Indigenous wisdom that sustainability leaders follow: *Seven Generations Ahead, Seven Generations Back.* Likewise, some of the oldest civilizations on Earth, India being one of them, also appreciate this synthetic flow of time and its importance to who we are now. One of the most important and successful voices of the 20th century for Sustainable Leadership was "Mahatma" Gandhi. Mohandas Karamchand Gandhi embodied certain Indian values, which reflected a civilization and understanding of the natural and built environments that are nearly 6000 years old (R. Gandhi, 2018; Lelyveld, 2011; Raghuramaraju, 2006; Wolpert, 2001; Prabhu and Rao, 1976; Easwaran, 1972; Erikson, 1969; M.K. Gandhi, 1927a). That these values and tactics have continued to be practiced on the ground throughout South Asia is a demonstration of the qualities of sustainability and leadership that Gandhi brought to the struggle. How might Gandhian ideas, values, tactics, and strategies possibly contribute to answers to some of the challenges of Sustainability Leadership in the 21st Century? Where might we find them?

Freedom fighters like Gandhi and others who followed him into the 21st century were, and are, deeply associated with ashrams. These spiritual and action centers, which have been the center of my research since 1977, speak not only for what the followers of Gandhians call *Movement Work* and *Constructive Work,* but of the spiritual foundations that are the overarching soul of Ashrams. During the colonial period in India, Gandhi founded two *satyagraha* (truth force, non-violence; see Rao, 2017, and Devji, 2012) ashrams, one at Sabarmati, Gujarat, and one later at Sevagram, Maharashtra. From these spread numerous other ashrams, centers of sustainability leaders. Payel Chattopadhyay Mukherjee (2021), moreover, has gone into considerable detail on ashrams and their ethical, moral, and action logics, which these two sages introduced so well as models for our own soul-searching, as have Lloyd and Susanne Rudolph earlier (2006).

Gandhian activists encourage vulnerability, humility, and empathy as central to their work in leadership, similar to the humble leadership of Edgar and Peter Schein (2018). Trust, collaboration, and cooperation are shown in daily practices and long-term strategies. Relational power, rather than transactional power, is central to their efforts of Movement Work and Constructive Work. The communities at these ashrams practiced, and still do practice, the *yamas* and *niyamas*. The *yamas* are about social ethics such as *ahimsa* (non-violence), *satya* (truth), and *aparigraha* (non-possessiveness). The *niyamas* are personal practice such as *tapas* (austerity), *svadhyaya* (self-study), and *shaucha* (cleanliness). Members are united in their beliefs in an ascetic and simple shared life, and in their practice of *satyagraha* they discover answers to their political and spiritual goals (Mehta, 2004, 2009; Raja, N.D.).

These activists live frugal lives; avoiding luxury, producing their own needs—food, agriculture, clothes, and *khadi* (handlooms, a symbol of resistance to colonial oppression). Gandhi's ashrams, thus, have not just been a return to the past—to a semblance of India's villages, which Gandhi saw as the "real eternal India,"— but are anchored in eternal values of compassion, commitment, and sustainability. What distinguishes Gandhian ashrams is their acceptance of all humans, irrespective of gender, caste, class or ethnicity as equals and their commitment to plurality. The new vision of society, which they embrace, aims for what Subash Sharma calls 'Harmonic Globalization, Harmonic Democracy, and Sacro-Civic Society' (2021). As sustainability leaders, they also understand that our survival as a species is threatened. More than one hundred years ago,

Gandhi and the revolutionary Aurobindo Ghose understood this, too, in their search for collective freedom and integral evolution. Later, Gandhi's economist, J.C. Kumarappa (Govindu and Malghan, 2016; Bandhu, 2011), whose ideas inspired E.F. Schumacher's *Small Is Beautiful*, helped orient this work to a sustainable village level (*gram*). Perhaps the most important factor in seeing Gandhian activists as sustainable leaders is their ability to recognize reality and practice, which are almost always local, but can then be scaled up fractally to regional, national, and international contexts. Supremely flexible, and with continuing impacts, Mahatma and Aurobindo were two of India's earliest Sustainability Leaders.

Transformational Leadership for Sustainability: Discovering Gandhian Values and Tactics in Revolutionary Indian Contexts

Recognizing and acting for the common good should be important goals for all societies if we are to attain Leadership for Sustainability. We can discover this common good or commons (Reid and Taylor, 2010) through research and practice, with an emphasis on emancipatory action and transformation. Healing the wounds and the fractures of society in order to move on is one of the goals of Gandhian leaders in South Asia today. Following Paulo Freire, all people have a right to agency and autonomy through a mutual and reciprocal process of dignity and respect (1970, 2000) as we attempt to discover "New Horizons of Sustainable Development" (Patnaik, 2021). Development, in this sense, connotes an overall capacity-building of the people, of "empowering human life to work for sustainable development," as she puts it. In other words, sustainability. Power, here, is seen not as domination of others by force, but as something shared in the community and as something which expands as it is shared. We are reminded of the work of the scholar of human evolution Michael Tomasello, who wrote *Becoming Human: A Theory of Ontogeny* (2019). Tomasello's long career of studying human children and great apes speaks to uniquely human cognition (social cognition, communication, cultural learning, and cooperative thinking) and a uniquely human sociality (collaboration, pro-sociality, social norms, and moral identity). We can see here reflections of Gandhi's actions as well: non-violence, truth, *satyagraha*, and integral theory.

What we are looking for, then, is a revolution in consciousness, an awakening into a new consciousness that combines Yoga and Dharma as Sri

Aurobindo and Mahatma Gandhi envisioned. As the great Gandhian scholar Sudarshan Iyengar shared with us in a 2020 Auroville Conference on *Swaraj & Sarvodaya* (Freedom and Service), "What is growth really? It is not the quantity of objects but a change of consciousness". This is, of course, the "Rethinking of Consciousness" of Paulo Freire (1996), something that can be seen on the ground in the 'Thoughtful 3rd Space' of Steve Brett and his colleagues in Konkan, India (2021), as well as Sharma's "New Social Vision" or holistic vision (2021). We are reminded, too, of Saji Varghese's spirituality of the environment (2021), Ananta Giri's integral development (2021), and of the American visionary Ken Wilber's Integral Theory. As Donna Haraway has related about the anthropologist James Clifford, "We need stories (and theories) that are just big enough to gather up the complexities and keep the edges open and greedy for surprising new and old connections" (2016, p. 101).

Case Study 1: Sustainable Transformative Leadership in South India: Krishnammal Jagannathan and S. Jagannathan

Since 1977, my own research has been centered around *Ullugaram Gramam* in Tamil, the Workers Home, which was founded by two visionary activists and their colleagues who walked with Mahatma Gandhi in the 1940s and Vinobha Bhave in the 1950s. These two activists, Krishnammal Jagannathan and S. Jagannathan, are called Amma and Appa, Father and Mother, by us (Coppo, 2005; Sarvodaya Ilakkiya Pannai, 2019). Humble souls, they are the recipients of the Right Livelihood Award, the Alternative Nobel Prize, the Padma Bhushan, and numerous other awards, and can be seen as the direct heirs to Gandhi and Vinobha Bhave, as Freedom Fighters. Gandhi considered Vinobha his chief disciple, and Vinobha, likewise, saw Krishnammal and Jagannathan as his heirs (Willis, 2014). The Workers Home has been one of two key bases for LAFTI, a successful Dalit and inter-caste based activist organization that has been working on behalf of Dalits and other oppressed communities in what has been one of the most severely downtrodden local areas in India. Their story is a signal one of courage, daring, and skills in the struggle against poverty, the caste system, and ecological oppression. What is especially critical, now, is how inclusion applies not only to communities, but the traditional idea of the balance of environment, ecology, and society as well, something activists in India are especially attuned to in their work at the local village level.

Fig. 12. Sustainability Leaders Appa and Amma - S. Jagannathan and J. Krishnammal, Workers Home, Gandhigram, South India (David Albert, 2006)

A venerable institution, the Workers Home has supported many activists concerned with sustainability and liberation, key themes of this chapter, including Martin Luther King Jr. and Representative John Lewis, who did training there in 1958 and took "good trouble" ideas on *satyagraha* back to the Civil Rights Movement struggle in America. Other luminaries such as Jawaharlal Nehru, Vinobha Bhave, Sunderlal Bahuguna, Dick Keithan, Coretta Scott King, David Ben-Gurion, and many others have trained or conducted trainings in the Workers Home. Similarly, Gandhian ashrams and communities in Sabarmati, Sevagram, Pondicherry, Madurai, T. Kallupatti, and New Delhi have been places in India where I have observed and experienced the possibilities of Sustainability Leadership for the 21st century. As the primary community for this Gandhian activism, those who are Dalits and other lower castes have utilized Gandhian ideas on Constructive and Movement Work to rise up against the barriers of caste and poverty. This is leadership from below, from the grass roots. The Workers Home has also been one of two key bases for LAFTI, a successful sustainable activist organization that has been working on behalf of Dalits in what has been one of the most severely oppressed and deprived stories in world history. How might we learn from these examples, and exemplars of values, meaning, and action? The historical and contemporary of Sustainability Leadership is being practiced through the Workers Home and the *Grama Swaraj* (Self-Rule) of the Sarvodaya Gandhian Movement.

Fig. 13. The Workers Home, Gandhigram, South India (David Albert, 2018)

The significance of the answers to these questions is that they bring new epistemologies and new perspectives on leadership, social injustice, human development, and human values to discourses long dominated by Western points of view. While traditional, qualitative studies in the form of monographs and journal articles emerge from research into these questions, there are also local sustainability outcomes on the ground for activists working for LAFTI, Khudai Khidmatgar, and many other groups supporting the poor and increasingly disenfranchised following passage of recent laws in India around citizenship and a national population registry. In the case of Amma and Appa, LAFTI's workers strike an interesting note as they can be considered sustainability leaders, which is especially important because they cause positive social change through their creativity, skills, and determination to transform an idea into reality (Ashoka; Bornstein, 2004). Possessing keen foresight, unflinching beliefs, and bold visions to build something new and to change institutions that have become outdated, they help us understand the strikingly different dimensions of Sustainability Leadership for the 21st century, where innovation and profits are not only economic and monetary, but are also social, civic, and political. They are, in fact, laying the groundwork for new conceptions of Sustainability Leadership in which the ties of oppression are replaced by a new citizenship that has been created, hopefully one beyond caste and class.

What we notice first about one of these Gandhian leaders, S. Jagannathan, is his capacity to transform himself and those around him during his life. Appa was the quintessential transformative leader. That he married this leadership with action was a hallmark of his life, often in ways that were perplexing, at first, to those around him. Over, and over again, he would discover the ways in which he could effect changes in a landscape of social injustice, bringing his and others service to humanity with the goal of "prosperity for all" (*Sarvodaya*; see Mehta, 2004, 2009). The guiding values of self-help, spirituality, and socio-ecological change were keys in Appa's struggles. In the story of Jagannathan's life (Coppo, 2002), we learn of a bright and curious boy from Ramnad who becomes a young man in college in Madurai, and aspires to be a member of the elite, dressing in fancy clothes to the delight of his Mother. After meeting a Scottish missionary, who became a Gandhian and who dressed simply and talked of revolution, Appa dramatically changed, to the consternation—but, we are sure, from what we know of her, the support, too— of his Mother. The goal of what would later be called *Sarvodaya* by Mahatma Gandhi had entered his life in powerful ways that began affecting all those around him.

Appa taught us, by example, that the work of social justice and emancipatory education needs to be done simultaneously, as we cross our own borderlands and those barriers that are right in front of our eyes. These questions, and the actions that need to be undertaken to begin to answer them, were his work and continue to be that of Krishnammal. Her efforts in the 1990s and 2000s enabled over 5000 families to receive land titles and housing for 4000 families in the women's names and collaboratively and cooperatively supported the sustainability of thousands of families. What lessons are to be learned from this couple and other activists for realizing a just world and for freedom in our own communities? One of the main lessons regards non-violence and the idea of "No Conflict, No Compromise": that one continues to work with and at the same time pressure those who oppose one's goals (Bondurant, 1958).

Fig. 14. Sustainability Leader-Activists at the Workers Home - R to L - P.V. Rajagopal, Jill Carr-Harris, Amma (Krishnammal Jagannathan), Vengopu, Sathya Jagannathan, S. Thanaraj, V. Shivakumar, Bhoomikumar Jagannathan (David Blake Willis, 2013)

The story of Appa and Amma is a signal narrative encompassing all of these insights for transformational sustainability leadership. There is no doubt that they have inspired many, motivating people to put their lives on the line during protests, fasts, and padyatras. All who have visited the Worker's Home and LAFTI can attest to the high morale and commitment of the workers, whose sense of identity and self are fully embodied in the struggle for social justice, a struggle which Appa was always identifying, sometimes in the most unexpected places. As a leader, he voiced a vision that reached far beyond the contemporary discourses of people and power, introducing striking and seemingly insurmountable goals that would, then, be met with action.

The collective identity of the workers, with Appa and Amma, is one that extends to the villages and hamlets they have aided over the years, in bringing land to the landless, and homes to the homeless. As role models, they have set standards and a high bar for social justice work that invites others into the struggle in body, heart, and mind. Appa's daily schedule included an early morning rising (4 am), the morning and evening prayers, the chanting of the 108 names of God, the Yoga exercises (for many years Appa would do 108 *Surya Namaskar* or Sun Salutations, every day), the spinning—always spinning— and the sharing of food together in a social atmosphere where people touch (remember, these are 'untouchables'). All of these signify a special sustainability community where significant change is being enacted. As David Albert wrote in his Introduction to their biography (Coppo, 2005), both Appa and Amma have "a feeling of abundance by owning virtually nothing."

Through their courage, daring, and skills in the struggle against poverty, caste, and ecological oppression, Appa and Amma have helped us to discover successful examples of liberation from the apartheid of caste and class. The inspired vision of Appa and Amma resulted in the training, agitating, teaching, and successful liberation of Dalit and other women, men, and children from the 1950s onward. Their work has helped us understand the place of the Gandhian struggle for liberation for the poor, and especially, the Dalits. The work of Amma and Appa continues to carry resonance at all levels of Indian society as it appeals to the idea of *swaraj* (self-rule, freedom) in all aspects of the struggle for liberation.

Appa also took up the charge of fighting environmental degradation and the horrors visited upon the poor by multinational corporations supporting tiger prawn farming, leading a firestorm of protests generated by LAFTI which greeted these predatory capitalists. The stories of the awful destruction generated by the multinational prawn aquaculture industry, in search of ever-greater profits, so that we may eat cheap shrimp, are tied to us all in developed countries (and now developing countries, including India, in the sense of new middle and upper classes). We, too, are complicit in the oppression of the poor, the downtrodden, and, in India, the Dalits, the former untouchables. This complicity is our responsibility, too, as Appa taught us, we are part of those rich countries and corporations, which continually seek new markets without heeding the consequences at the local level. Appa's struggles against the multinationals led to a Supreme Court of India case, which Appa won, requiring a significant environmental stewardship to be followed. These are paths of service and progress for all, *Sarvodaya*, with the goal of *Swaraj,* the freedom of self-rule. Yet, quite a different, new generation of Sustainable Leaders are now emerging in India, following these traditions and taking them to the next significant level.

Case Study 2: The Need for a Different Leadership in Sustainability: Dalit Activists in Nalanda Academy

My meeting with Nalanda Academy colleagues took place on February 24, 2020. We first heard the social activist Anoop Kumar's story; then, the stories of his colleagues Vishal Sarpe, Nilesh, and Kapil Wankhede; and then, the history of Nalanda Academy, an impressive effort to support Dalit, Tribals, BCs (Backward Castes), SCs (Scheduled Castes), Muslims, and other marginalized young people from across India in their quest for Higher Education in India and abroad. I should note that the Dalits constitute nearly 20% of India's population or over 200 million people (Willis and Rajasekaran, 2007; Charsley and Karanth, 1998). They come from a range of castes and subcastes united by their oppression in a system that can be described as a severe apartheid. One of these caste names, Paraiyar/Paraiyan, derived from a traditional drum they played called the *parai,* has entered the English language as pariah.

Seemingly forever condemned to the lower reaches of the caste/*jati* system in India, the various communities which the Dalits consist of have strengthened their voices, and actively campaigned for change at the local and national level in recent years. Dalits have long been victims of poverty, as well as historical, and continuing, acts of extreme violence. The tragedy of Kilvenmani in Thanjavur District, Tamil Nadu in 1969, was one such massacre, drawing national attention in India to the situation of the Dalits. In this atrocity, 42 Dalits, including children, were burned alive in a small building, an answer from upper caste landlords to their strikes for higher wages. The aftermath of this tragedy was personally witnessed by Krishnammal, who told me that Kilvenmani was the driving force behind her beginning a massive and very successful campaign of land redistribution and the building of housing for Dalit communities. Not much has changed since that time, and the story of Anoop Kumar echoes this atrocity.

As a response to such severe discrimination, Anoop decided on a path toward a different kind of social and educational leadership, which would sustainably nurture and support the poorest, yet brightest, Dalit students from villages across India. The values of community and engagement brought to Anoop's work are similar to those of Krishnammal, herself Dalit— even as Dalits are wary of calling themselves Gandhians, preferring to see themselves as Ambedkarites. Founded in 2015, Nalanda Academy was Anoop's answer for a new generation. The Academy has had a 100% success rate in helping students enter Higher Education institutions, often with full support of their education, as first-generation students from extremely poor families. It is a new example of Sustainability Leadership, established to support and nourish the community first, the community of Dalits, the most down-trodden people in India. Nalanda Academy began with Anoop Kumar teaching 22 village girls at a Marathi medium college in Wardha in 2013, that his friend had recommended to him as a collective experience, after the turmoil of many years of Anoop's activism in Kanpur and New Delhi. The local Buddhist Dalit community offered a broken-down, two-story Buddhist *Vihar* as a facility for Nalanda Academy in 2015, which has been considerably enhanced by Nalanda Academy, including a small temple space for Dalit Buddhists and others. Many Dalits in Western India, it should be noted, converted to Buddhism from Hinduism in the 1940s under the leadership of B.R. Ambedkar, the author of India's Constitution, a Dalit, and a revolutionary leader with Gandhi. Anoop's success with these students led him to believe that he could do something more, hence the founding of Nalanda Academy. He realized that he could help these marginalized students change their whole life in a matter of months. The students are at Nalanda Academy from 9am-6pm every day with no holidays until they complete their term. The students are determined, committed, and passionate, as they are the next generation of Dalit leaders.

Fig. 15. Nalanda Academy Students, Wardha, India. "Our icons who are also pioneers in field of education for lower castes in India - Savitri Phule, Dr Ambedkar and Jyotirao Phule" (Anoop Kumar with David Blake Willis, 2020)

Nalanda Academy began with 20 students and has been responsible for the achievements of 450 students. There are at present 250 students, ages 17-22, studying in the Nalanda Academy community. The effort is supported entirely by Anoop's friends and networks. There is no exam to enter, nor is entrance based on merit. Instead, through two days of interviews they select their incoming class with the goal of creating new leaders, 50% of whom are girls and 90% of whom come from rural areas. Word of mouth brings many parents and their children to Wardha in the third week of June to seek admission. As Anoop said to us, "With the first batch of students the story spread." The first term includes senior students as interns, and many graduates have returned to offer service in teaching and in other ways as well. Anoop also founded the Dalit magazine *Insight* at Jawaharlal Nehru University in the early 2000s, an immediate success that spread widely to 80 universities around India. The magazine depicted experiences and struggles from a Dalit point of view, and the many enthusiastic supporters of *Insight* have formed the core of Anoop's and Nalanda Academy's supporters.

Fig. 16. Anoop Kumar, Dalit Sustainability Leader, Nalanda Academy, and Admirers, Wardha, India (David Blake Willis, 2020)

Now, Nalanda Academy has grown dramatically, and there is a plan not only for a new facility but also for a community center in the countryside, which will further enhance the students learning as they become new leaders in their communities. It is the vision of Nalanda Academy to expand to a six-acre donated plot of land about 20 minutes east of Wardha. Their land donor, Kapil Wankhede's father, worked this land, which was traditionally in his family and associated with a nearby village. Kapil was anxious to support Nalanda Academy after his own experiences of being able to go to the United States for his graduate education in Chicago, and then, later, working for a year and a half in New York City. He is now looking for some way to return to the US for work, so that he can provide further support for Nalanda Academy, beyond the donated land. Nalanda Academy is committed to "A Principled Stand," and has consistently refused requests from the BBC, and other Indian and international mainstream media, to portray what they have done. As Anoop said to us, "We will tell our own stories." With this in mind, *Nalanda Tales*, a book, will be coming out soon.

Case Study 3: Joining the World Is Not a Choice: P.V. Rajagopal, Jill Carr-Harris and *Jai Jagat*

A *padyatra* or *yatra*, a traditional march of protest, is one of the important vehicles of dissent in India, as was seen by Gandhi's Salt March against British imperialism in 1930, and then the *yatras* of Vinobha Bhave and Appa in the 1950s-1980s. In October 2007, the front page of India's national newspaper, *The Hindu*, had photographs of the Janadesh March sponsored by the activist organization Ekta Parishad. The Janadesh protestors, composed of Dalits, members of the Other Backward Class (OBC), and tribals, all poor and landless, walked over a period of more than a month from Gwalior to New Delhi. The Janadesh March was large and impressive, with over half a million protestors and walkers at the end of the yatra. It succeeded in its initial goal of bringing the attention of the world to the plight of the poor in India, as well as a commitment by the government to investigate and address these problems of poverty and landlessness. Along with *ahimsa*, is the search for truth (*satya*) and the pressure or truth force (*satyagraha*) which it can bring to bear on these difficult social contexts, something A. Annamalai, the Director of the Gandhi Museum in New Delhi, has spoken of (2018, 2020). *Ahimsa* is the means, the vehicle to reach the goal, which is truth, liberation and freedom (Cortright, 2006). Mutual aid and cooperation are the key, again: "No Conflict, No Compromise." Two of the great contemporary practitioners of this are P.V. Rajagopal and Jill Carr-Harris with their 2019-2026 *Jai Jagat* (Victory for the World) yatra.

These leaders of the Janadesh and Jai Jagat movements were inspired by Gandhi and the techniques of non-violent protest. The work of Appa was a signal example for them. What we are seeing from these activities is an increasing awareness of what come next, a politics based on the conflict between haves and have-nots. Increasingly, Dalits, Muslims, and other marginalized communities are at the core of this movement in India, in alliance with middle, and some upper, caste members. Where this will all go is being indicated by what is happening on the streets of many cities around the world. A change is in the wind. Gandhi and his fellow activists began with projects of decolonization (Villanueva, 2018; Tuhiwai Smith, 1999), another essential tool leading to sustainability. Possessing keen foresight, unflinching belief, and bold visions to build something new, or to change institutions that have become outdated, these Gandhian activists, or those who have adopted Gandhian principles, have helped us to understand the transformative dimensions of social change and social action for the 21st century, where innovation and profits are not only economic and monetary, but social, civic, and political. They have been, in fact, laying the groundwork for a new conception of sustainability as *swaraj* in which the ties of oppression are replaced by a new citizenship beyond caste and class.

Like the great visionary Soedjatmoko of Indonesia, the founder of the United Nations University (Soedjatmoko, 1994), they have awakened us to what could be done to make the world a better place. For our world today, as Edmund O'Sullivan has described, four levels of consciousness need to be awakened (1999, p. 34):

1. A pre-conscious non-reflective level
2. An emergent survival-conscious level
3. A critical conscious level
4. A level of visionary consciousness

Mahatma Gandhi, Martin Luther King Jr., Appa, Amma, Anoop, PV Rajagopal, Jill Carr-Harris, and other great transformational leaders began with the first, and, then, led us all to the last. Their activism for critical consciousness put survival as paramount for all, followed by a recognition that our current form of economic "development" consistently moves wealth upwards to a smaller and smaller elite group while leaving the vast majority of the people of the world increasingly destitute. In the context of globalization, the global market mentality

Fig. 17. Rajagopal speaking at the 2007 Janadesh March for Land and Environmental Justice, Gawlior, India (Photo by Ekta Parishad/Wikimedia)

that is taking hold even overshadows nation-state loyalty, this mentality has also shared with us visions for the future in the struggle against predatory capitalism. It is now up to us to do our part, in however small a measure, because these add up, to alleviate whatever suffering we see, to raise and spread a deeper awareness, and, above all, to further the cause of peace.

I write this chapter in the midst of the great pandemic of 2020, a humbling and terrifying event in human history which may well result in dramatic transformations at the structural and institutional levels. The American and Canadian Activists Angela Davis and Naomi Klein emphasized the importance of taking care of each other and the planet during this precious moment we are in now (Rising Majority, 2020); of international solidarity, and of the transformative power of crisis. Such a transformative power is the foundation of our common dream of human liberation, what the Gandhian leaders I have been studying have taught us above all: *a sustainable activism based on love and justice.* One of the most effective demonstrations of Sustainability Leadership in our world today can be found in the Right Livelihood Award, the Alternative Nobel Prize, headquartered in Sweden. Every year, they select a range of visionary activists who have done much for the planet and people in their respective contexts, including the occasion of Amma's 95th birthday on June 15, 2020. *"JAI JAGAT!!"* was written on the birthday cake, shared amongst ourselves and members of the Right Livelihood Team, demonstrating the unanimity of Amma's love and compassion. As Amma shared with us, 'Jai Jagat' needs to echo the world over, especially when global peace is threatened by pandemic, racism, violence and climate change issues.

Gandhian activists like Amma and those inspired by Mahatma Gandhi are people who want to create a new culture— a more humanistic, and more sustainable culture. Their work has been very much about ending colonialism, what one the great women's activist of India, Gabrielle Dietrich, calls *internal* and *external colonialisms*. There is a colonialism of the mind and heart that has been especially devastating for oppressed peoples. Finding ways of addressing and resolving these problems has been their life's work. The opposition or taboo against transcaste marriage, of which Amma and Appa are one example, is also part of this lifework; even as there are always the echoes of purity and pollution, of caste and outcaste.

Moreover, there are lessons to be discovered in transformative learning in the Gandhian contexts of self-help, spirituality, and socio-ecological change as exemplified by Ekta Parishad. The ancient wisdom of India has been melded with the steely activism and clear eye of social entrepreneurs, who clearly intend to help provide, together with the workers, homes for the homeless and lands for the landless. PV Rajagopal's life and work are powerful and successful examples of liberation from the apartheid of caste and class through LAFTI's radical Gandhian strategies for human and organizational development. *Ahimsa* (non-violence) transcends time and space, something the American activist Gene Sharp (1973, 2002) wrote about in *Politics of Non-Violent Action* and *From Dictatorship to Democracy*, whose words inspired the Arab Spring and Occupy Movements: OTPOR in Serbia, Kmara in Georgia, Solidarity in Poland, PORA in Ukraine, the Velvet Revolution in Czechoslovakia, and particularly, the work of Dolores Huerta and Cesar Chavez with the United Farm Workers in the United States. What these movements and their leaders reveal is how what had once been unspeakable conversations, reflecting divided communities and parallel societies, can be transcended by action. As Dolores, who is now 88 and still active in social movements, told me during a conversation in January 2020,

"Every moment is an opportunity for activism."

Colonizers and native modernizers alike have continued to replace pre-modern sustainability with psychological and physical borders that have sustained the tropes of difference, fear, and nationalism. Yet, borders and borderlands can be surprising, indeed, in their creative production and as the location of emergent, transformative change (Willis and Murphy-Shigematsu, 2008; Willis and Rappleye, 2012). Leaders like P.V. Rajagopal and Jill Carr-Harris, whose many *yatras* have brought Gandhian ideas and ideals back to the forefront, in their support of the needs of the poorest and most marginalized sectors of society show that resistance means new lessons as moral positioning values as sustainable and continuing to have power. Their foresight has been captured by scholars as diverse as Sri A. Annamalai, Director of the National Gandhi Museum in New Delhi, whose wonderful digital compilation of the works of Mahatma Gandhi (2018) will echo for generations to come, and Lloyd and Susanne Rudolph (2006) who saw Gandhi as postmodern prophet of 'the modernity of tradition' in his understanding of situational truth. Our own experiments with truth, as a human species, require us now, more than ever, to stand on the shoulders of these giants of identity and liberation to establish a leadership for sustainability. How might we best understand the lessons they left for us as we face the chaos of globalization, and what will surely be multiple coronas?

Transformational Leadership for Sustainability: The prescient power of Gandhian Values and Action

What I began to discover from speaking with these many activists and learning from their leadership over the years, is similar to the work on leadership by James MacGregor Burns (1978), reflecting at its heart the concept of leaders and followers working together tirelessly in unison towards common goals. Morals, motivation, and morale are joined together in this conceptualization, through an inspired vision of change that dramatically alters the perceptions, expectations and actions of both the followers and the leaders themselves. The next steps in the development of this concept of Transformational Leadership came in the 1990s with the research of Bernard M. Bass, an American scholar, who found that transformative leaders are given not only admiration and respect by their followers and others, but they also create circles of trust among their followers. Bass and his colleagues identified the following characteristics of

Transformative Leadership:

Transformational Leadership: Key Principles

1) Motivation, Morale, Performance of Followers Enhanced
2) Sense of Identity and Self Committed to the Work
3) Leader Articulates Energized Vision and Challenging Goals
4) Organization Has a Collective Identity
5) Leaders: Role Models for Followers, Inspiring Them to Further Work
6) Followers Share Deeply in the Work
7) Significant Change Through Example and Work as a Team

(Burns, 1978; Bass, 1990; Bass & Riggio, 2008; Bass & Bass, 2008)

Monica Sharma has followed this research with her own book on *Radical Transformational Leadership* (2017) that echoes the values and tactics of on-the-ground Gandhian leaders today in its emphasis on the power of transformational leadership for sustainability. Key to the strategies are, what she describes as, compassion, equality, and human capability, all of which describe India's current Gandhian activists. As Peter Senge of MIT and the Academy for System Change has commented on Sharma's work (2017), "The new field she describes as 'radical systems and cultural transformation' constitutes a kind of invisible renaissance emerging around the world of understanding the entwined inner and outer nature of genuine systemic change." Sharma emphasizes three innate intertwined attributes, which describe what Gandhian leaders in ashrams and villages in India are accomplishing today: the universal heart of compassion, an empathetic burning for fairness, and a discerning eye for seeing patterns. One of the most interesting aspects of Sharma's work is her emphasis on systems and fractals, which enables a vision of scaling up possibilities for both whole systems transformation and for sustainability leadership for measurable change (2017, p. 210). Her 'learning-in-action' programs follow what Gandhian leaders in India have followed from the beginning of resistance to colonialism and the depredations of modern industrialism. Sustainability is a key goal at the village or *gram* level for these programs. Gandhigram University professor-activist G. Palanidurai and Wardha educator-activist Anoop Kumar both reported to me, during my interviews, on their active program of seeking out and fostering transformational leaders at the village level, the former for political consciousness-raising, and the latter for transforming caste relationships, particularly for Dalits. These young leaders are a groundswell of change in India that has largely gone unnoticed in the media, which is so focused, as it has been, on traditional politics, while their work has been at the village level. Yet, it reflects a commitment to transformation with results, as Sharma calls it. We can see, too, in the work of Khudai Khidmatgar, Faisal-Bhai, and Inamul Hassan, what Sharma calls "an architecture for equitable and sustainable results" (2017).

The Yoga of Sustainability Leadership: Relearning, Reimagining, and Resistance

What we discover with Amma, Appa, Nalanda Academy, and Jai Jagat follows in the footsteps of Aurobindo and Gandhi, then is a reimagining, not only with the 20th century in mind, but with the 21st century in mind as well, especially now that the Coronavirus has upended many traditional notions of structure and agency. Gandhi and Aurobindo can be seen in a fresh light, too, as Sangeetha Sriram, Divyanshi Chugh, Manoj Pavitran, and Naveen Vasudevan of Auroville envisioned when they created "Indian Renaissance: Swaraj & Sarvodaya," a conference in Auroville in early March 2020, with a collection of distinguished activists and scholars that directly examined Sri Aurobindo and Mahatma Gandhi together, perhaps for the first time, in a serious and engaged way.

Their work and our conference, together in Auroville, continued what Bindu Mohanty calls the "Social Practices of Citizenship" of Gandhi and Vinobha Bhave and what has often been called cosmopolitan citizenship (Appiah, 2006). Many of the speakers emphasized the ideal of human unity and the quest for an evolution of human society, which Sri Aurobindo so eloquently explored and what became the basis for the Mother's original project, extending these ideas into a human society: Auroville. This conference spoke for the *sadhana* (spiritual practice) of these two giants as an important confluence, forcing us to realize that any approach to social phenomena, even when it came to these two great individual leaders, needs to be multilateral, multipolar, and multicultural. With mixing, mashing, and hybridities, what they brought to the stage were, in fact, what we can call 'creolizations' that have asserted themselves (Willis, 2001). Like the Dance of Shiva, called the *Tandava*, there is dancing as newness springs up, too. The leaders of the conference and its participants were (and are) "staying with the trouble," as Donna Haraway calls it (2016), seeking survival strategies, as we all are, of rational, resourceful, and human behavior and unexpected new connections to support these strategies (following Ursula Le Guin's and Bruno Latour's praise for Anna Tsing's book in 2015). Like Haraway, Gandhi and Aurobindo realized the clarity and call of sym-poiesis, or making-with, rather than auto-poiesis, or self-making.

"Relearning, Reimagining, and Resistance" were very much part of the makeup and strategies of Aurobindo and Gandhi. Relearning is both about the lessons these two great leaders took from their actions and, especially for Sri Aurobindo after his withdrawal to the Ashram in Pondicherry, their contemplations. Instead of an advance, a liberation and a relative embracing of others by society, what they both experienced was a return to tropes of past eras that appear and disappear throughout Indian history. In that sense, like them, we need to relearn what our place is in this circular drama, where performance, spectacle, and commotion (disruption in the current parlance) are all revisited. As Ganesh Devy has said, Sri Aurobindo and Gandhi are "children of a shared time." We may, in fact, note the complexity of reimaging the present moment, which appears as chaos, but is actually notable for its multiple cores and multiple peripheries.

The coronavirus has revealed these multipolarities. We have, in a sense, then, a more complicated World Systems theory, where enclaves of enlightenment clash with peripheries of prejudice and isolation. Just as the core has been captured by one kind of periphery, as in the American election of 2016 or the Indian election of 2019, the traditional periphery of the marginalized is being occupied by new Others. Thus we have multiple centers and complex systems operating at the same time. This byzantine era is problematic and convoluted for its members, but understandable, too, in the context of a larger imperial decline, not only of the United States, but of the structural and political hegemonies of that other great republican nation, India. Their fates interwoven by pandemic braiding and deep racisms or casteisms, the United States and India would do well to heed the teachings of both Sri Aurobindo and the Mahatma, whose wisdom and action give us collective promises for what Anna Lowenhaupt Tsing has called "the possibility of life in capitalist ruins" (2015) and Rebecca Solnit has named as "Hope in the Dark" (2016).

Like Solnit, they understood the uses of uncertainty, the importance of the stories we tell, and resistance. People do indeed have the power. Debashish Banerji and Robert McDermott note something similar, how "...patchwork solutions are no longer effective and if we are to rise to the challenge of our times, we need what Thomas Kuhn called a paradigm shift. Gandhi and Sri Aurobindo were radical thinkers, and we need to study their contributions once more for what they may offer to a postcolonial, postmodern and posthuman world."(2021) "Swaraj as inclusive freedom," as Nishant Kumar (2021) terms it, is what we discover here, the spiritual quest for human unity or the "Self and Swaraj" as Payel Chattopadhyay Mukherjee refers to it (2021). All of this speaks to what should be a rallying cry for the 21st century: *Decolonization.*

Like the coronavirus, the historical roots and routes of these cultures are now deeply intertwined with who we are in the world. This 'grassroots globalization' (Appadurai, 2000) thus implicates us more than it first appears to. As Arundhati Roy has shared with us, 'The Pandemic Is a Portal' (2020). The 'habitus of homogeneity' of Harumi Befu (2001) is thus continually disrupted by innovation and newness as these intrusions challenge and pressure us to transform. Aurobindo and Gandhi understood this and gave us "a preview of the coming attractions." Resisting and relearning, as these two great sages enacted them in their lives are, in this sense, strategies for dealing with difference and newness. Permeability (relearning) and immunity (resisting) are always at work in a complex dance of systems and circulations (Willis and Rappleye, 2011).

What both Gandhi and Aurobindo realized was the need to pay special attention to emergent strategy as they "shaped change and changed [the] world" (Brown, 2017). Not only did they emphasize intentional adaptation, but they understood interdependence and decentralization, who we are and how we share. The pathways of change of Gandhi-Ji and Sri Aurobindo were also nonlinear and iterative, realizing again the power of circular approaches to societal change; *Swaraj as Sarvodaya* – Freedom for All. Their charge to us, more than one hundred years on, is, indeed, "New Lamps for Old."

For Amma, Appa, PVR, Jill, Anoop, and the many brave souls who have worked as social change activists, the *Bhagavad Gita* can be seen as *Satyagraha,* the truth force of dharma, of our duty, and of non-violent resistance, as paramount in our lives (Sundaresan and Chandrapaul, 2008; M.K. Gandhi, 1927b). Binod Kumar Agarwala speaks of this as a 'theory of revision of institutions' (2021), just as Ramesh Chandra Pradhan emphasizes the yoga and spiritual practice as integral to Sri Aurobindo and the action logics or *karmayoga* of Mahatma Gandhi (2021). Certainly, the *Gita* has been and continues to be a touchstone that is wide-ranging for all Indian activists, inasmuch as its soul-searching is reflected in everyone in what Agarwala calls a 'new hermeneutics of self and social transformation' (2021).

What, then, are our responsibilities as educators for this new world we have joined? Like the modern environmental movement, which was dramatically moved to action by the photograph of "Earthrise," we look, as educators, to this simple and powerful image for inspiration; for our perception of being in this together, that globalization is not only economics, that we all have a responsibility to open our hearts and minds to cross the borders of fear, ignorance, and desperate poverty. Global warming, the threat of nuclear weapons, and environmental destruction are pressing on us like never before. This is a call for a cosmopolitan citizenship, a transnational global citizenship, a call for a flexible and activist orientation.

It is now time to re-invoke that famous Latin saying for educators and students of *Carpe Diem!* ("Seize the Day!") along with its Sanskrit corollary: *Jai Jagat!* ("Victory for the World!").

Questions for Discussion

1. How might Sustainability Leaders utilize Gandhian ideas and values for their next steps in transitioning to a balance that will empower and support the rest of the planet?
2. What will it take for humanity to support those core Gandhian strategies for constructive and collaborative change?
3. How can the larger lessons of Gandhian constructive work and movement struggle be shared with the rest of the world?
4. What Gandhian tactics might be employed to bring all parties into the circle of change required for sustainability?
5. How will Sustainability Leaders respond to future pandemics as well as racial and environment crises, learning from the examples of Gandhian movement work in South Asia?

Acknowledgments

A special thanks to Fielding Graduate University, Dr. Katie McGraw, Dr. Monique Snowden, and Dr. Katrina Rogers for support of my research 2018-2021 as well as earlier grants from Fielding Graduate University. Searching for the origins of the voices and roots of Gandhian leadership, I began conducting interviews with key figures in the Sarvodaya movement from 2006, many of whom I had known since living in India in the mid to late 1970s. These activists have been associated with the Worker's Home, Gandhigram, ASSEFA, LAFTI, and other organizations. Along with my academic and intellectual co-researcher J. Rajasekaran of Madurai, I have delved deeply into a movement that is similar to the work of Nelson Mandela in South Africa. These voices include those of Appa's and Amma's son and daughter, Sri Bhoomikumar and Smt. Sathya and of their colleagues and co-workers Sri K.M. Natarajan; Sri Mariappan; Dr. M.P. Vasimalai; Sri Gautam Bajaj; Dr. S. Narayanasamy; Dr. G. Palanithurai; Dr. V. Raghupathy; Dr. M. William Baskaran; Dr. Vino Aram; Dr. T. Ravichandran; Dr. G. Pankajam; Dr. N. Markandan; Sri M.R. Rajagopalan; Sri K. Sivakumar; Sri S. Loganathan; Smt Gabriele Dietrich; Smt. V.A. Vidya; Sri M. Vannikali; Smt. Pondammal; Dr. M.A. Arasu; Dr. M.P. Vasimalai, Dr. Umarani, Dr. Gurusamy, and many others of Dhan Foundation; Sri Shankar; Rev. Jim Jesudoss; Dr. S. Muthulakshmi; M. Pamayan; and of key figures directly involved in the activism through Krishnammal's actions: Sri K. Natarajan, Sri Vengopu, Sri Veerachamy, Sri Thamba, Sri Gandhi, Smt Kannagi, Smt Jothi, Sri Anbuselvan, Sri Muniyan, and many more. Beyond Gandhigram and Madurai have been the powerful voices of Sri P.V. Rajagopal and Dr. Jill Carr-Harris of Ekta Parishad and the Jai Jagat Movement; Sri T. Kannan and Smt. Nedya of Coimbatore; Sri Rejendran and others in T. Kallupatti; Sri Nanda Kumar; Sri Inamul, Sri Musthafa, Sri R. Ilyah Kumar, and Sri Faisal-Bhai of Khudai Khidmatgar; Dr. A. Annamalai of the Gandhi Museum, New Delhi; the many thoughtful activists of Auroville including Sangeeta Sriram and Ram Subramanian; organic farmers like Sivakumar and Ananthu of Chennai; Dr. Bijay Mahajan of the Rajiv Gandhi Institute of Contemporary Studies; venerable Gandhians Jyotibhai Desai and Daniel Mazgaonkar of Baroda; Mr. and Mrs. Ganesh N. Devy; Arun Bhai Bhatt; Dr. and Mrs. Sudarshan Iyengar of Gujarat Vidyapeet; Sushuma Sharma and Adwait S. Deshpande of the Nai Talim School, Gandhi's Ashram, Wardha;

Anoop Kumar and colleagues at Nalanda Academy, Wardha; and of academics who have helped me make sense of the contexts and times, especially Dr. Ananta Giri of the Madras Institute of Development Studies.

About the Author

David Blake Willis, Ph.D., is Professor of Anthropology and Education at Fielding Graduate University and Professor Emeritus of Anthropology at Soai Buddhist University in Japan. His interests in anthropology, sustainability, social justice, and immigration come from 37 years living in traditional cultural systems in Japan and India. He researches and writes on transformational leadership and education, human development in transnational contexts, the Creolization of cultures, comparative education, citizenship, transcultural communities, transnational diaspora, transformative adult education, and Dalit/Gandhian liberation movements in South India. His publications include *World Cultures: The Language Villages (Leading, Learning, and Teaching on the Global Frontier)* with Walter Enloe (Tertium Quid, 2016); *Reimagining Japanese Education: Borders, Transfers, Circulations, and the Comparative* with Jeremy Rappleye (Oxford Studies in Comparative Education, 2011); *Transcultural Japan: At the Borders of Race, Gender, and Identity* with Stephen Murphy-Shigematsu (Routledge, 2007); and *Japanese Education in Transition 2001: Radical Perspectives on Cultural and Political Transformation* with Satoshi Yamamura (Adelaide Shannon, 2002).

References

Agarwala, Binod Kumar. (2021). Interpretation of the *Bhagavadgita* During the Freedom Struggle in India and the Theory of Revision of Institution in It: Understanding Gandhi and Sri Aurobindo, in Ananta Kumar Giri (Ed.). *Mahatama Gandhi And Aurobindo.* Routledge.

Annamalai, A. (Ed.) (2018). *Special Digital Multi Media Kit on Mahatma Gandhi.* National Gandhi Museum.

Annamalai, A. (2021). "Empowering People Through Non-Violence," in Ananta Kumar Giri (Ed.). *Mahatama Gandhi And Aurobindo*. Routledge.

Appadurai, Arjun. (2000). Guest Editor. *Globalization.* Special Issue of Public Culture, Millennial Quartet, 12 (1) Winter.

Appiah, Kwame Anthony. (2006). *Cosmopolitanism: Ethics in a World of Strangers,*

New York:

Ashoka. (2020). Ashoka envisions a world in which everyone is a changemaker, https://www.ashoka.org/en-us/about-ashoka

Bannerji, Debashish, and McDermott, Robert. (2021). Afterword, in Ananta Kumar Giri (Ed.). *Mahatama Gandhi And Aurobindo.* Routledge.

Bass, B. M. (1997). Does the Transactional–Transformational Leadership Paradigm Transcend Organizational and National Boundaries? *American Psychologist*, Vol. 52, No. 2, pp. 130-139.

Bandhu, P. (2011). *Back to Basics: A J.C. Kumarappa Reader.* Kozhikode: Gitanjali Press.

Bass, B. M. (1985). *Leadership and Performance Beyond Expectation.* Free Press.

Bass, B. M. (1990). From Transactional to Transformational Leadership: Learning to Share the Vision. *Organizational Dynamics,* (Winter): 19-31.

Bass, B. M. and Riggio, R. E. (2008). *Transformational Leadership.* Lawrence Erlbaum Associates, Inc.

Bass, B. M., and Steidlmeier, P. (1999). *Ethics, Character and Authentic Transformational Leadership.* Leadership Quarterly, Summer, Vol. 10, Issue 2, pp. 181-217.

Befu, Harumi. (2001). *Hegemony of Homogeneity: An Anthropological Analysis of Nihonjinron.* Trans Pacific Press.

Bondurant, Joan V. (1958). *Conquest of Violence. The Gandhian Philosophy of Conflict.* Princeton, Princeton University Press.

Bornstein, D. (2004). *How to Change the World: Social Entrepreneurs and the Power of New Ideas.* Oxford University Press.

Brett, Steve. (2021). Gandhi, Aurobindo and Second World War, in Ananta Kumar Giri (Ed.). *Mahatama Gandhi and Aurobindo*. Routledge.

brown, adrienne maree. (2017). *Emergent Strategy: Shaping Change, Changing Worlds.* AK Press.

Burns, J. M. (1978). *Leadership*. Harper and Row.

Charsley, S. R., & Karanth, G. K. (eds). (1998). *Challenging Untouchability*. Sage.

Coppo, L. (2005). *The Color of Freedom*. Common Courage Press.

Cortright, David. (2006). *Gandhi and Beyond: Nonviolence for an Age of Terrorism.* Paradigm.

Devji, Faisal. (2012). *The Impossible Indian: Gandhi and the Temptation of Violence.* Harvard University Press.

Easwaran, Eknath. (1972, 2011). *Gandhi the Man: How One Man Changed Himself to Change the World.* Nilgiri Press.

Erikson, Erik. (1969). *Gandhi's Truth: On the Origins of Militant Nonviolence*. Norton.

Freire, Paulo. (1970, 2000). *Pedagogy of the Oppressed.* Continuum.

Fischer, Louis (Ed.). (1962). *The Essential Gandhi: An Anthology of His Writings on His Life, Work, and Ideas.* Vintage Books.

Gandhi, M. K. (1927a). *An Autobiography or My Experiments with Truth.* Navajivan Publishing House.

Gandhi, M. K. (1927b). *Non-Violent Resistance (Satyagraha).* Schocken Books by arrangement with the Navajivan Trust.

Gandhi, Rajmohan. (2018). *Modern South India: A History from the 17th Century to Our Times*. Aleph.

Giri, Ananta Kumar (Ed.). (2021). *Mahatama Gandhi and Aurobindo*. Routledge.

Gorringe, H. (2005). *Untouchable Citizens: Dalit Movements and Democratisation in Tamil Nadu.* Sage.

Govindu, Venu Madhav, and Malghan, Deepak. (2016). *The Web of Freedom: J.C. Kumarappa and Gandhi's Struggle for Economic Justice*. Oxford.

Haraway, Donna J. (2016). *Staying with the Trouble: Making Kin in the Chthulucene.* Durham: Duke University Press.

Haraway, Donna. (2015). Anthropocene, Capitalocene, Plantationocene, Chthulucene: Making Kin, *Environmental Humanities*, vol. 6, pp. 159-165 www.environmentalhumanities.org ISSN: 2201-1919

Kumar, Nishant. (2021). Gandhi, Aurobindo and the idea of Swaraj as 'inclusive freedom,' in Ananta Kumar Giri (Ed.). *Mahatama Gandhi and Aurobindo.* Routledge.

Lelyveld, Joseph. (2011). *Great Soul: Mahatma Gandhi and His Struggle with India.* Alfred A. Knopf.

Mehta, Subhash. (2009). *A Hand-Book of Sarvodaya (Part One): Gandhi, Vinobha and Jayaprakash – The Triumvirate of Sarvodaya (Their Lives in Brief).* Geeta Prakashan.

Mehta, Subhash. (2004). *A Hand-Book of Sarvodaya (Part Two): Gandhi, Vinobha and Jayaprakash – The Triumvirate of Sarvodaya (Their Lives in Brief).* Geeta Prakashan.

Mohanty, Bindu. (2021). Social Practices of Citizenship Based on Gandhian and Aurobindonian Thoughts, in Ananta Kumar Giri (Ed.). *Mahatama Gandhi and Aurobindo.* Routledge.

Mukherjee, Payel Chattopadhyay. (2021). A Meeting That Never Happened: Unheard Dialogues Between Sri Aurobindo and Mahatma Gandhi, in Ananta Kumar Giri (Ed.). *Mahatama Gandhi and Aurobindo.* Routledge.

O'Sullivan, E. (1999). *Transformative Learning: Educational Vision for the 21st Century.* Zed Books.

Patnaik, Sanghamitra. (2021). Gandhi, Sri Aurobindo, and New Horizons of Sustainable Development, in Ananta Kumar Giri (Ed.). *Mahatama Gandhi And Aurobindo.* Routledge.

Prabhu. R. K., & Rao, U. R. eds. (1976). *The Mind of Mahatma Gandhi.* Ahmedabad: Navajivan Publishing House.

Pradhan, Ramesh Chandra. (2021). Interpreting Bhagavadgītā: Mahatma Gandhi and Sri Aurobindo, in Ananta Kumar Giri (Ed.). *Mahatama Gandhi and Aurobindo.* Routledge.

Raghuramaraju, A. (Ed.) (2006). *Debating Gandhi: A Reader*. Oxford University Press.

Raja, K.C.R. (Ed.) (N.D.). *Gandhigram Thoughts and Talks of G. Ramachandran.* Gandhigram.

Rao, Koneru Ramakrishna. (2017). *Gandhi's Dharma.* Oxford University Press.

Reid, Herbert, and Taylor, Betsy. (2010). *Recovering the Commons: Democracy, Place, and Global Justice.* University of Illinois Press.

Riggio, R.E. (2009, March 24). Are You a Transformational Leader? *Psychology Today.* Found online at http://blogs.psychologytoday.com/blog/cutting-edge-leadership/200903/are-you-transformational-leader

The Rising Majority. (2020). Movement Building in the Time of the Coronavirus Crisis – Angela Davis and Naomi Klein, April 2, https://therisingmajority.com/events/movement-building/

Roy, Arundhati. (2020). 'The Pandemic Is a Portal," *The Financial Times*, April 3.

Rudolph, Lloyd I., and Rudolph, Susanne Hoeber. (1967). *Postmodern Gandhi and Other Essays: Gandhi in the World and at Home.* University of Chicago Press.

Sarvodaya Ilakkiya Pannai (2019). *A Pilgrimage Towards Gramswaraj: In the Footsteps of Gandhi, Vinobha and Jayaprakash – Collection of Speeches, Articles from the Sarvodaya Day Seminars, 2014-19.* Madurai: Sarvodaya Ilakkiya Pannai.

Schein, Edgar H., and Schein, Peter A. (2018). *Humble Leadership: The Power of Relationships, Openness, and Trust.* Berrett-Koehler Publishers.

Sharma, Monica. (2017). *Radical Transformational Leadership: Strategic Action for Change Agents.* North Atlantic Books.

Sharma, Subhash. (2021). Towards A New Earth Sastra: Gandhi, Sri Aurobindo and New Horizons of Human Development and Social Transformations, in Ananta Kumar Giri (Ed.). *Mahatama Gandhi and Aurobindo*. Routledge.

Sharp, Gene. (1973). *The Politics of Non-violent Action, Part I: Power and Struggle.* Boston. Peter Sargent.

Sharp, Gene. (2002). *From Dictatorship to Democracy: A Conceptual Framework for Liberation.* New York: Albert Einstein Institute.

Soedjatmoko, with Newland, K. & Soedjatmoko, K. C. (Eds). (1994). *Transforming Humanity: The Visionary Writings of Soedjatmoko.* West Hartford, CT: Kumarian Press.

Solnit, Rebecca. (2016). *Hope in the Dark: Untold Histories, Wild Possibilities.* Chicago: Haymarket.

Sundaresan, R., and Chandrapaul, J. (2008). *Silent March of the Invisible Force.* Sarvodaya Action Research Centre.

Tomasello, Michael. (2019). *Becoming Human: A Theory of Ontogeny.* Harvard University Press.

Tsing, Anna Lowenhaupt. (2015). *The Mushroom at the End of the World: On the Possibility of Life in Capitalist Ruins.* Princeton: Princeton University Press.

Tuhiwai Smith, Linda. (1999). *Decolonizing Methodologies: Research and Indigenous Peoples.* London: Zed Books.

Varghese, Saji. (2021).Towards Spirituality of the Environment: A Perspective from Sri Aurobindo and Gandhi, in Ananta Kumar Giri (Ed.). *Mahatama Gandhi and Aurobindo.* Routledge.

Villanueva, Edgar. (2018). *Decolonizing Wealth: Indigenous Wisdom to Heal Divides and Restore Balance.* Oakland: Berrett-Koehler.

Willis, David Blake (2001). 'Creole Times: Notes on Understanding Creolization for Transnational Japan-America,' in Takeshi Matsuda (Ed.) *The Age of Creolization in the Pacific: In Search of Emerging Cultures and Shared Values in the Japan-America Borderlands,* Hiroshima: Keisuisha.

Willis, David Blake. (2014). A remarkable life: The transformative leadership and

Gandhian challenge of S. Jagannathan, *Sarvodaya Journal,* January 2014

Willis, David Blake. (2018). Resist and Relearn: Comments on Circulations and Escapes in a Barbaric Age, Afterword in Blai Guarné and Paul Hansen, *Escaping Japan: Reflections on Estrangement and Exile in the Twenty-First Century* (2018). Routledge.

Willis, D. B., and Rajasekaran, J. (2007). "Dalits: The Changing Contexts of Caste, Culture, and Class in South India," in the Series, *Race and Caste in India and America: Case Studies of Power, Community, and Psyche. Soai Daigaku Kenkyu Ronshu (Annual Research Report of Soai University)*, Vol. 23.

Willis, David Blake, and Murphy-Shigematsu, Stephen (Eds.) (2008). *Transcultural Japan: At the Borderlands of Race, Gender, and Identity.* London: Routledge.

Willis, David Blake, and Rappleye, Jeremy (2011). *Reimagining Japanese Education: Borders, Circulations, and the Comparative.* Oxford: Symposium Books.

Wolpert, Stanley. (2001). *Gandhi's Passion: The Life and Legacy of Mahatma Gandhi.* Oxford.

CHAPTER 12

Collaborative Support Networks for Sustainability Leadership

Sergej van Middendorp
Miles Ahead
Laurence Habib
Faculty of Technology, Art and Design, Oslo Metropolitan University
Agnes Dewi Hartkamp
Foundation for Innovations in Horticulture (SIGN)
Flávio Mesquita Da Silva
Marie Fielder Center, Fielding Graduate University
Frederick Steier
Fielding Graduate University

Preamble

The subject of this chapter. This chapter addresses how theories, methods, and practices using collaborative support networks as a form of organizing can help address issues of sustainability leadership in a variety of contexts. We start by sharing our definition of sustainability leadership and then introduce collaborative support network theories, methods and practices. We place both in the context of the literature to help you orient yourself and become familiar with these ideas. Then, we share examples from the practice of the authors in applying collaborative support networks in different countries, cultures, and settings. We end by sharing challenges and questions that you can consider while applying the ideas from this chapter to your learning and practice.

The nature of this study. Our examples come from a merger between two Norwegian academic institutions with the aim of becoming a professional university, a project to develop a method for systemic workplace innovation in the Dutch horticultural sector that employees use to design and implement solutions themselves, and a project that brought thousands of children, parents, and teachers from hundreds of schools in Brazil together to explore peace through a dialogical process. These will illustrate that collaborative support networks, as a conscious form of organizing, afford ways to see similarities and differences in these varying contexts as one way to use collaboration to lead towards more sustainable practices.

The outcome of this chapter. After having read this chapter, you will be able to connect your own stories to ours and you will gain an understanding of how collaborative support networks could help you address issues of sustainability leadership. You will also be able to define sustainability leadership challenges, identify collaborative support networks, and understand how collaborative support networks can help lead towards sustainability. You will also be able to further develop your own ideas guided by the living systems perspective that we provide you with and the questions that we share at the end of the chapter.

From Sustainable Development to Sustainability Leadership

Sustainable development has been defined as "development that meets the needs of the present without compromising the ability of future generations to meet their own needs" (Bruntland et al., 1987, p.43). The inherent vagueness of the term "sustainable development" has been criticized for failing to address environmental and ecological issues (Buchdahl & Raper, 1998). The definition of the word "needs" is itself the subject of debate and alternative understandings of what individuals and societies "need" have been suggested, for example, in Jackson's (2009) book "Prosperity without Growth."

How can societies develop ecologically and socially sustainable practices? In order to achieve the sustainable development goals, there is a need for societies to radically transform a wide variety of social and economic areas: consumption, production, transport, living, education, and healthcare, just to name a few. Those transformations require new, systemic, inclusive, and progressive forms of leadership.

While there is a rising concern for the issues related to ecological and social sustainability, the question of how to concretely translate knowledge into action remains surprisingly elusive. Although it is evident that the climate crisis has increasingly dire consequences for inequality, poverty and health, there seems to be little concerted leadership effort across the globe to address the urgent need for action. If we want to understand why calls for unified action are mostly absent from political discourse and national policies, we may need to take a closer look at the notion of leadership itself.

The dominant leadership approach that developed in the past hundred years is characterized by top-down, policy- and data-driven approaches to economic and social development. For example, Heizmann and Liu (2018), in their analysis of an Australian sustainability leadership centre, describe how identity narratives are constructed to promote leadership as an individualist project, where heroism plays a defining role in the identity of the sustainability leader. They call for a new understanding of sustainability leadership that breaks away from the heroic, individual narratives and that relies more heavily on relational concepts such as collaboration, dialogue, and closeness to practice. With this, they echo the ideas promoted in the critical leadership studies literature (Caroll et al. 2008; Fairhust & Uhl-Bien, 2012; Raelin, 2016).

When we take such an organic and comprehensive approach to sustainability leadership, we also realize that leadership is just as relevant at the local level as at the global level. Economics and social affairs have typically been treated as belonging exclusively to the realm of national governments, which often ignore the global backdrop that both enables and constrains their endeavors. Going forward, ad hoc, local initiatives must be included in a truly global perspective that acknowledges, but also transcends, national and regional idiosyncrasies.

We suggest that *collaborative support networks* are a powerful means for enabling sustainability leadership as defined by this approach, as they offer an alternative to the antiquated picture of leadership where a tiny minority (the leaders) go forward and show the way, and the vast majority (all those who are not leaders) choose to follow (or not). As we will see in the next section of this chapter, collaborative support networks afford the emergence of a new type of leadership, where collaboration, dialogue, and practical support are the defining elements. In a sense, collaborative support networks are bound to promote the idea of *leadership in* the network rather than *leadership of* the network. Also, collaborative support networks offer the possibility to work across local, regional, national, and global levels, helping to scale leadership to help address sustainability challenges at all levels and scopes.

Sustainability leadership calls for a more organic approach that recognizes that sustainable development is dependent on broad participation and support. Although taking action is central to sustainable development, sustainability leadership is as much about taking action as it is designing for action. In all the cases that the authors have worked on, and that will be described in this chapter–dialogue on university design, workplace process innovation, and peace–action is enabled by broad participative processes of learning together and joining forces to imagine and shape sustainable futures. In practical terms, sustainability leadership means co-designing a process that holds together a dynamic web of constructive and empowering relationships between participants. Through reflection, dialogue and action, those participating in such networks are learning and enacting what they have learned, thereby empowering themselves and each other.

Another key concept of sustainability leadership is vulnerability, or, more precisely, how individuals learn to accept and deal with their own vulnerability, and the vulnerabilities in nature and society. In the sustainability literature, the concept of vulnerability often refers to ecological vulnerability: vegetation patterns, animal species, water resources are all vulnerable to climate change and variability. The terms vulnerability is also used to refer to broader societal phenomena that include economics, health and gender equality. The prospect of mass human migration due to climate change brings up issues of vulnerability both for the displaced populations themselves, and in terms of infrastructures, social configurations and political structures.

If we are to take vulnerability seriously, we also need to understand why it is seldom discussed in leadership studies. One way to address the question is to look into the notion of risk and, more importantly, risk aversion. Risk aversion is a distinct trait of human nature and has been discussed in the context of leadership. For example, Carmelli & Scheaffer (2009) found that risk aversion and self-centeredness amongst leaders was significantly related to organizational decline. Similarly, when developing sustainable leadership, risk aversion and hesitation to accept vulnerability may limit new possibilities that opening up to learning could bring, such as the possibility for "trial and error".

As we can see now, sustainable development covers a whole range of interrelated actions that range from the local to the global level. There is a need, more so than in the past, to rise above institutions, organizations, hierarchies, and geographical boundaries. And for this, we need a new form of leadership. A leadership open to vulnerability and learning. A leadership in networks that is collaborative, dialogic, supportive, and close to practice.

Collaborative Support Networks

What are collaborative support networks? And how do they relate to sustainability leadership? In this section, we introduce collaborative support networks as a new way of seeing and organizing. A way that fits well with the notion of sustainability leadership as developed in the section above.

The term collaborative support network emerged in the literature from 1999, when the term was first used to argue for the purposeful creation and improvement of such networks in education to help "foster the development of collaborative relationships and, in a broader sense, collaborative communities" (Walther-Thomas et al., 1999, p. 1). Several authors have used the term since, but none has developed a distinct theory of collaborative support networks.

According to Borgatti and Halgin (2011), network theory aims to theorize about the underlying principles of how networks support individuals and organizations to achieve certain outcomes. Theories of networks, conversely, are meant to support individuals and organizations in creating networks aimed at achieving certain outcomes. Network theory and theories of networks are interrelated, and the scholarly literature about both concepts co-evolved and refers to each other regularly. Over the decades since network theory was first mentioned in the literature, there has been much development in the subject. Network theory, for example, helped us to understand how contacts, links, ties, relationships, channels, resources and value function in networks (Andriessen & Gubbins, 2009). Based on this knowledge, many different theories of networks were developed for different settings and purposes. Today, almost every field of human practice has its own theory of networks, framed in a language that is fitting to that field. From the amount and the diversity of network theory and theories of networks available, we can infer how important networks as a form of organizing have become in our social worlds.

But, much of the development in theories of networks is rooted in the paradigm that Schön (1983) called 'technical rationality.' According to Schön, technical rationality emerged when universities codified the knowledge of the professions in their curricula and research to offer conceptual rigor, semantic certainty, and a rational understanding of how these professions work. But when doing research into how professionals actually work in practice, Schön found that the real work of professionals is much more improvisational, interactional, and messy than technical rationality implies. Technical rationality separates research from practice, thinking from doing, and man from nature. Technical rationality thus fails in a context where "complexity, uncertainty, uniqueness, and value-conflict" (Schön, 1983, p. 39) shape the problem setting.

The artificial separations underpinning technical rationality also provide one way of understanding how human action may have come to be unsustainable in the first place. Seeing man as separate from nature and autonomously independent has engendered much progress over the past few centuries, but has also resulted in negative impacts on our social and ecological environment. The nature of our sustainability issues is complex, uncertain, unique, and full of value-conflict, and the more integral theory and research of the past few decades provides converging evidence for the continuity and integration of body, mind, and environment. An embrace of complexity and ambiguity, and a renewed appreciation for how messy and improvisational our human lives truly are, may well help us change our ways towards regenerative and sustainable futures. The requirements that sustainability leadership set resonate with this view, and collaborative support networks provide a theory of networks that fits it well.

One way of achieving integration of the kind that Schön (1983) suggested for dealing with the challenges of technical rationality is to achieve an awareness of how metaphors enable or hinder our ways of seeing a problem. When we sub-consciously use metaphors to frame a problem, we cannot see that we may choose other ways of "seeing-as", which is the term Schön introduced to make us aware of the generative potential of metaphors. When we consciously choose a metaphor, and use its entailments to generate coherence to the abstract concept or to the new future that we are trying to understand, the seeing-as that the metaphor affords us may lead to new insights regarding possible solutions.

To help us make the paradigm shift away from technical rationality, we suggest that we base the theory of collaborative support networks on Verna Allee's Value Network Theory (Allee, 2008). Value Network Theory embodies two generative metaphors: a network is a complex of roles engaging in value conversions of tangible and intangible assets, and a network is a living system. With these two metaphors, Value Network Theory integrates both social and living systems theory. Allee defines a value network as "any set of roles and interactions in which people engage in both tangible and intangible exchanges to achieve economic or social good" (Allee, 2008, p. 6). In her work, *intangible exchanges* include employee expertise and the relationships they have built outside the company, while *tangible exchanges* concern "financial resources and other capital-based resources that are controlled by the firm" (p. 6). In Allee's model, a value network is actually a value-conversion network, i.e.- a network that transforms tangible value into intangible value and vice-versa.

In addition to *value,* Allee also wove *living systems* theory into the fabric of her work. In *The Future of Knowledge,* Allee (2003), follows Capra's (1996) suggestion that there are three criteria for systems to be living systems: pattern, structure and process. A *pattern* is a set of relationships existing amongst a system's components that allows it to be recognized as what it is. In nature, there are definite patterns for what constitutes a leaf, a tree or a forest. In society, they may be patterns for what constitutes an organization or a family. The *structure* of the system is "the physical embodiment of its pattern of organization" (Alee, 2003, p. 50). For example, within a dog pattern, there are a number of structures which characterize what kind of dog it is. Within an organization pattern, there are different structures such as a government, a religious organization, or a healthcare organization. Finally, *processes* are what links patterns and structures. Those three elements - structure, pattern and process - are inherent to the metaphor of living systems.

Using these elements, we can see collaborative support networks as living systems whereby support is the pattern, the network is the structure, and collaboration is the process that connects these two in a living system for sustainability leadership. This living systems metaphor for networks has the power to transcend and include both human and natural systems and can thus be used at any level of complexity and scale. By this, collaborative support networks based on Allee's theory of value networks enable forms of leadership that are collaborative, dialogic, supportive, open to vulnerability, and close to practice.

Bateson's Binocular Vision

In the above sections, we used ideas from value- and living systems to see how collaborative support networks afford sustainability leadership. In the next section, we turn to practice by sharing three cases. This means attending to what can be learned from programs featuring collaborative support networks in local contexts, while also realizing their interconnectedness, and what might be learned from patterns across local settings. Our focus is to create, for the reader, possibilities to learn across contexts.

For this, we invite you to use Gregory Bateson's idea of the importance of binocular vision, and his related concept of double description. Bateson develops this most clearly in his 1979 Mind and Nature: A Necessary Unity (Bateson, 1979). A focus on the depth that is gained from binocular vision and double description can foster learning for sustainability leadership at multiple levels, and guide anticipation of sustainable futures.

Bateson develops the importance of double description, and multiple description, by posing the question: "What pattern connects the crab to the lobster and the orchid to the primrose, and all four of them to me? And me to you?" (p.8). By posing this question, Bateson sets up an ecological form of inquiry that rests on seeing what emerges from patterns that connect. Indeed, Bateson invites us to consider "multiple versions of the world" by bringing to our attention "a number of cases in which two or more information sources come together to give information of a different sort from what was in either sort separately" (p. 22). It is this process of pattern making that Bateson calls double description. It is important to note that what emerges from double description is, thus, not the same as two, or more, different descriptions, but what emerges from the pattern that connects them.

The particular sources of our binocular vision and double description are programs of sustainability that generate new futures through collaborative support networks. We offer three cases involving collaborative support networks as key to sustainability. These cases vary in scale and show the concepts in collaborative support networks at work inside a single organization in The Netherlands, in the merger of two educational institutions in Oslo, Norway, and in a network of hundreds of schools in the state of Ceará, Brazil.

We invite the reader to learn from a brief description of each case and to think about what emerges from bringing the three together. This emergence is key.

The Practice of Sustainability Leadership in Collaborative Support Networks

Case no. 1: A new type of educational institution. One of the authors has been working in academic management in Norwegian higher education for the past 10 years, and has witnessed a trend whereby professional education and research-oriented institutions have converged to shape a new type of educational institution: the professional university.

This type of integration is different from the hostile takeovers in business, as this involves a cooperative, mutually beneficial evolution over time. In many ways, this new construct, the professional university, is unique as it combines elements of traditional institutions, such as professional colleges, on the one hand, and research universities on the other hand. Although research-orientation and profession-orientation are not mutually exclusive, the trend raised criticism both from "purist" circles that disapproved of research being "watered down" in profession-oriented educational programs and from practice-focused circles that resisted an "academization" of professional education. In some sense, the two traditions, which had existed side by side for decades without needing to acknowledge each other, suddenly entered a kind of competition, due to becoming closely involved. Despite being the target of much criticism, and the focus of much dissent, "professional universities" in Norway have had a unique opportunity to redefine themselves and their mission, in accordance with a changing society where practical skills and critical sense go hand in hand. In those universities, practice-oriented educators and researchers joined forces in collaborative support networks that enabled honest and constructive dialogue across fields and traditions; which, in turn, reinforced feelings of empowerment in the quest for a novel, more socially sustainable educational form.

This case illustrates a type of *value conflict* that is deeply rooted in education's history and in its traditions; whereas, colleges emphasized practice as their core value, universities considered research to be theirs. The apparent competition between research and practice may have been the result of a perspective that is highly reliant on technical rationality (Schön, 1983). Joining both these core values into one (practice-based research) might be considered heretical, and certainly brings about an unknown degree of ambiguity for those who take the risk of spearheading a new way of thinking, and a new way of taking action. The new, profession-oriented university, as a living system, redefined itself as a new type of ecosystem, in which both types of value system co-exist. This was achieved through faculty members and students alike taking the initiative not only to accept, but also to actively promote their university as something novel and ground-breaking, thereby demonstrating shared leadership in their discourse, as well as in their actions. When observing this through the lens of

Allee's (2003) Value Networks, we can see the education system as the *pattern*, and the new university as a *structure* within this pattern. What connects the structure to the pattern is the *process* of reinventing the meaning of higher education, using collaboration between various traditions and various ways of working, in order to make the structure acceptable within the evolving pattern. The pattern itself is supportive of the structure, despite the structure being novel and, to some extent, challenging. In this example, we see how sustainability leadership is as much about *taking action* (i.e. creating a new type of university), as it is about *designing for action* (i.e. providing a blueprint for other institutions to follow suit, by reinventing themselves as a different type of institution than the established types).

One example of a *collaborative support network* within the university was the introduction of a mentoring program for academics, who aimed at becoming professors at the new university. One of the interesting elements of this program is that it catered to two very different types of academics - as the English-language term "professor" refers to two different career paths in Norway, one primarily based on research ("professor" in Norwegian), and one primarily based on educational development ("dosent" in Norwegian). Having both "professor" candidates and "dosent" candidates in the same program gave an important signal, both within the organization and to the outside world, that research and education were valued equally at the university. If we look more specifically into what this program represents, we can see it as a *structure* within the university. It can also be argued that the underlying *pattern* for this program is the existence of two parallel career paths in higher education, which seems to be rather unique to Norway. The *process* might be the actual mentorship that took place, often across the demarcation line between the two career paths, with academics with a "dosent" status mentoring "professor" candidates, and vice versa.

Case no. 2: Optimizing work process organization in production settings. This case demonstrates several key aspects of sustainable leadership development through collaborative support networks that evolved in the workplace settings of the Dutch Horticulture sector. Organizing work processes, collaboration, knowledge management and communication between employees in an increasingly non-hierarchical work culture is a key to success in the Horticulture sector. The sector faces increasing complexity in dealing with issues of social and ecological sustainability. From 2014-2016, two of the authors introduced the non-hierarchical WorkisPlay methodology for team collaboration in organizing work and finding solutions to problems in the collaborative work process.

WorkIsPlay assumes that we make our physical and social worlds in interaction and that all employees are knowledge workers (Alexander, 1979; (Pearce, 2007). All employees are capable of designing solutions for complex problems in their workplace, especially when there is room for a non-judgmental, playful exchange of apparent details in the differing perspectives on what causes these situations. The cycle of using WorkisPlay to generate solutions consists of four steps that can be repeated as often as desired:

1. Sharing stories. WorkIsPlay considers stories to be the most reliable means to understand people's experiences from different perspectives.
2. Identifying forces. Forces are what shape, form, and cause stories to be what they are. WorkIsPlay encourages the players to name as many forces as they can see in a story without judging or analyzing the forces.
3. Co-creating and implementing solutions that coherently balance the body of forces that are found in the stories.
4. Evaluating the changes that implemented solutions make in how the stories are experienced.

By sharing experiences and identifying numerous forces that play a role in the stories, a deep and shared insight emerges in the causes and consequences of workplace issues. In this way, solutions, that balance a complex of multiple forces, can be co-created. Because these solutions are co-created, and thus supported by all members of the team, they are more likely to be adopted after implementation. Teams were given a mandate to implement solutions they designed within a small set of boundaries, such as "can be implemented without large company investment." Visualization of the 'playing board' of stories, forces and solutions encouraged continuous involvement of employees and led to continuous design of solutions. Teams of employees in the horticulture industry independently implemented a large number of solutions to work organization of the collaborative processes (Van Middendorp & Hartkamp, 2016).

In one example, after 18 months of growing, potted orchid plants are selected, categorized into different quality levels, labeled, packed and prepared for transport. Fairly fixed teams of two people work together to execute the tasks. Two teams of Dutch employees have worked together for 10-15 years, two other teams of Eastern Europeans exist, working together, and occasionally teams with temporary workers are hired to cope with peaks in demand. Some days of the week such as Monday, Thursday and Friday, are much busier than others. There are issues with packaging 'B' quality and cleaning up utensils after work. One team works efficiently by simultaneously packing A-quality orders, while directly packing B-quality orders and putting it ready on containers. Other teams do what they interpret to be their task: only pack the quality requested for the customer order. The quality not required is left for the end of the day, and in the case of high pressure or high workload, are left for the next day, where it is not always picked up in the next shift. There are several irritations towards each other. But, the situation is accepted as characteristic of different working ethics of the different duo-teams. Management does make rules on working swiftly and neatly, but after some time these disappear into the background. Through the WorkisPlay methodology employees were allowed to design solutions that had previously been left as a responsibility of management.

After sharing perspectives and analyzing underlying forces, solutions were designed and suggested by the whole team of packers, such as: rotating team composition to make teams of different backgrounds and experiences, according to varying workload or pressure, changing workplace design. These include using new utensils and making packaging containers for the lesser quality orders available for every team, visualization of the ideal tidied up workplace situation expected at the end of the day, circulating responsibility of "expert" available to help less experienced workers, etc.

Ilona from Poland explains: "Suddenly, we came up with solutions no-one thought would be accepted by either management or employees. As we realized, everyone's story is true to them, and we took time listening to their underlying thoughts. After sharing perspectives, two things became clear to me: 1) there are a lot of issues we normally don't discuss that lead to different interpretations of our tasks, responsibilities, and how we relate to each other; 2) we all wanted the same thing: to execute our work on time and to contribute to the success of the company. How could we get the job done together and make the process more enjoyable? We were stimulated to think through our own actions and of those of others on the team, and which knowledge or decision-making was lacking. Opening up to each other's perspectives was really, very valuable, it really helped us connect and work together."

Through applying WorkIsPlay, employees developed leadership in a collaborative process of work organization and designing of solutions, created a network for feedback and support while following a pattern of coexistence and symbiosis instead of competition, and better adapting to constantly changing work processes and environments.

The implementation of the methodology guided teams within the company to become micro-*collaborative support networks.* Investment in employee involvement, diversity of worker perspectives and relationships, and the in-depth analysis of underlying work processes, led to a better understanding of the individual qualities of other team members within which *collaboration* evolved as a process. Participating in WorkIsPlay had a strong positive effect on joint network identity and responsibility, creating room for specific roles–as opposed to fixed tasks– of individuals that fit personal preferences for autonomy, mastery and purpose (Pink, 2011). As a result, new, more naturally sustainable *patterns* to work process organization were implemented based on strengths, like the *support* of individuals to function as a whole. Teams became aware of the possibilities and changing roles in different work situations, thus creating a flexible *network structure,* transforming their work experience from being parts of a machine to being adaptive organisms in a living system.

The case demonstrated in practice aspects of sustainable leadership development of individuals within collaborative support networks:

- Moving away from heroic, individual narratives of an operations manager towards discovering qualities and natural tendencies of individuals to balance solutions.
- Moving away from technical rationality of top-down solutions towards embracing a more organic systems approach with social and natural forces to help shape sustainable solutions.
- Moving away from risk aversion and hesitation that closes individuals off from the *collaborative process* and therefore limiting the possibilities of designing solutions that are supported by the

whole group.

- Sharing individual and joint values in teams as a starting point for the development of collaboration within the network.
- Giving room for every employee to design solutions for action and to realize sustainable leadership for workplace improvement.
- Moving away from fixed task orientation towards joint responsibility for collaborative design for improvement and action.
- Teams nurtured collaboration and adapted to increasing complexity of work process organization.

We saw collaborative support networks evolving as a living system that was better adapted to complexity and uncertainty of day-to-day work processes, balancing individual versus group dynamics through sustainable leadership as reflection in action.

We would like to argue that sustainable leadership and collaborative support networks in the workplace are needed for a sustainable future. In what way could opening up to different perspectives, analyzing underlying forces, designing solutions through collaborative support networks and utilizing sustainable leadership development in each of us, contribute to flexibility and balancing solutions for complex global challenges?

Which analogies of collaboration support networks and sustainable leadership development in the workplace do you regard useful in the context of addressing the ecological challenges we face?

Case no. 3: Generation of Peace. The Generation of Peace project, in Brazil, a cooperation between the State Department of Education of Ceará (SEDUC), and the United Nations Educational, Scientific, and Cultural Organization (UNESCO) had its focus on the co-creation of networks of cultures of peace through dialogue within more than 700 schools, which involved thousands of students, education professionals, families and communities. The adoption of the World Café (Brown, Isaacs, & Community, 2005) as a dialogic form of meeting, designed to bring together large groups of people in small, close conversations, served as the leading *process* that afforded a period of six years of project execution. From 2010 to 2016, one of the authors acted as a UNESCO strategy consultant responsible for both the project's design and coordination.

The project's *pattern of organization* comprised the principles that reified a new order as to where education is "done," with the school being the center of the system, not the "edge". In the same way, this pattern embodied the concept of peace as a phenomenon of systemic wholeness, with its own inherent value: peace as peace, instead of peace as an opposite of, say, violence. The *structure* involved the work's focus, its path and direction; the students and their protagonism and emancipation supported by a culture of cooperation, solidarity and service, and schools' integrated curriculum and shared management. The *process* contained the methods chosen to make concrete steps in the project, like the World Café method mentioned earlier, which was used to create what the project called Peace Café's. (Mesquita da Silva, 2017).

The World Café brought this conceptual framework to life thanks to its participatory and transformative nature. Accordingly, the meaning-making, inquiry and knowledge co-production process fostered by the World Café brought forth a sense of purpose, shared values and goals, which allowed for the co-creation of consensus around what mattered to participants, and to those they represented. Based on the principles and the focus found in the project's framework, the World Café encouraged all participants to address their previous perceptions and understandings, and at the same time, review their positions, regardless of the variety of themes they had dialogued with other people. According to Mesquita da Silva (2017), participants of the Peace Cafés stated that people "suddenly began to listen to each other in another way, with a more attentive ear, and more open-hearted!" (p. 9).

The breadth of the project followed the premise that a culture of dialogue precedes a culture of peace, as well as understanding that network, leadership, and sustainability are interdependent and overarching entities of the same system. These entities proved invaluable to the success of the project as both Collaborative Support Networks and sustainability leadership thrived simultaneously. The major indicators of success of the project were:

- 509 schools (73% of the total) approved into the Certification Program by showing evidence of systematic, daily practices towards the generation of a culture of peace.
- The leadership of the State Department of Education of Ceará (SEDUC) gathered in a World Café, "The World Café: Dialogues for a Generation of Sustainable Networks of Peace," designed and

facilitated to evaluate the project and plan its institutionalization in the educational system. After some refinement, it culminated in the following statement that translates the idea of Collaborative Support Networks and Sustainability Leadership:

> "The participants support the implementation of the culture of peace as a mission of the beings that comprise the educational system of Ceará. We need to transform the Generation of Peace into a mark present in everything: in the curriculum, in the management processes, in pedagogical material, in the formation / training, in the projects and programs, in the collegiate organisms, in the events and in the physical spaces, and also, into the mission of each public servant of the system: the doorman, the cook, the teacher, the principal, coordinators, etc.

The three cases illustrate an important aspect of sustainability leadership: if sustainability issues are to be addressed seriously, individual actions and actions in ad-hoc groupings, no matter how brave or heroic, might not suffice to bring about enduring change. To ensure the impact of actions and their sustainability over time, we urgently need to cultivate the natural leadership that resides in each one of us, and to conjugate it with the natural leadership of others, not in a competitive way (as is often the case in professional organizations), but in a collaborative manner. Through collaborative support networks, we can liberate ourselves from the myth of leaders as fairy-tale heroes with superhuman powers and build a new narrative, where everyone is empowered with enough knowledge, skill and motivation to scaffold change.

Traditional research, like traditional leadership, is often classified as deductive (looking back at patterns), inductive (generalizing based on limited observations), or abductive (forming a conclusion based on incomplete data). In this chapter, we proposed a new and organic way of approaching sustainability leadership through participation in *collaborative support networks*. Participating could provide a structure, a process and a pattern for a journey of discovery, based on practices and experiences, and on learning by doing. In the same spirit, we invoke a sustainability research, which takes questions and connections as the starting point for exploration.

We regard asking powerful questions as a key to creating the kinds of change to how we think about and act with regard to sustainability leadership. While we often think of questions as having a straightforward answer, questions can also create movement and afford new ways of thinking. It is with this latter frame of questions that we invite the reader to understand the questions we offer.

Questions for Discussion

1. Are you able to identify a collaborative support network either from your own work practice or in your extracurricular activities? In what way are they collaborative? What processes of collaboration do they support? In what way are they supportive? What patterns of support are consciously enacted? In what way do they qualify as "networks"? What aspects of network structure are visible in your practice?
2. Are you currently participating in a form of collaborative support network? How would you describe this network? How would others in the network describe it? How would you explain any differences? Are there existing networks that you could join and contribute to in order to boost your own work? Would you consider joining collaborative support networks that are unknown to you? How would you go about finding or creating one?
3. What would you expect to gain from collaborative support networks? What kind of insights can you gain from participating in these networks? In what way does collaborating with others in such networks broaden your horizons and/or enrich your perspective? What kind of support can you feel that you need in order to believe in your own leadership and ability to address sustainability challenges?
4. How will you go about giving yourself enough room to learn in collaborative support networks even after graduating from your program?
5. We invite the reader to think of questions that might be brought from one of our stories to another, to invite learning across the different cultural contexts. For example:
6. What might be the ways that a World Cafe process from the Generation of Peace project might be brought to organizing a new educational institution? How might participants be invited into a World Cafe in this different setting?
7. How might lessons learned from considering work settings be brought to questions asked in a World Cafe?
8. How might the variety of ways of thinking about learning spaces, so important to designing a new educational institution, be brought to how we consider new

work settings? And how might each of these allow for a deeper understanding of collaborative support networks?

About the Authors

Laurence Habib is a Professor in Information Technology and Learning and currently the Chair of the Department of Computer Science at the Faculty of Technology, Art and Design at OsloMet – Oslo Metropolitan University, Norway. She has conducted research in a variety of areas including domestic technologies, the pedagogical and organizational aspects of learning technologies, assessment, educational development, engineering education and universal design of information and communication technologies.

Sergej van Middendorp, while searching for ideas that support the design and development of systems that help create wholeness, came across the theory of organizational improvisation. For several years, together with a jazz band and with the help of many colleagues and clients, he explored the metaphor of jazz improvisation in both theory and practice. Today, he combines the experience from systems design and improvisation to help create systems that are alive, and that help their users achieve a 'groove' in their performance. With his crew in Miles Ahead, and a collaborative support network of people and organizations in The Netherlands he is trying to help the Dutch health system evolve to become more whole through a more positive, constructive, integrative, integral, and digital approach.

Flávio Mesquita da Silva is a World Café international practitioner. Peace activist and researcher. Consulting, training, counseling and coaching since 1978 in Brazil, USA, Canada, Spain, United Kingdom, Mexico, and Colombia in the areas of Human, Social, Environmental, Educational, and Organizational Development for not-for-profit organizations, universities, communities, governments and corporate businesses, and the United Nations. Honor to Merit for relevant work in the Service of Peace, Education Commission of the Chamber of Deputies, Brasilia, Brazil. Research Scholarship Award (studies and research on the World Café), Institute for Social Innovation, Fielding Graduate University, California, USA. M.A. & Ph.D. Human and Organizational Systems; Dissertation: "Generation of Peace Dialogues: How the World Café Approach to

Community Understanding Led to Cultures of Peace". Marie Fielder Graduate Fellow, Marie Fielder Center for Democracy, Leadership & Education. Fielding Graduate University.M.A. Whole Systems Design, Project: A Holistic Approach to Peace: a Case for Design. Antioch University Seattle.

Agnes Dewi Hartkamp is currently working as program manager at the Foundation for Innovations in Horticulture (SIGN). Connecting disciplines and organizations for healthy food, wellbeing and healthy work environments through strategic horticultural innovations. Before her position at SIGN, she worked as policy advisor for the Dutch Agriculture Ministry on sustainability, economics and agricultural policies and European regional development programs. Before that, she worked for the Farmers Association and Cereal industry on biotechnology, food safety, quality systems, and research coordination for cereal breeding, production and processing. She did her PhD research at CIMMYT, the leading international Institute for Maize and Wheat Research. Her research focused on designing sustainable maize cropping systems for Latin America, through combining GIS, climate interpolation techniques, crop modeling and consultation with regional stakeholder networks. Ph.D. Production ecology Wageningen University, (2002) Dissertation: Learning from biophysical heterogeneity: inductive use of case studies for maize cropping systems in Central America.

Frederick Steier, Ph.D, is Professor in the School of Leadership Studies at Fielding Graduate University. His work focuses on systemic approaches to social/ecological systems, with attention to learning, communication, and design. He has directed participatory action research programs in a wide variety of settings, ranging from government institutions, including NASA, to science centers, such as the Museum of Science and Industry (MOSI), in Tampa, Florida, where he was also a Scientist-in-Residence. He is the editor of the volumes, *Gregory Bateson: Essays for an ecology of ideas* (2005), and *Research and Reflexivity* (1991), and is a Past-President of the American Society for Cybernetics. He has been on the faculty of the University of South Florida (where he was also Director of Interdisciplinary Studies Programs), Old Dominion University (where he was also Director of the Center for Cybernetic Studies in Complex Systems), the University of Oslo (Norway) and the University of Pennsylvania. He has also had the honor of being King Olav V Fellow with the American-Scandinavian Foundation, and recently (2019) received the Norbert Wiener award for lifetime achievement from the American Society for Cybernetics. Dr. Steier received his doctorate from the Wharton School of the University of Pennsylvania, in Social Systems Sciences, in 1983.

References

Alexander, C. (1979). *The timeless way of building.* Oxford University Press.

Allee, V. (2003). *The Future of Knowledge: Increasing Prosperity through Value Networks.* Oxford: Butterworth-Heinemann.

Allee, V. (2008). Value network analysis and value conversion of tangible and intangible assets. *Journal of Intellectual Capital, 9*(1), 5–24.

Andriessen, D., & Gubbins, C. (2009). Metaphor analysis as an approach for exploring theoretical concepts: The case of social capital. *Organization Studies,* 30(8), 845–863. https://doi.org/10.1177/0170840609334952

Bateson, G. (1979). *Mind and nature: A necessary unity.* Dutton.

Borgatti, S. P., & Halgin, D. S. (2011). On network theory. *Organization Science, 22*(5), 1168–1181. JSTOR. https://www.jstor.org/stable/41303110

Brown, J., & Isaacs, D. (2005). *The World Café: Shaping our futures through conversations that matter* (1st ed.). Berrett-Koehler Publishers.

Brundtland, G. (1987). Report of the World Commission on Environment and Development: Our Common Future. United Nations General Assembly document A/42/427.

Buchdahl, J. M., Raper, D. (1998). Environmental ethics and sustainable development. *Sustainable Development, 6,* 92–98. DOI: 10.1002/(SICI)1099-1719(199808).

Capra, F. (1996). *The Web of Life - A New Scientific Understanding of Living Systems.* New York: Anchor Books.

Carmeli, A., & Sheaffer, Z. (2009). How Leadership Characteristics Affect Organizational Decline and Downsizing. *Journal of Business Ethics,* 86(3), 363–378. https://doi.org/10.1007/s10551-008-9852-7

Carroll, B., Levy, L. & Richmond, D. (2008) Leadership as practice: Challenging the competency paradigm. *Leadership, 4*(4), 363–379.

Fairhurst, G.T. & Uhl-Bien, M. (2012). Organizational discourse analysis (ODA): Examining leadership as a relational process. *The Leadership Quarterly, 23*(6), 1043–1062.

Heizmann, H., & Liu, H. (2018). Becoming green, becoming leaders: Identity narratives in sustainability leadership development. *Management Learning, 49*(1), 40-58. https://doi.org/10.1177/1350507617725189

Jackson, T. (2009). *Prosperity without Growth: Economics for a Finite Planet.* London: Earthscan.

Mesquita da Silva, F. (2017). *Generation of peace dialogues: How the World Café approach to community understanding led to cultures of peace* [Ph.D., Fielding

Graduate University]. http://search.proquest.com/docview/1936354743/abstract/EC409A5C8D7A425DPQ/1

Pearce, W. B. (2007). *Making social worlds: A communication perspective.* Blackwell Publishing.

Pink, D. H. (2011). *Drive: The surprising truth about what motivates us.* Riverhead Books.

Raelin, J. (2016) Imagine there are no leaders: Reframing leadership as collaborative agency. *Leadership, 12*(2), 131–158.

Schön, D. A. (1983). *The Reflective Practitioner: How Professionals Think in Action.* Aldershot: Avebury [Ashgate].

Van Middendorp, S., & Hartkamp, D. (2016). Workisplay: Facilitator's guide. http://workisgaming.nl/files/FacilitatorGuide_WorkIsPlay.pdf

Walther-Thomas, C., Korinek, L., & McLaughlin, V. (1999). Collaboration to support students' success. *Focus on Exceptional Children, 32*(3), 1–18. http://search.proquest.com/docview/224045032?pq-origsite=summon&accountid=33310

CHAPTER 13

Afterword:
What Can Leaders Learn about Tackling Wicked Problems in Sustainability

Frederick Steier and Jean-Pierre Isbouts
Fielding Graduate University

As we noted in the Introduction, our purpose in writing this book is to provide leaders with case studies and tangible ideas for building a more sustainable future—not only in their organizations, but also in society and indeed, the world at large. In doing so, we set out to emphasize the critical role of leadership – not only how sustainable leaders can be effective, but also how such leadership can sustain itself in the long run. Doing so requires a systems approach, which is why many chapters in this book are founded on systemic theories and solutions.

In Chapter 1, for example, we set the stage with an overall framework for understanding ecological and social issues. Chapters 2 and 3 depicted the urgency of current ecological challenges, not only in terms of climate change but also in terms of the ongoing destruction of animal and natural habitats that continue to erode the principal fabric of nature. Chapters 4 through 7 then turned to the pivotal role of leadership in grappling with these crises, based on case studies of intervention in a variety of settings and organizations.

In the second part of the book, we looked for new ways to frame the discussion of sustainability leadership, using such concepts as the Sustainability Mindset Model, the Environmental Activism Propensity Scale, and the need to move from a Eurocentric worldview to a more inclusive and indigenous perspective. The idea that the debate around sustainability should not be limited to an American perspective was then continued in Chapter 11, which looked for inspiration from Indian social activists, and Chapter 12, which analyzed collaborative support networks in Norway, the Netherlands and Brazil.

What these chapters tell us is that sustainability leadership needs to recognize the variety of cultures within which successful strategies can evolve. That certainly includes national cultures, but it also involves organizational or even professional cultures. This variety is key. In fact, the preservation of cultural diversity in the face of changing environments may be a central principle of sustainability leadership.

In this Afterword, we would like to conclude with some ideas that reinforce key patterns present throughout the book. These three ideas – ecosystemic approaches, wicked problems and frame dilemmas - allow us to go one level up from the concrete examples and case situations offered in the various chapters. At the same time, they share a connection to the practical wisdom needed for sustainability leadership. It is that link to practice that we want to emphasize here.

One is the recognition of the importance of ecosystemic approaches (Wilden, 1972). This means that we must rely on interconnections and interdependencies in managing stability and change in the face of ecological change. If there is one thing that characterizes the postwar period, it is the growing interconnectivity between key elements of our society—a process that ultimately produced what is now known as the global economy. In a world where much of human activity is driven by just-in-time protocols, any form of disruption in the human productivity chain can lead to a cascade of consequences—as vividly illustrated by the abrupt blocking of the Suez Canal, the artery of human commerce, by a wayward container ship in March of 2021. That means that leaders must recognize the implications of their decision-making beyond the walls of their organization, and reflect on the greater impact in their community, their marketplace, and the delicate fabric of human dependencies at large. That is why leadership in sustainability is above all about having the desire to understand the greater context –or what in the Introduction we called the "second order learning process".

An Ecosystemic Approach

At the core of this willingness to learn is our recognition that we live in a participatory universe. In other words, when we speak about sustainability and sustainability leadership, we do so as participants in those worlds we are trying to sustain. We are not external to those situations. We also recognize the value of others – including non-human others – as participants in bringing about sustainability, even as we recognize the different perspectives that others may bring to our quest. Thus, we are speaking about sustainability of our home (as in *oikos*, the Greek word that became, through the pioneering work of Ernst Haeckel (1876), the basis for the eco in ecology) as well as nature's home.

In his article "Ecology, Planning and the American Dream," Geoffrey Vickers (1968) notes four key ideas of systems approaches that fit with what ecologists do; how ecologists understand worlds, and then act with worlds. The principles that Vickers offers are: interdependence, attention to recurring patterns, change, and regulation. For example, from a systems approach, we see not only the interconnections between parts, but also how they mutually influence each other – their interdependencies. Change in one part of a system will influence, and in turn be influenced by, change in another part. Vickers' attention to pattern is also important because it encourages us to see connections not only within a situation, but also across situations, which is central to learning. The couplet of change and regulation encourages us to realize the importance of how we develop processes to balance identity and stability with change and transformation. For example, if we consider riding a bicycle, we would generally like to maintain as stable a position as possible relative to the ground – we do not want to fall down. At the same time, in adjusting for wind, incline, speed, we want to be able to change our position on the bicycle, while still remaining upright. Having flexibility to do so becomes key – and it is that same flexibility, while holding on to variety, that is central to systems and sustainability.

Vickers' focus on the relationship between systems and ecology also invites us to recognize the importance of a systems approach to our organizations. When we speak of our system, in eco-systemic terms, we stress the relational aspect, because to destroy our environment would also mean destroying ourselves. How we make a differentiation between what is inside our system and what is outside matters, because from an ecosystems perspective, the two are intertwined.

Ecosystemic approaches also recognize the value of different voices, or even different species. What might be essential to the sustainability – or even the identity – of a system may vary from different perspectives. The viewpoints offered in this book focus on bringing those different voices together, while also identifying the challenges at hand.

As Eriksen (2016) noted in his introduction to the Overheating Project – itself an interesting model of appreciating the systemic nature of sustainability leadership – the connections are not necessarily smooth, nor are they seamlessly integrated. An appreciation of the roughness of the interconnections is one aspect of the challenges of sustainability leadership.

Wicked Problems

In a number of chapters, we addressed the fact that for many, ecological change is irreversible, and that humankind is essential powerless to stop it. These voices believe that the challenge of sustainability is a *wicked* problem – a problem too difficult to solve, either because of the lack of know-how, the high cost involved, the complexity of the problem, or simply because we lack a consensus on how to tackle it. This idea of "wicked problems" is now increasingly being cited in areas ranging from local and regional planning to the design of future programs and spaces (Sweeting, 2018). In our introduction to this volume, we showed that many issues facing sustainability leaders can likewise be understood as wicked problems. What is important, however, is to recognize that there is a big difference between wicked problems and hard problems. Wicked problems do not lend themselves to being solved, but rather encourage us to recognize *that we need deal with them differently*. For example, landing the Perseverance spacecraft on Mars was a hard problem – a very hard problem. But it was not a wicked problem in the sense that Rittel and Webber (1973) understand the term. What they suggest is that wicked problems are distinct because of the difficulty for stakeholders to understand their complexity.

In response, Rittel and Webber offered ten points, but we will only focus on three that are particularly relevant for our discussion:

(1) there is no definitive formulation of a wicked problem;

(2) wicked problems have no stopping rule, and

(3) every wicked problem can be considered to be a symptom of another problem.

Sweeting (2018) elaborates on Rittel and Webber's ideas in ways that nicely resonate with sustainability leadership. For example, on the question of how we formulate wicked problems, Sweeting notes that wicked problems are often presented in a highly ambiguous and incomplete manner. That means that any attempt to more clearly define a wicked problem will often result in another problem – one that will fundamentally challenge the way we understand the problem in the first place. Indeed, dealing with wicked problems often rest on appreciating their ambiguity, and not trying, in the words of Webber and Rittel, to "tame" them in ways that lose their integrity.

So what does that mean for us? In terms of sustainability, it means we need recognize that there is always going to be some pushback on a perceived solution, whether from ourselves or from other participants. Indeed, it is the recognition of our environment as a continuously changing system that forms the basis for any successful approach to sustainability.

One reason why wicked problems are so thorny is that attempts to solve the symptom as a problem can often lead to a more serious and related problem in another. For example, efforts to promote social sustainability by creating self-regulating working conditions has now produced a multi-billion dollar compliance industry that is beholden to the firms that hire them. What that means is that, when compliance firms interview workers about wages or safety issues, these employees often fear that if they reveal any deficiencies in the organization, they risk losing their job. In other words, the solution to the problem has actually produced another and more pernicious problem.

One program that can serve as a good example of tackling wicked problems, is the previously cited Overheating Project led by Thomas Hylland Eriksen (2016). As we saw in the above, Eriksen recognized that the interconnections central to systemic understanding are not necessarily smooth. Among others, he notes how rights and opportunities are unevenly distributed, and how the capitalist world system is riddled with contradictions that often hold the seeds of severe crises. For example, policy makers who express concerns about environmental issues often advocate strong economic growth, without apparently understanding the inherent conflict.

The Overheating Project identifies three parallel crises of our planet: a crisis of identity, of climate change, and of economics. The three crises share a cybernetic feedback concern with how, in the public domain, different positions on opposite sides of the issue get into a relationship of positive feedback loops. Thus, "overheating" also refers to the process of how these issues are dealt with in different public settings. At the same time, many issues at play can be understood as either an economic issue, an environmental issue, or one where national identity is at stake; and indeed, the very identity of the issue itself. Case studies range from places like Gladstone, Australia, where Eriksen investigated issues around coal-mining, to the Fort MacMurray area in northern Alberta, where Lena Gross explored issues for First Nations groups around tar sands extraction. In each case, the underlying issue was not only one of economics and jobs, but also environmental concerns and even group or national identity. Eriksen also showed how the change at play in each of these local contexts is also growing at an accelerating rate, leading to overheating in yet another sense. Yet at its core, a key feature of this project was its recognition of what we can see as wicked problems involves overheating in many senses.

What this means is that situations can be viewed from different frames, for example, is this an environmental issue or an economic one? Further, who has the right to dictate what frame is the one we need to be using? How those different frames are dealt, or even acknowledged by those with a differing perspective, is itself a concern that brings overheating to sustainability leadership. Such dilemmas, what Schön and Rein (1994) referred to as frame dilemmas, becomes an important aspect of our volume.

Frames and Frame Dilemmas

In his article, "A Theory of Play and Fantasy," Gregory Bateson (1972) developed the concept of frame, and of framing, to recognize the variety of ways in which we classify and make sense of experience. He wondered how an act that would ordinarily be perceived as aggression might actually be an invitation to play. In developing this dilemma, Bateson realized that there must be what he called a "metacommunicative act" – communication about the communication process – that tells, at another level, how the action asks to be understood by a recipient. Bateson noted that all messages require a context to be understood. Yet, that understanding assumes a shared context that may or may not be there. Bateson chose the word "framing" to illustrate the concreteness of our so doing, in much the same way that a frame for a painting calls attention to what might be within its borders that is different than what we might otherwise assume. Erving Goffman (1974) made the process of how we recognize frames—and disagreements about what that frame might be—a cornerstone of his Frame Analysis. Building on their work, Don Schön and Martin Rein (1994) noted the importance of realizing that participants in policy discussions often find that the intractability of their situation is rooted in the fact they are operating from different frames. They referred to this process as frame dilemmas. Jorgenson and Steier (2013) extended this work even more bringing recognition of frame dilemmas at the heart of misunderstanding at meetings, even those intended to offer possibilities for dialogue. In fact, as they note, even raising the possibility that participants are operating from different frames itself requires a frame of understanding that may not be there. Having a flexibility to appreciate, recognize and operate from different frames (Steier, 2005) is required.

The idea of frame dilemmas is central to sustainability leadership. Indeed, one can see an affinity between frame dilemmas and wicked problems in that many situations involving sustainability, such as those in the Overheating Project, involve participants who are quite literally operating from different frames, without an acknowledgment that the frame of the other is a legitimate frame, or at least one that has the merit of their frame. In extreme situations, the possibility of creating a dialogic frame is itself understood as a choice that negates the desired frame of a participant. This is truly a wicked problem rooted in communication about issues that might be central to sustainability. What is it that we would like to sustain? What is it that we would like to change? Who are the "we" who are making these distinctions? What are the consequences of the choices we make in dealing with these systemic dilemmas for those who do not have a voice?

Continuing the Conversation

In bringing together ecosystemic approaches, wicked problems, and the issue of framing, a final thought might be: sustainability leadership is also about improvisation. There is no script to be followed, other than the need to be attentive to process and to the multiple frames that might be possible in a situation. In that sense, there is no question that new metaphors of sustainability leadership are needed, and we hope that the chapters in this volume have offered some possibilities. Might the geographical metaphor from Martin Buber (1966), in his work on dialogue offer some hope- that of the *narrow ridge* where we find a way to hold to our position while still opening space for another? This is a wicked ecosystemic problem indeed.

We hope that this volume has inspired your thinking about sustainability leadership, and we invite you to contact us with any thoughts you may have about your experience. As we said before, sustainability leadership is about an ongoing process of adapting to change—and we very much like to have you join the conversation.

References

Bateson, G. (1972). *Steps to an ecology of mind.* New York: Ballantine Books

Bateson. M. C. (2005). *Our own metaphor: A personal account of a conference on the effects of conscious purpose on human adaptation*. Cresskill, NJ: Hampton Press

Buber. M. (1966). *The way of response.* New York: Schocken Books.

Eriksen, T.H. (2016). *Overheating: An anthropology of accelerated change.* London: Pluto Press

Goffman, E. (1974). *Frame analysis: An essay on the organization of experience.* Boston, MA: Northeastern University Press.

Haeckel, E. (1876). *The History of Creation*. New York: D. Appleton and Co.

Jorgenson, J. & Steier, F. (2013). Frames, framing and designed conversational processes: Lessons from the World Café. *Journal of Applied Behavioral Science 49*, 3, 388-405

Rittel, H. and Webber, M. (1973). Dilemmas in a general theory of planning. *Policy Sciences*, 4, 155-169.

Schön, D., & Rein, M. (1994). *Frame reflection: Toward the resolution of intractable policy controversies.* New York, NY: Basic Books.

Steier, F. (2005). Exercising frame flexibility. *Cybernetics and Human Knowing, 12*, 1-2, 36-49

Sweeting, B. (2018). Wicked problems in design and ethics. In P.H. Jones & K. Kijima (Eds.), *Systemic design: Theory, methods and practice,* 119-143. Tokyo: Springer Japan.

Vickers, G. (1968). Ecology, planning and the American dream. In *Value Systems and Social Process.* London: Tavistock Publications.

Wilden, A. (1972). *System and structure: Essays in communication and exchange.* London: Tavistock Publications.

Made in the USA
Monee, IL
27 February 2022